THE YOUNG OXFORD BOOK OF
CINEMA

THE YOUNG OXFORD BOOK OF

CINEMA

David Parkinson

OXFORD UNIVERSITY PRESS

CONTENTS

To Alan Smithee and P. H. Vazak

Oxford University Press, Walton Street,
Oxford, OX2 6DP

Oxford New York
Athens Auckland Bangkok Bombay
Calcutta Cape Town Dar es Salaam Delhi
Florence Hong Kong Istanbul Karachi
Kuala Lumpur Madras Madrid Melbourne
Mexico City Nairobi Paris Singapore
Taipei Tokyo Toronto
and associated companies in
Berlin Ibadan

Oxford is a trade mark of Oxford University Press
© David Parkinson 1995

ISBN 0 19 910071-3

A CIP catalogue record for this book is available
from the British Library

Printed in Spain by Mateu Cromo, S. A. Pinto-Madrid

Front cover *King Kong* (1933)

**Some of the films mentioned in this book should not
be watched by younger viewers without the
permission of an adult. They have been included to
present the reader with the fullest possible account
of film history and contemporary cinema.**

1

SILENT CINEMA

PLAYER'S CIGARETTES

Greta Garbo   (M.G.M.)

2

CINEMA: SOUND TO CDI

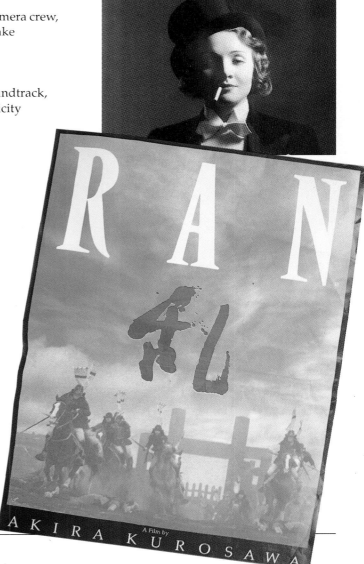

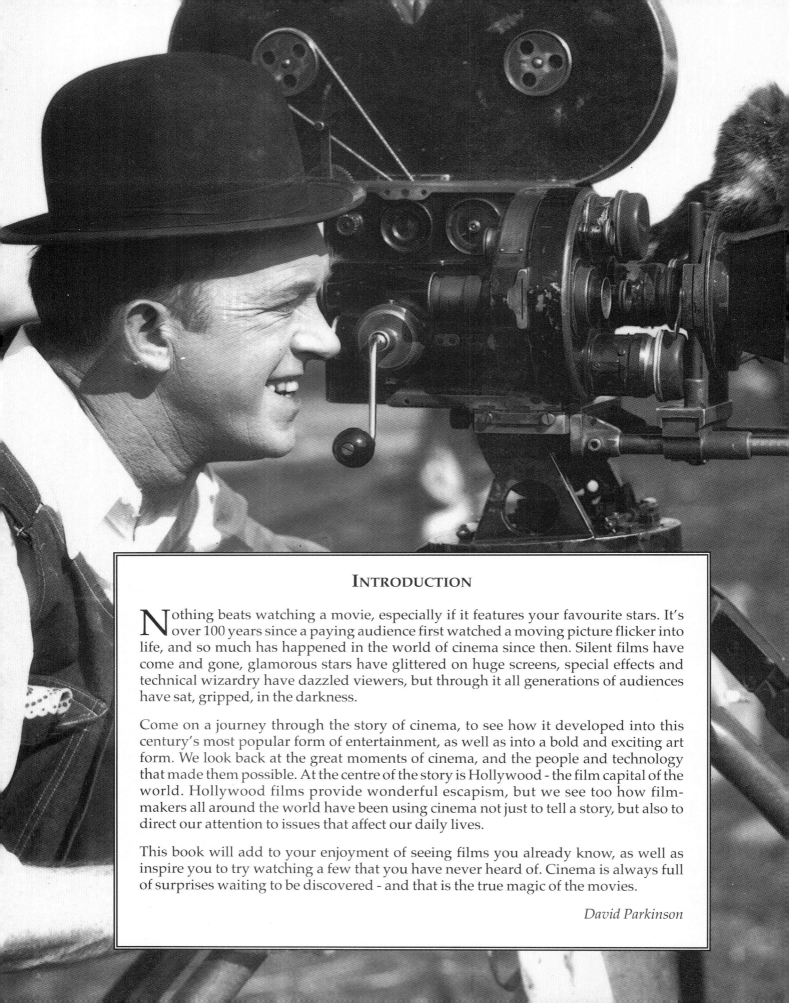

INTRODUCTION

Nothing beats watching a movie, especially if it features your favourite stars. It's over 100 years since a paying audience first watched a moving picture flicker into life, and so much has happened in the world of cinema since then. Silent films have come and gone, glamorous stars have glittered on huge screens, special effects and technical wizardry have dazzled viewers, but through it all generations of audiences have sat, gripped, in the darkness.

Come on a journey through the story of cinema, to see how it developed into this century's most popular form of entertainment, as well as into a bold and exciting art form. We look back at the great moments of cinema, and the people and technology that made them possible. At the centre of the story is Hollywood - the film capital of the world. Hollywood films provide wonderful escapism, but we see too how film-makers all around the world have been using cinema not just to tell a story, but also to direct our attention to issues that affect our daily lives.

This book will add to your enjoyment of seeing films you already know, as well as inspire you to try watching a few that you have never heard of. Cinema is always full of surprises waiting to be discovered - and that is the true magic of the movies.

David Parkinson

SILENT CINEMA

The story of cinema begins, amazingly, with the ancient Greeks and moving shadows. Centuries later, in the 1800s, inventors and entertainers came together to produce moving pictures packed with magic tricks and thrills. The earliest movies were animations, but soon photographic images were also being used. Hollywood was born and the silent stars were created. Although films had no sound, they could be shaped by talented film-makers into enjoyable entertainments and works of art.

MAKING PICTURES MOVE

Imagine a cold winter's Saturday evening over 100 years ago: you have paid one franc to join the small audience seated in a darkened room in the Grand Café in Paris. A machine flickers into life and the photographic image of a set of heavy wooden gates appears on the screen before you. Suddenly the gates open and a crowd of factory workers floods out into the street...

It is 28 December 1895, and you are watching the very first cinema show.

Only 35 tickets were sold that day, but by the end of the week vast queues were forming along the Boulevard des Capucines to see the moving pictures produced and presented by Louis and Auguste Lumière's camera-projector – the Cinématographe.

The ten short films that made up that first programme might not seem very exciting to today's cinemagoers, but those simple images were as thrilling to that first audience as virtual reality is to us today.

Similar entertainments – shadow dramas, illuminated drawings and other optical displays that appeared to show movement – were already popular and playing in Paris at that time. But the realism of moving photographic images had never been witnessed before.

Although the Lumière brothers presented the first cinema show to a paying audience, they did not invent the motion picture. Films evolved over many centuries. The story of cinema development is one of separate discoveries rather than a single-minded quest, involving scientists, showmen and artists. Each new development occurred as a result of either curiosity, observation, experiment, coincidence, or even pure accident.

The earliest picture shows

Since the time of the Ancient Greeks, people have been fascinated by tricks of light and shade. Around 360 BC, the Greek philosopher Plato described in his book *The Republic* the movements made by shadows thrown on to the wall of a cave by the glow of a camp fire. Some film historians consider this description of the 'Cave of Shadows' to be the first reference to moving images.

◁ An advertising poster for the Lumière brothers' Cinématographe camera-projector, with which they gave the first cinema show on 28 December 1895. The picture on the screen is *L'Arroseur arrosé* (*The Sprinkler Sprinkled*). It was based on a newspaper cartoon, and was the first fictional film in movie history.

◁ Telling of kings and queens, magicians and monsters, Javanese shadow shows often last up to eight hours. They are still popular with locals and tourists today.

Puppeteers in medieval Java, China and India used light and shade to cast the shadows of delicately decorated leather puppets on to translucent screens in order to tell epic tales based on local myths and legends. Similar puppet shows were introduced into Europe in the late 18th century during the period of intellectual curiosity known as the Enlightenment. Shows, such as Dominque Séraphin's 'Chinese Shadows', remained popular for over a century.

Illuminated entertainments

In the 1780s a Scottish showman, Robert Barker, devised another form of visual entertainment called the Panorama. This used ingenious lighting to animate vast paintings depicting dramatic battles or busy street scenes. At the same time, the artist Philippe de Loutherbourg introduced his Eidophusikon, a 'theatre of effects' which used imaginative lighting to make pictures appear three-dimensional.

But the most ingenious illuminated picture display was the Diorama, presented by Louis Daguerre and Claude-Marie Bouton in 1822. Using blinds and shutters to control the amount of light reaching a large semi-transparent painting, the Diorama treated its audiences to a dazzling display of ever-changing views, including the passage of day and night.

Although illuminated displays were very fashionable, the entertainment with the widest appeal was the magic lantern. Showmen travelled around Europe delighting and amazing young and old, rich and poor alike with their lanterns' colourful images (see page 12).

The most famous lanternist was Étienne Robert (known as Robertson), whose *Phantasmagoria* (1798) was the forerunner of the horror film. Staged in a theatre eerily decorated like a ruined chapel, this terrifying show used a moving lantern to make supernatural images appear and vanish in the smoke-filled air.

As the public demanded greater novelty, the showmen began to use multiple lanterns to achieve 'dissolving views', in which images slowly faded into or out of sight, or were 'superimposed', that is, overlapped one another. Later, mechanical slides made it possible to move figures or objects within the picture itself. The development of moving images coincided with the 19th-century fascination with machinery and movement. If trains and steamships moved, why shouldn't magic lantern images?

▷ Robertson's *Phantasmagoria* opened in Paris during the French Revolution. By placing magic lanterns on small trolleys, he was able to make ghosts, skeletons and monstrous faces grow and diminish on translucent screens placed around a ruined monastery chapel. He also used shutters to make them vanish in a terrifying flash of lightning.

THE MAGIC LANTERN

The magic lantern was one of the most important machines in the story of the cinema – an ancestor of both the movie camera and the projector.

CAPTURING IMAGES

Its origins lay in 8th-century China. A group of scientists observed that light passing through a small hole in a window blind cast an inverted, or upside down, image of the scene outside on to the wall of the room in which they were sitting. Six hundred years later, the great Italian painter and inventor Leonardo da Vinci designed the *camera obscura*, (which means 'dark room') using this observation. The first practical *camera obscura* was built by Battista della Porta in 1558. Artists were soon using the device to trace realistic backgrounds and dimensions for their paintings, and later it was used as a new form of entertainment.

The first *camera obscuras* were light-proof boxes, but later examples were darkened rooms equipped with mirror lenses which cast, or projected, scenic views on to a screen placed on a tabletop. Over the next 250 years, scientists attempted to make lasting impressions of the images held inside the *camera obscura*, experimenting with a variety of light-sensitive chemicals. The first permanent pictures were produced by Nicéphore Niepce in 1826, although photography did not become widely popular until Louis Daguerre perfected a process using metal plates 11 years later. In 1840 William Fox Talbot devised a method of reproducing photographs from negatives which were then printed on specially prepared paper. Eventually these images were called photographs and the ingenious box that 'captured' them became known simply as the camera.

PROJECTING IMAGES

In the mid-17th century a priest named Athanasius Kircher described, in his book *The Great Art of Light and Shade*, how the main parts of the *camera obscura* could be brought together in a single device to project images from a transparent slide on to a wall or screen.

Kircher's idea was developed by a Dutch scientist, Christiaan Huygens, who in 1659 added focusing lenses to ensure that the images were as clear and as bright as possible. In 1666 Thomas Walgenstein gave the first magic lantern show in Denmark. It would take another 200 years for inventors to discover how the magic lantern could be modified to project moving pictures.

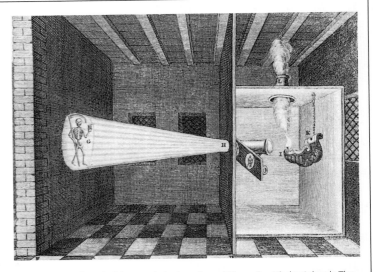

△ A drawing of a primitive magic lantern from Athanasius Kircher's book *The Great Art of Light and Shade* (1671). He based his ideas on his observation that an object placed on a mirror cast a faint shadow when a light was shone upon it. But his apparatus had no lens, which suggests that he did not fully understand the principles of projection.

▷ Magic lantern shows were a popular form of entertainment for over 250 years. By the 1880s highly sophisticated shows were being staged by teams of operators using lanterns with up to three separate lenses. These shows continued to attract audiences until the 1920s, long after the coming of films.

Persistence of vision

Try waving a torch around in a darkened room; can you see the trail it leaves behind? Similarly, stare at a window or a bright object and then close your eyes; can you see a momentary image of whatever you have been looking at?

This illusion had first been observed by the Ancient Egyptians. They believed that the eye retained an image of an object for a fleeting moment after it had been removed from sight (in fact we now know that it is the brain and not the eye that has this ability). In 1765 a French physicist, the Chevalier d'Arcy, whirled a torch made from a glowing piece of coal to demonstrate this observation.

This phenomenon was first called 'persistence of vision' in 1824 by Peter Roget, the author of the famous *Roget's Thesaurus*. Persistence of vision allows us to see a series or sequence of separate still images as a single, continuous action. The whole process of making and watching films depends on this principle.

In the 19th century, scientists in Europe made use of persistence of vision to make drawings appear to move by running them together in rapid succession. Many produced delightful optical toys which showed comic or acrobatic scenes (see pages 14 and 15). These toys were too expensive for most children, however, as many of them had to work for their living in factories or mines.

Projecting pictures

Today it is hard to imagine that simple toys like the Thaumatrope, Phenakistoscope and Zoetrope could have played such a key role in the coming of motion pictures, particularly as they could only be viewed by a few people at a time. Yet showmen and inventors alike were soon seeking ways of combining them with magic lanterns.

An Austrian baron, Franz von Uchatius, was the first to project moving pictures in 1853. However, his Projecting Phenakistoscope produced blurred images. The problem was solved by L. S. Beale, who devised a six-frame slide called a Choreutoscope. This slide briefly held each picture before the projecting lens and then used a shutter to block the light until a system of gears slid the next image into place. Incredibly, nothing has since been found to better this stop-start process – known as intermittent movement – and it is still employed in even the most up-to-date cameras and projectors.

A French artist Émile Reynaud pioneered an alternative projector called the Praxinoscope. Based on the Zoetrope, it used mirrors placed at the centre of the drum to project images on to miniature stage sets. In 1892 he constructed a full-size version, with which he presented his Illuminated Pantomimes at the Optical Theatre in Paris. Complete with musical accompaniment, these charming shows are considered to be the earliest animated films. His first programme was made up of *The Clown and his Dogs*, *Poor Pierrot*, and *A Good Glass of Beer*. Each 15-minute story required hundreds of hand-drawn colour pictures, which took weeks to complete. It was Reynaud's misfortune that, just when he was perfecting his technique, other inventors were exploring ways of producing more realistic moving images using photographic sequences.

◁ Reynaud's Optical Theatre show opened in Paris in 1892 with three hand-drawn short films. Although he later made photographic films, he could not meet the demand for new pictures and went out of business. Shortly before his death, he smashed his apparatus and threw his films into the River Seine.

OPTICAL TOYS AND HOW TO MAKE THEM

Despite their complicated names, the toys described here relied on the simplest optical illusions, which you can easily recreate.

THE THAUMATROPE

The first and simplest optical device to go on sale was the Thaumatrope (meaning 'spinning wonder'). It was invented by Dr John Paris in 1826, and was made up of a cardboard disc with a picture on each side and string handles at either end. When the disc was spun round, the separate drawings merged into a single image.

TO MAKE YOUR OWN THAUMATROPE

1 Copy the drawings here and stick one on to each side of a cardboard disc – making sure that the umbrella remains upside down!
2 Carefully punch holes through the two small circles at each side of the disc and thread a piece of wool or string through them to form the handles.
3 Spin the card on the handles and the woman will appear beneath her umbrella. Try it again with your own drawings.

THE PHENAKISTOSCOPE

Produced by Joseph Plateau in Belgium in 1832, the Phenakistoscope (meaning 'untruthful spinner') was a disc with notches around its outer edge beneath which were a series of drawings. When the disc was rotated and viewed in a mirror through the notches, the pictures gave the impression of animated action. An Austrian scientist, Simon von Stampfer, who knew nothing of Plateau's work, designed a similar device, which he called the Stroboscope. This was made up of two discs. One had a sequence of drawings, the other had a series of slots at its centre. When the discs rotated the drawings appeared to move when viewed through the slots.

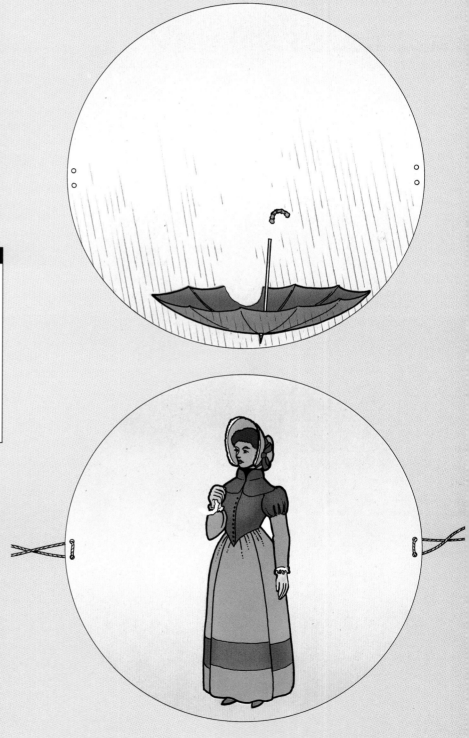

THE ZOETROPE

Originally called the Daedalum by its inventor William Horner, the Zoetrope (meaning 'live spinner') went on sale in the 1860s. This replaced the notched disc of the Phenakistoscope with a strip of drawings which appeared to move when viewed through the slots of a rotating drum.

TO MAKE YOUR OWN ZOETROPE

1 Trace Strip A on to three separate pieces of card each with a 5 mm tab at the right-hand edge.
2 Carefully cut out the slots and form the three strips into a drum shape by sticking the left-hand edges on to the tabs.
3 Trace the drawings on Strips B on to a piece of paper. If you want to produce your own design, make sure that each frame shows a slightly different stage of the action you wish to depict.
4 Form this into a circle so that it fits inside the slotted drum.
5 Ask an adult if you can use the turntable on their music system. Place the drum (with the illustrations inside) on the turntable and switch it on.

As the drum rotates look through the slots. The series of drawings seems to form a single continuous action.

THE FLICK BOOK

The earliest flick books appeared in the 1860s, and contained dozens of drawings showing the varying stages of an action. Following the success of Edison's Kinetoscope (see page 17) a number of photographic devices based on the flick book went on sale in the 1890s, including Henry Short's Filoscope and the Lumières's Kinora.

TO MAKE YOUR OWN FLICK BOOK

1 Find a small notebook containing about 30 pages.
2 Cut out the body, arms and legs of a figure from cardboard.
3 Firmly fix the limbs on to the body with paper fasteners.
4 Trace the outline of your figure close to the edge of page one of your notebook.
5 Slightly adjust the figure into the next stage of the action you wish to depict.
6 Trace this on to the second page and so on until you have filled the book.
7 Flick the pages of the book from the front to watch your 'film'.

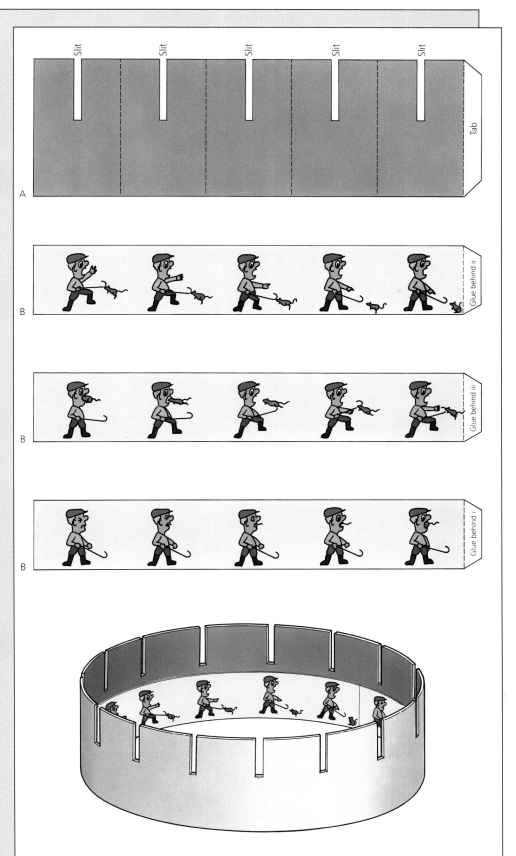

THE RACE TO PROJECT

Although photography had existed since the late 1820s, the development of a camera capable of taking enough photographs to record a continuous action was to be extremely difficult.

In 1870 the inventor Henry Heyl did recreate the illusion of movement with his Phasmatrope, but only by carefully posing each picture in much the same way that you would adjust a cut-out figure for a flick book. Soon afterwards, an English eccentric named Eadweard Muybridge and a French ornithologist, Étienne-Jules Marey (see below), working separately, succeeded in accurately recording movement by series photography.

Muybridge and Marey were primarily interested in natural history, and only experimented with photography to further their research. However, once it became clear that moving pictures had the potential to make large sums of money, inventors and showmen were soon in competition to produce a reliable camera-projector. The invention of strong and supple celluloid film (see box on page 18) greatly speeded up the race to record, reproduce and project photographs in rapid succession.

As with many other developments in early cinema history, it is difficult to credit such a machine to a single person. An English lawyer called Wordsworth Donisthorpe had designed a movie camera as early as 1878, but he ran out of money before he could perfect it. A similar fate befell William Friese-Greene whose story is told in the 1951 British film *The Magic Box*. In 1888 Louis Le Prince, a French engineer working in England, did manage to produce moving images of traffic passing over a bridge in Leeds, using a specially treated paper strip. But he mysteriously vanished in 1890 leaving his work unfinished. Claims have also been made on behalf of many other European and American inventors.

Enter Edison

But it was Scotsman William Dickson, an assistant to the famous American inventor Thomas Edison, who produced the first

---

PHOTOGRAPHING MOVEMENT

In 1872 a stills photographer, Eadweard Muybridge, was asked to discover whether, at some point, a galloping horse lifted all four hooves off the ground at once. Six years later, after many experiments, he succeeded in proving this was the case by positioning 12 cameras along the finishing straight of a Californian racetrack. As the horse passed by it broke threads stretched across the turf, which triggered electromagnets that opened and closed the camera shutters. When the pictures were viewed through a projector based on the Phenakistoscope, the horse appeared to move. Muybridge later developed his own projector called a Zoopraxiscope, and published 20,000 photographs of animals in motion in a series of books.

One man inspired by Muybridge was Étienne-Jules Marey. In 1882 he invented a gun-shaped camera called a 'photographic rifle' which was capable of capturing 12 images in sequence on a disc that revolved when he pulled the trigger. By 1889 he was using the new celluloid strip known as 'film' (see page 18), that enabled him to record 100 images per second.

▷ This picture shows how Muybridge photographed movement. As the horse broke each thread in the row, it set off the camera attached to it.

◁ Étienne-Jules Marey only turned to filming to study birds. Dissatisfied with his 'photographic rifle', he perfected the 'chronophotographic camera' in 1888, which enabled him to superimpose multiple images on to a single frame of film.

1895: the birth of cinema

Leading the way were Louis and Auguste Lumière who demonstrated their Cinématographe projector at a scientific conference in March 1895. Later that spring, Major Woodville Latham showed a boxing film to a paying crowd on Broadway in New York. In August, Birt Acres and R. W. Paul projected several shorts with the Kineopticon in London.

The following month Americans Thomas Armat and Francis Jenkins presented their Phantascope in Atlanta. Finally, just weeks before the Lumières's Grand Café première, Max and Emil Skladanowsky exhibited their Bioscope in Berlin.

Any of these inventors could justifiably claim to have projected the first moving pictures, but the majority of film experts now agree that cinema began with the Lumières's show on 28 December 1895.

movie camera in 1891 (see box on page 19). Edison hoped that a picture machine would have the same commercial success as the light bulb and the Phonograph which had earlier been developed by his laboratories.

Using a camera, which he called the Kinetograph, Dickson shot one of the earliest motion pictures of a man raising his hat and bowing. Two years later he completed the Kinetoscope, a viewer that employed a stop-start motion to wind films past a peephole situated in its lid. These machines were first available to the public only at fairgrounds and amusement arcades, but their popularity eventually led to the opening of special Kinetoscope parlours throughout America.

In order to satisfy the demand for moving pictures featuring vaudeville (or music-hall) stars, comedians and boxers, Edison built the world's first film studio. This was called the Black Maria, because it looked like an American police wagon of the period. Inside this cramped room Dickson photographed such influential early films as *Fred Ott's Sneeze* and *The Rice-Irwin Kiss*.

Convinced that moving pictures would be merely a passing novelty, Edison decided to ignore projection and make a quick profit from his Kinetoscopes. But most people preferred to be entertained as part of an audience or a crowd, whether they were at a sporting event, a theatre, a shadow play, or a lantern show. Others recognized this and continued working towards creating a projecting machine.

▷ The Kinetoscope was a coin-operated viewer that presented 'shows' lasting up to 20 seconds.

Cinema learns to tell stories

Let's return to the first cinema show: the audience has just seen the workers at the Lumière factory passing through the gates for their lunch break.

The next nine shorts followed in quick succession depicting a baby's mealtime, a goldfish swimming round a bowl, a game of cards, a man bathing in the sea, a boat coming into dock, a street scene, blacksmiths working in their shop, and a wall collapsing. Louis Lumière was a skilled stills photographer and shot the action for these moving pictures from an angle that increased their realism. The view of a train pulling into a station was so convincing that the audience was supposed to have scattered in terror thinking that they would be crushed.

The undoubted hit of the show was *L'Arroseur arrosé* (*The Sprinkler Sprinkled*), in which a small boy tricked a gardener into soaking himself in the face with his own hosepipe.

Throughout the following year, the Lumières sent projectionists around the

world, not only to demonstrate the Cinématographe, but also to film views of famous landmarks for later showings in theatres, fairgrounds, lecture halls and

◁ The Lumières's Cinématographe combined a camera, printer and projector, and so brought about the birth of cinema. But it also earned cinema much bad publicity. In 1897 a projectionist at a charity bazaar in Paris accidentally set light to his film stock and 140 people were killed in the fire.

town squares in places as diverse as India, China, Japan, Egypt and Australia, as well as Europe. By 1903 they boasted over 2,000 titles, ranging from domestic scenes to records of news events.

The success of these shows made Edison realize his mistake in neglecting projection in favour of arcade peepshows. He bought the rights to a projector called the Phantascope, renamed it the Vitascope, and launched it as his own invention on 23 April 1896 as the last item on a music-hall programme in New York. However, he soon had competition from many rival companies, including Mutoscope and Biograph, which had been founded by his former assistant, William Dickson. This rivalry was to lead to a series of business wars for control of the emerging American film industry in the early 1900s.

FILM STOCK – FROM GLASS SLIDES TO CELLULOID

The first images to be projected were the pictures painted on to magic lantern slides. These were made out of glass so that the light could pass through the picture and cast it, via the projecting lens, on to a screen. The earliest movie projectors, such as Muybridge's Zoopraxiscope, used a similar method to project subjects from glass discs.

However, inventors soon learned that moving pictures only looked realistic if a minimum of 16 frames passed before the lens each second. Glass frames were not only too heavy to move at a sufficient speed, but also too fragile, and often shattered as they ran through the mechanism of the camera or projector.

In 1885 George Eastman, founder of the Kodak photographic company, suggested that rolls of light-sensitive paper might be more suitable. In addition to being cheaper, the rolls could also capture more consecutive pictures than discs or plates, and offered pioneers, such as Louis Le Prince, the opportunity to shoot lengthy sequences rather than

single actions. However, they also tended to rip, especially when they encountered the sharp teeth of the gears that wound them past the lens.

Eastman then introduced a film roll, or strip, made from a tough, transparent, flexible material called celluloid, which was first used in Marey's camera in 1888. Later that year William Dickson added perforations called 'sprocket holes' along the outer edges of the strip, which the gears caught hold of, to regulate its movement through the camera or

projector and produce a sharp image.

Rolls of celluloid 35 mm wide, known as 'film stock', were used during the silent era. However, such film had certain disadvantages. The earliest stock was made from a chemical compound called cellulose nitrate, which was highly flammable and often caught fire in overheated projectors. It was also very unstable and, if not properly stored, deteriorated into a jelly-like substance. Sadly, many old pictures were lost for ever in this way.

△ Film stock ranges from 8 mm and 16 mm (usually for amateur film-making) and 35 mm (the standard size for much of cinema's history) to 55 mm, 65 mm and 70 mm (for widescreen projection).

THE FIRST MOVIE CAMERA

The Kinetograph, built in 1891 by William Dickson, was the first reliable movie camera. A clever combination of elements from a number of existing machines (including those of Muybridge and Marey), it used a stop-start mechanism. Like other early cameras it was worked by a handle called a crank.

How film passes through a camera has altered little in over a century. A toothed wheel, called a sprocket, catches hold of the perforations at the edge of a film strip and pulls it with great precision through the camera so that each frame stops exactly before the lens. When the frame is in position, a semi-circular disc, called a shutter, rotates out of the way to allow light to enter through the lens and reach the film. Once the photograph has been taken, the shutter drops back into place to prevent any further light from hitting the strip until the next frame has arrived before the lens.

Dickson had to run his film through the Kinetograph at a speed of 40 frames per second (fps) to make a realistic record of an action. Later silent cameras only needed to operate at 16 fps, although the rate increased to 24 fps with the introduction of sound. Most movie cameras still work at this speed today.

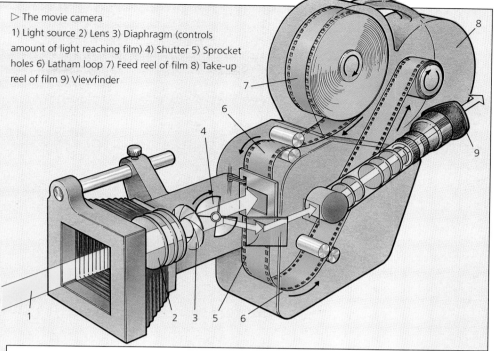

▷ The movie camera
1) Light source 2) Lens 3) Diaphragm (controls amount of light reaching film) 4) Shutter 5) Sprocket holes 6) Latham loop 7) Feed reel of film 8) Take-up reel of film 9) Viewfinder

HOW A PROJECTOR WORKS

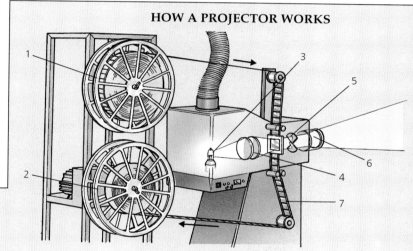

Louis Lumière always claimed that he invented the Cinématographe in the course of a single night when he was kept awake by nightmares and a headache. As with Edison's Kinetograph, he based it on many other machines.

The basic mechanism allows film to pass at regular intervals through the projector, in much the same way as it runs through the camera (see above). However, when the shutter rotates clear, light from inside the projector passes through the strip and casts an image, via the lens, on to the screen. Thanks to persistence of vision (see page 13), the images overlap to give the impression of a single, continuous picture.

A gear in the shape of a Maltese Cross plays a vital part in creating this illusion. It controls the shutter so that it covers the lens while a new frame slides into place. As most early projectors were operated by a crank handle, this shutter often moved too slowly to prevent the black line between each frame appearing on the screen, causing the picture to flicker. Indeed, this was such a common occurrence that movies were nicknamed 'flickers' and many people still call them the 'flicks'.

The first films were usually only as long as the celluloid strip or roll itself. Kinetograph pictures lasted about 20 seconds, while those produced with the Cinématographe ran for up to a minute. The running time could not be extended because longer strips snapped when they

△ The projector
1) Feed reel 2) Take-up reel 3) Powerful lamp
4) Condenser lenses (direct light on to film)
5) Shutter 6) Lens 7) Film strip

were pulled through the camera-projector. The solution was found in the late 1890s by Woodville Latham, who added extra sprockets above and below the lens to force the film into a loop. This eased the tension placed upon it.

Without this 'Latham Loop' it would never have been possible to make longer movies, and cinema would certainly never have developed into the complex form of art and entertainment that it is today.

Méliès – cinema's first storyteller

In the audience at the Lumière première was Georges Méliès, a magician who believed films could be useful in his act. While Méliès was impressed with the realism of Louis Lumière's records of people, places and events, he felt they were short on entertainment. After all, stage plays, lantern shows and Reynaud's Illuminated Pantomimes had taught audiences to expect stories in which they could become involved. So, while he also made actualities (documentaries) and re-enactments of historical incidents, Méliès preferred to produce short dramas in which he attempted to link individual scenes into simple narratives.

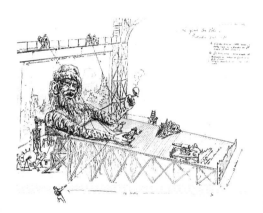

△ Georges Méliès's diagram showing how his moving model for 'The Giant of the Pole' would be operated. *The Conquest of the Pole* (1912) was one of Méliès's most ambitious pictures and shows the lengths to which even the earliest film-makers would go to achieve dazzling special effects.

Méliès was not only the cinema's first storyteller, but also the originator of such popular film styles as horror and science fiction. In making a range of trick films and fantasies, he introduced numerous special effects. Some, like fades and superimpositions, were borrowed from lantern shows, while others, such as stop-motion photography, were unique to the movies. This latter technique allowed the director to stop the action and re-adjust a scene before the cameras began shooting once more. The effect could be highly dramatic, as in *The Vanishing Lady* (1896), in which a woman was transformed in an instant into a skeleton.

Between 1896 and 1914 Méliès made almost 1,000 short films ('shorts'). He appeared in many of them, designed their elaborate sets and was often cameraman, as well as scriptwriter and director. By 1902 his Star Film Company was the biggest in the world, even releasing some of its films in hand-coloured versions. Sadly, only 140 of Méliès's delightful pictures still survive.

The plot develops

The Lumières and Méliès shot their films using a distant, stationary camera to record the action. This technique was soon to become outdated as other film-makers started to explore how cinema could tell a story in its own, unique way.

G. A. Smith and James Williamson, two Englishmen who were part of the Brighton School of film-makers, began moving the camera to follow the action and editing separate shots together into scenes to emphasize a key expression or detail. In *Grandma's Reading Glass* (1900), for example, they included a shot of the old lady's eye to suggest that the action was filmed solely from her viewpoint. This was the first close-up in cinema history.

◁ Frames from Georges Méliès's *A Trip to the Moon* (1902). Loosely based on a novel by Jules Verne, the story follows a crew of astronomers on their voyage through the stars to the moon. The film was made up from 30 separate scenes called 'tableaux'. These were joined together by 'lap dissolves', in which the old scene slowly faded away as the new one appeared on the screen.

▽ The screen's first close-up, from the British film *Grandma's Reading Glass* (1900).

◁ Edwin Porter's *The Great Train Robbery* (1903) transformed the art of film editing. It also contained several other innovations. Porter filmed the action from a variety of unusual angles, and also moved the camera in a sweeping shot called a 'pan' to follow the bandits as they escaped.

In *Fire!* (1902), Williamson became the first film-maker to combine indoor studio scenes with outdoor shots in order to add realism and suspense to the drama. A few months later in America, Edwin S. Porter employed a similar technique in *The Life of an American Fireman*. The following year, in *The Great Train Robbery*, Porter showed that it was possible to edit or 'cut' between shots showing events happening at identical times but in different places, without breaking the sense (or 'continuity') of the plot. This editing technique became known as 'cross-cutting'. It is still the basic method of constructing a screen story.

Another British producer, Cecil Hepworth, applied the techniques of continuity editing to his 1905 film *Rescued by Rover* – an exciting picture about the rescue of a kidnapped baby by a dog.

Hepworth added to the tension of his tale by ensuring that the action moved across the screen in a consistent direction, so that the viewer always knew how close Rover the dog and his master were to catching the kidnapper. The French producer, Ferdinand Zecca, used the same technique in a series of frantic comic chases.

For audiences used only to seeing action filmed in one continuous shot, or 'take', cross-cutting within scenes was at first rather puzzling. For film-makers, however, it was regarded as a major breakthrough in screen storytelling. One man, in particular, recognized that cinema was only just beginning to develop its unique narrative power. In the course of the next decade, D. W. Griffith was to transform the motion picture from a novelty entertainment into a form of art.

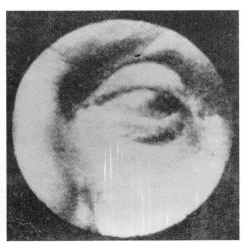

▷ Cecil Hepworth's skilful use of real locations and movement across the screen, and the smoothness of his cutting between scenes, made *Rescued by Rover* (1905) one of the most sophisticated and exciting films of its day.

HOLLYWOOD IN THE SILENT FILM ERA

In 1907 David Wark Griffith was offered the chance to appear in Edwin Porter's *Rescued from an Eagle's Nest*. Although he originally disliked cinema, within a year Griffith had directed 61 short films and was regarded as one of America's most promising film-makers. By the end of 1913 he had completed over 450 motion pictures and was hailed as the 'Shakespeare of the screen'.

Although his work is rarely shown today, Griffith is considered a film-making genius who developed the visual language that most mainstream directors used until the 1960s.

'The father of film technique'

Improving on the techniques discovered by the pioneers of screen storytelling, Griffith broke scenes down into many different shots, varying the distance and angle from which the camera recorded the action to make it more dramatic. He also added to the tension of a scene by gradually increasing the speed or rhythm of the cross-cutting so that it reached a thrilling climax. This method was particularly effective for last-minute rescues, which became a Griffith trademark.

Griffith was an innovator in the field of film acting. He understood that the camera tended to magnify every gesture a performer made, which made them appear to be over acting. The result was often rather ridiculous, especially in supposedly sensitive scenes shot in close-up. Griffith's insistence on a more subtle acting style made his films far more convincing.

Griffith was also prepared to introduce elements from other art forms to improve the quality of his work. He rejected the painted backdrops commonly used in the earliest films, in favour of solid sets similar to those used in the theatre. These not only created a more realistic impression, they also allowed the camera to move between the figures and objects (or 'props') contained within it. This increased the audience's feeling of involvement in the story. As a great admirer of Victorian art, Griffith also tried to compose each shot as a painter would a canvas, filling the screen with items that helped the viewer to understand a character's personality or actions. When he wished to stress a particular object or gesture, Griffith often used a device called an 'iris', in which the entire screen was blackened out apart from the area containing the significant detail.

Although Griffith specialized in making melodramas (see page 88) he also produced several comedies, costume dramas, thrillers, Westerns, romances and 'social message' films, as well as adaptations from the Bible and literature.

The Birth of a Nation

By 1913 Griffith had grown tired of producing films of only one reel, which he felt offered him little scope to demonstrate his mastery of technique. Most producers believed that cinemagoers could not concentrate on a picture for more than 15 minutes, but Griffith was convinced that they could. A year earlier he had watched the audience's reaction to the French film *Queen Elizabeth*, which ran for about 50 minutes, and later the Italian epic *Quo Vadis?*, which lasted for almost two hours. Following a row over the length of his four-reel, 42-minute *Judith of Bethulia* (1913), Griffith resigned from the American Biograph Company to begin work on his first feature film, *The Birth of a Nation*.

Everything Griffith had learned about film-making he now used on this three-hour epic. Tracing the relations between two families during the American Civil War and the period of reconstruction that followed, *The Birth of a Nation* (1915) was easily the most ambitious film so far attempted in America. The battle sequences were particularly spectacular,

▷ D. W. Griffith shouting directions through a megaphone. Checking the lens is his regular cinematographer, Billy Bitzer.

◁ Members of the racist organisation the Ku Klux Klan attack black soldiers in a dramatic scene from D.W. Griffith's controversial film *The Birth of a Nation* (1915).

with long shots juxtaposed, or edited together, with close-ups of the soldiers, in order to place the viewer at the centre of the action. Several scenes were also shot on specially coloured or tinted film stock to heighten their mood.

The Birth of a Nation was such a success that it had made a profit within two months of its first showing. It earned the cinema a new social and intellectual respectability as audiences of all classes flocked to see it. However, it was also openly racist in its depiction of black characters and a storm of protest blew up around it, causing the film to be banned in many American cities.

Intolerance and after

Deeply wounded by this criticism, Griffith hoped to restore his reputation with a complex film called *Intolerance*, which he released the next year. The film contained four stories set in different times and places – ancient Babylon, the time of Christ, 16th-century France and modern New York – and attempted to show, using cross-cutting techniques, how 'truth' had been threatened by violence and injustice throughout history. But the picture was far too confusing for audiences who were only just getting used to feature films, and it did badly at the box office.

Griffith spent the remainder of his career paying for its failure. While later features like *Broken Blossoms* (1919) were successful, he rarely experimented with film technique, and his work became increasingly old-fashioned and sentimental. In 1948, 18 years after directing his

last picture, he died utterly forgotten (like Méliès and so many other cinema pioneers) by the medium he had done so much to create.

The movie wars

When Griffith first entered the film industry in 1907 it was on the verge of chaos. It was still largely controlled by the inventors who had been involved in the race to project. Many of these people were now engaged in a feud known as the Patents War, to decide who had the legal ownership (or patent) of the camera-projector. This legal battle had broken out in 1897 but, in spite of countless court cases, it could not be satisfactorily

concluded as so many individuals had contributed ideas to the machine. In 1909, however, Thomas Edison called a truce so that he could deal with a greater threat to the American cinema – piracy.

When moving pictures played in travelling fairgrounds and amusement arcades, the showmen and women who exhibited them bought each movie at so many US cents per foot of film. However, when the first permanent theatres – called nickleodeons (see page 27) – were opened, the exhibitors could no longer afford to purchase pictures outright if they were to present the varied range of programmes the public demanded. A new player now came on the scene – the distributor – who bought films from the production companies and then rented them to the exhibitors. This three-tier system of producer-distributor-exhibitor ensured the producer's films were screened and that the exhibitor could afford to rent a variety of films. It is still in effect today.

For Edison and the other film producers, back in 1909, the main worry was that there was nothing to stop distributors, or exhibitors, from making illegal copies of popular pictures and showing them without paying anything to their original producers. So, to prevent this practice, Edison and eight of his competitors formed the Motion Picture Patents Company (MPPC). This organization refused to rent films to any distributor

◁ Belshazzar's feast from the Babylonian segment of *Intolerance* (1916). This magnificent set was inspired by 19th-century religious art and the Italian 'superspectacle', *Cabiria* (1914).

THE STUDIO SYSTEM

When World War I broke out in 1914, production in many countries was disrupted because many artists and technicians joined the armed forces. But America did not enter the war until 1917 and Hollywood took advantage of the lack of competition to dominate the film industry worldwide. To complete pictures on time and within budget, the studios began to follow the pattern established by producer Thomas Ince in the late 1910s and operated as film 'factories', shooting feature films with detailed scripts and tight schedules.

Over the next few years the Hollywood-based independent producers used these unexpected wartime profits to purchase their own theatre chains. They were then sure of having American outlets for their pictures and could swallow up smaller production companies. By the mid-1920s five studios dominated Hollywood: Metro-Goldwyn-Mayer (MGM), Paramount, Fox, Universal and Warners. Each of these studios was managed by a chief of production who had made his fortune during the Trust War: Louis B. Mayer, Sam Goldwyn, Adolph Zukor, William Fox, Carl Laemmle and the Warner brothers. These men were nicknamed the 'movie moguls' and they were to control the fortunes of the American cinema throughout most of what is known as the Studio Era which lasted until the early 1960s.

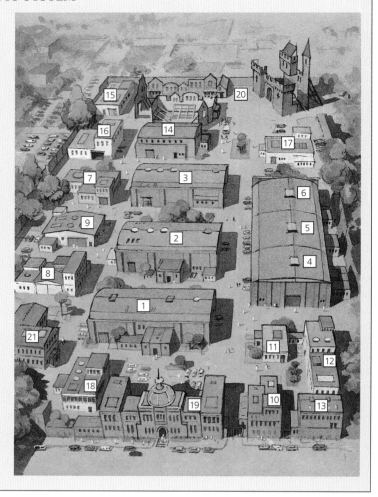

▷ The Studio
1, 2, 3, 4, 5, 6) Sound Stages 7) Paint shop 8) Carpenter's shop 9) Plasterer's shop 10) Administration building 11) Cutting room 12) Laboratory 13) Projection room 14) Rehearsal studio 15) Lighting room 16) Electrical room 17) Props 18) Cafeteria 19) Front office 20) Back lot 21) Writer's office

who dealt with pirates, or handled films made by companies that were not MPPC members.

In response to this, several distributors went 'independent' and began producing their own films. In 1910 these Independents formed their own organization and took the MPPC to court for trying to control all aspects of the film business illegally, through what is known as a monopoly or a trust. The Trust War that followed was one of the most colourful episodes in American film history, with armed MPPC gangs roaming the country with orders to intimidate Independent film crews and confiscate their equipment. According to cinema legend, the film industry only settled in Hollywood – a town known best for growing oranges and olives – because it was close enough to Mexico to allow the Independents to leave the country before the MPPC thugs caught up with them.

In fact, Hollywood offered film-makers many other advantages. It had plenty of sunshine and was within easy reach of a wide range of scenery – mountains, valleys, islands, lakes, beaches, deserts and forests – that could be used to evoke locations just about anywhere in the world. Land was cheap too, and there was a large workforce to draw on for the building and running of the studios. By 1915, 60 per cent of American production was based in Hollywood, and over the next five years its Studio System grew up enabling it to become the film capital of the world (see box above).

Enter the genre

The movie moguls wanted to produce the highest quality entertainment, but they were not keen to risk making films that might not earn any money. To minimize such risks, they began to concentrate on

groups of films called genres. These reused the most popular plots, characters, locations and themes to guarantee box-office success.

Among the most popular genres were crime, horror, comedy, melodrama, action adventure and the Western. The development of each of these genres from the silent era to the present day is covered in Section 3: Subjects and Stories (see page 72). The most important pictures were backed by cleverly targeted advertising and mass publicity campaigns, which focused on the film stars who, by the 1920s, had become the cornerstone of the entire Hollywood system.

The biggest stars of the silent era were Mary Pickford and Douglas Fairbanks. Among the highest paid performers in the world, they were treated as Hollywood's equivalent to royalty after their marriage in 1920. Mary Pickford was known as 'America's Sweetheart'. She usually played innocent young girls in films like *Rebecca of Sunnybrook Farm* (1917). Indeed, her popularity declined when she took on more varied roles because audiences refused to accept that she had grown up. Douglas Fairbanks rose to fame in a series of social comedies, but his charm and athleticism were better suited to such swashbuckling adventures as *The Black Pirate* (1926). In 1919 the couple joined with comedian Charlie Chaplin and director D. W. Griffith to form their own film distribution company, United Artists.

Film in the Jazz Age

America underwent a dramatic change after World War I as the motor car, the radio, the tabloid press and a new style of music called jazz all became part of daily life. The younger generation saw the 1920s as a fresh start and were keen to abandon many of the moral and cultural attitudes that had existed before the war. A key aspect of this social revolution was a more relaxed approach to sex and morality, which Hollywood was quick to exploit.

Actresses like Theda Bara were presented as 'love goddesses' whose private lives were supposedly as stormy as their affairs on the screen. Eventually the glittering lifestyles enjoyed by the top stars earned Hollywood the nickname 'Tinsel Town'. Yet in the early 1920s it was rocked by a series of scandals involving some of its biggest celebrities. Politicians called for an inquiry into the running of the film

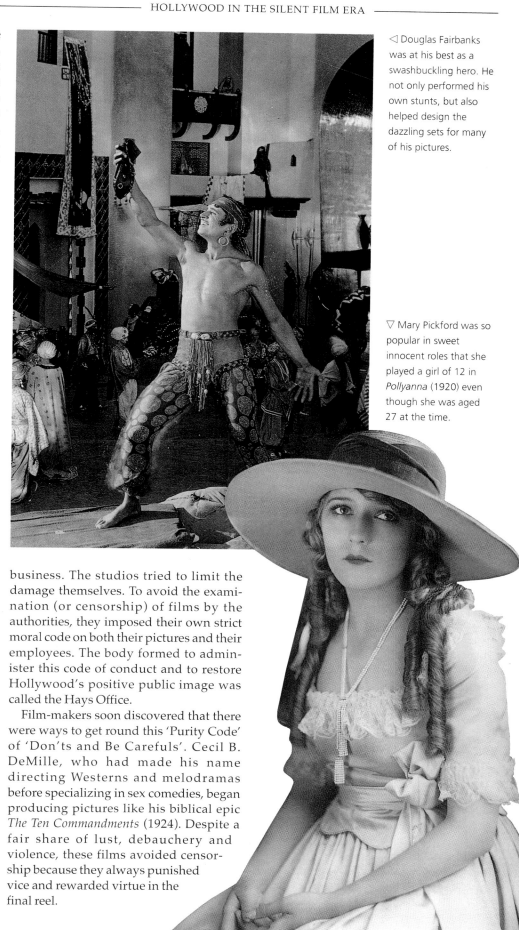

▷ Douglas Fairbanks was at his best as a swashbuckling hero. He not only performed his own stunts, but also helped design the dazzling sets for many of his pictures.

▽ Mary Pickford was so popular in sweet innocent roles that she played a girl of 12 in *Pollyanna* (1920) even though she was aged 27 at the time.

business. The studios tried to limit the damage themselves. To avoid the examination (or censorship) of films by the authorities, they imposed their own strict moral code on both their pictures and their employees. The body formed to administer this code of conduct and to restore Hollywood's positive public image was called the Hays Office.

Film-makers soon discovered that there were ways to get round this 'Purity Code' of 'Don'ts and Be Carefuls'. Cecil B. DeMille, who had made his name directing Westerns and melodramas before specializing in sex comedies, began producing pictures like his biblical epic *The Ten Commandments* (1924). Despite a fair share of lust, debauchery and violence, these films avoided censorship because they always punished vice and rewarded virtue in the final reel.

▽ Robert Flaherty showed how screen storytelling methods could be used to add power to documentary films like the influential *Nanook of the North* (1922).

THE STAR SYSTEM

The earliest American actors and actresses had appeared in films with no mention of their names on the screen. Even the most popular performers were known to audiences only by nicknames like 'The Vitagraph Girl' or 'Little Mary'. But in 1910 the Independent producer Carl Laemmle signed up 'The Biograph Girl' to his IMP (Independent Motion Picture) studio and, by circulating false rumours of her death created such public interest that Florence Lawrence (her real name) was transformed overnight into America's first film star.

Stars soon became vital to box-office success, with their screen images carefully shaped to appeal to the public. The most popular actress types were exotic temptresses, or 'vamps', such as Theda Bara and Pola Negri; frivolous high-society girls or 'flappers' like Colleen Moore and Louise Brooks; worldly women, including Gloria Swanson and Greta Garbo; innocents like Lillian Gish; and girls like Clara Bow who had 'It' – a 1920s term for sex appeal.

Fewer actors achieved equal fame apart from comedians like Charlie Chaplin, Buster Keaton and Laurel and Hardy. However, among the best-known male stars were exotic lovers like Rudolph Valentino and Roman Novarro, fresh-faced 'boys-next-door', such as Richard Barthelmess and John Gilbert, horror specialist Lon Chaney, and cowboys like William S. Hart and Tom Mix. There were also many popular child stars including Jackie Coogan, and animal favourites like the Alsatian dog hero Rin Tin Tin.

The larger-than-life image of these film superstars was reinforced by new movie magazines like *Photoplay*, which kept fans up to date with the careers of their favourite stars, and revealed the 'secrets' of their luxury homes and glamorous romances.

▽ Cigarette cards were popular with cinemagoers from the silent era. Most cards gave details of a star's career and their glamorous romances.

In contrast to DeMille's rather excessive style was the subtle approach of the German director Ernst Lubitsch, who had been invited to Hollywood by Mary Pickford. Equally refined was the Austrian-born Erich von Stroheim, a former assistant to D. W. Griffith who had become known as 'the man you love to hate' during World War I as an actor who often played brutal German officers. As a director he was renowned for sophisticated studies of adultery and satires on Viennese high society that used a technique called *mise-en-scène*. Literally meaning 'putting in the scene', *mise-en-scène* was a further development of Griffith's method of moving the camera around the set to draw the audience's attention to significant or symbolic details.

In order make his films as naturalistic as possible Von Stroheim insisted on great realism, but his studio bosses thought this was extravagant and ordered a number of his pictures to be cut. His masterpiece, *Greed* (1923), was subjected to particularly drastic editing, with only 10 of its original 42 reels being shown to the public. Although the changes did disrupt the film's storyline, it remains one of the cinema's finest achievements thanks to Von Stroheim's visual artistry.

▷ A romantic moment from Cecil B. DeMille's *Forbidden Fruit* (1921). DeMille was one of the few silent directors with box-office appeal. He played a key role in making Hollywood the world's film capital.

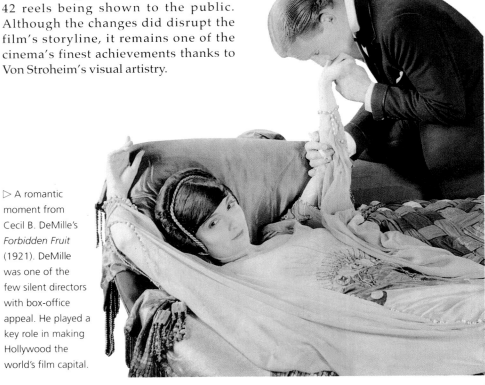

◁ Gowland Gibson and Jean Hersholt in Erich von Stroheim's *Greed* (1923). The original nine-hour version remains the longest film ever produced in Hollywood.

Silence in decline

With the coming of sound in 1927, interest in silent cinema disappeared virtually overnight. The sudden decline of silent film-making has no parallel in any other art form. The public never abandoned classical music, for example, when rock-'n'roll arrived. But the idols of the silent era almost are forgotten and, apart from slapstick comedy and a few epics, their films are now rarely shown.

Yet the pictures produced in Hollywood at this time are some of the most ingenious in its history. Although silent film-makers often used printed cards, called captions or intertitles, during or between scenes to convey important pieces of information, they relied chiefly on visual images not only to tell a story, but also to express the ideas and emotions of the characters. Audiences had to learn the meaning of these signals, but soon understood the significance of certain gestures or objects.

The making of feature films in the 1920s was, therefore, a demanding task and the people who produced them needed to be skilful communicators, as well as entertainers. Although the Studio System offered little opportunity for experiment or personal expression (in contrast to much European cinema) it did support many talented directors. Some, like John Ford and King Vidor, became major figures during the sound era, while others like James Cruze, Rex Ingram, Lois Weber and Fred Niblo faded into history.

The American movie moguls were impressed by the sophistication and artistry of European cinema, and invited continental directors, technicians and performers to Hollywood. The influence of German film-makers in particular shows in the lighting, decor and cinematography of the classical Hollywood style of the 1930s. But few stayed there permanently because they could not adapt to the studios' production-line methods. They returned to make important contributions to film-making in their own countries.

NICKELODEONS TO DREAM PALACES

Cinema spent much of its first decade as a fairground attraction or an item on a music-hall bill. But in 1905 Harry Davis and John P. Harris converted a disused Pittsburgh shop front into a movie theatre, to which they charged five cents – a nickel – admission. Within three years there were 5,000 of these 'nickelodeons' throughout America.

With their hard wooden seats packed tightly together, nickelodeons were far from comfortable. As there was no dialogue to listen to, audiences usually talked throughout performances, cheering and applauding the action sequences.

By 1910 film-going had become a national pastime with the poorer classes, and up to 26 million tickets were sold each week. But it was not until longer films gave cinema the same status as the theatre that the middle classes began to attend regularly.

As the content of films became more sophisticated, so did the places where they were screened. From the early 1920s nickelodeons were replaced by elaborately decorated theatres. The most famous of these 'dream palaces' was Grauman's Chinese Theatre in Hollywood itself.

▷ The Egyptian Theatre was opened by Sid Grauman in Hollywood in 1922. The columns beside the screen were covered with hieroglyphics, while above it ran bands of pictographs.

◁ Grauman's Chinese Theatre in Hollywood boasts a pavement containing the hand and footprints of top performers, including dog star Rin Tin Tin.

EXPERIMENT AND EXPRESSION IN EUROPE

While Hollywood was emerging as the centre of American film-making, European cinema was severely disrupted by World War I. Many countries were forced to stop making pictures between 1914 and 1918, and this helped Hollywood to confirm its position as the film capital of the world.

Georges Méliès was France's leading film-maker during the early 1900s, but his Star Films company soon faced serious competition. The Pathé Brothers became one of the world's largest producers, distributors and exhibitors of the silent era. Their company boasted the talents of the influential comic Max Linder and producer Ferdinand Zecca. Méliès's other major rival, Gaumont, employed Alice Guy-Blaché, the first female director, and Victorin Jasset, a pioneer of the film serial.

◁ An atmospheric poster for Louis Feuillade's serial *Fantômas*. In five adventures made between 1913 and 1914, the master criminal Fantômas (known as 'the Master of Terror') escaped the clutches of the police detective, Juve.

FANTOMAS

Serials and art films

Louis Feuillade was not only one of the first but also the best maker of film serials (in which a complete adventure was screened over a number of weekly episodes). *Fantômas* (1913-14), for example, made eerie use of locations around Paris. Such crime serials looked quite different from the longer, theatre-inspired 'art' pictures produced by the Film d'Art Society. This company was founded in 1908 and filmed important plays for the screen to encourage the upper classes to attend the cinema. Some of France's top theatre performers took part in these expensive *films d'art*.

Films d'art, such as *Queen Elizabeth* (1912) tended to be over-acted and to look stagey and old-fashioned. But they did attract the attention of such top directors as D. W. Griffith. He was also deeply impressed by feature-length costume dramas being produced in Italy just before the war. Following the release of *The Last Days of Pompeii* (1913) directors attempted to outdo each other in the length, splendour and thrilling action of their films. Among the most influential of these 'superspectacles' were *Quo Vadis?* (1913) and *Cabiria* (1914).

The effects of war

With the outbreak of World War I many European film studios were closed down

◁ The great French actress Sarah Bernhardt in Louis Mercanton's important *film d'art*, *Queen Elizabeth* (1912).

▷ In *The Phantom Carriage* (1921), a drunkard promises to reform after seeing the Carriage of Death. Director Victor Sjöström used skilful lighting and trick photography to give the carriage its ghostly look.

because few politicians were able to see that cinema could help boost morale, and, therefore, help the war effort. Instead film materials were confiscated, as some of the chemicals required to make movies were also vital to the manufacture of weapons. Many interesting films were also destroyed as a result.

As Sweden did not take part in the fighting its film industry continued to prosper, producing many inventive pictures. Victor Sjöström's *The Phantom Carriage* (1921) and Mauritz Stiller's *The Atonement of Gösta Berling* (1924) were among the first films to try to show the thoughts and feelings of their characters through visual images. Sjöström and Stiller, as well as actress Greta Garbo, were eventually invited to Hollywood. The leading Danish director, Carl Dreyer, also experimented with bold new techniques. In *The Passion of Joan of Arc* (1928) he used extreme close-ups and dramatic camera angles to show the suffering of France's famous heroine.

▷ The stage star Renée Falconetti in Carl Dreyer's *The Passion of Joan of Arc*. She gave a fine performance, but found film acting so exhausting that she refused to make another picture.

German cinema ... out of the shadows

Germany had made little impact on international cinema before World War I. But in 1917 the government set up a production company called UFA to raise the standard of German films. It was also ordered to show that German people were not the wartime brutes that Hollywood films made them out to be.

UFA's first successes were lavish historical dramas. The best of these were directed by Ernst Lubitsch. In features like *Madame Dubarry* (1920) he showed how the story could be developed by simple and often witty imagery. But these escapist films went out of fashion in the early 1920s when Germany began to experience a severe economic depression. Many new artistic groups emerged whose work reflected this crisis. Among them were the Expressionists, who, like the Scandinavian film-makers before them, attempted to express a character's emotions by means of distorted or unexpected visual images.

Yet only one truly Expressionist film was made – *The Cabinet of Dr Caligari* (1919, see box below). Nevertheless, its disturbing use of light, shade and angular scenery inspired a series of horror fantasies called 'shadow films'. These reflected the mood of despair that existed in Germany at that time.

One of the most influential shadow films was the screen's first vampire story, *Nosferatu* (1922), directed by F. W. Murnau. But the genre's most versatile director was Fritz Lang, who introduced a note of menace into fantasy, crime, legend and science-fiction pictures. The popularity of shadow films faded as the depression lifted. Many of those who had worked on them later went to America, where they had a major influence on Hollywood horror movies.

The camera as performer

The Cabinet of Dr Caligari was co-written by the leading German screenwriter Carl Mayer. He also believed that Expressionism could be used to explore more realistic subjects. He wrote a series of films called 'chamber plays', which explored the hardships facing the lower classes. The finest example was *The Last Laugh* (1924). This followed the misfortunes suffered by a pompous hotel doorman when he is forced to take the post of lavatory attendant.

In *The Last Laugh* Mayer and the director F. W. Murnau used the camera to record events as if they were being witnessed through the eyes of a particular character. This technique was called 'subjective camera'. To achieve it they moved the camera on a bicycle, a fire-engine ladder and even on overhead cables to suggest the doorman's actions. They also used superimposed images, unfocused lenses and distorting mirrors to allow the audience to experience the doorman's bruised pride and, at one point, blurred vision caused by his drunkenness.

Murnau's discovery that the camera could act as a performer was seized upon by Hollywood. So too was the technique of 'invisible editing' pioneered by the director G. W. Pabst. He would cut to a new camera angle while a figure or object moved across the screen. This not only helped to make the cut less obvious but also made the action flow more smoothly. Pabst first used invisible editing in 'street films' like *The Joyless Street* (1925). Such films also relied on detailed studio sets to examine the problems of the poor with gritty realism.

More experimental techniques were explored by 'avant-garde' film-makers like Viking Eggeling, Hans Richter and Oskar Fischinger. They specialized in animated films using moving lines, patterns and shapes. Walter Ruttmann used a similar technique in his documentary *Berlin – Symphony of a Great City* (1927).

THE CABINET OF DR CALIGARI

(Germany, 1919) Director: Robert Wiene

The Cabinet of Dr Caligari tells of an asylum director who hypnotizes one of his patients to commit murders on his behalf. However, as the narrator of the story is also being treated by the doctor, the truth of his tale is open to doubt.

To suggest the narrator's disturbed state of mind, Robert Wiene hired Expressionist artists to produce sets full of distorted shapes and exaggerated angles. They also painted unnatural patterns of light and shade on to the backdrops and used thick layers of make-up to give the performers a more sinister appearance.

The picture was considered an artistic triumph, with one critic comparing it to 'painting in motion'. Although no one tried directly to copy its experimental style, the film's influence can be seen in many German horror pictures of the early 1920s.

Impressionism and Surrealism

The French film industry was in ruins at the end of World War I and had lost its place as a leader of international cinema. But several critics and directors were determined to restore France's reputation for inventive cinema. Chief among them was Louis Delluc. He believed that French cinema techniques had become outdated. He urged directors like Germaine Dulac, Jean Epstein and Marcel L'Herbier to learn from the skilful editing of Griffith, Ince and Chaplin, as well as from the inventive visual style of the Scandinavians and the German Expressionists.

But some artists thought even Delluc's ideas were too traditional. They belonged to the Dada group, which challenged all accepted ideas about art. Their films did not always tell stories. Some were made up of unrelated photographic images. Others consisted of abstract patterns and rhythms that had been painted or etched directly on to the film strip. Examples of this 'pure cinema' were Man Ray's *Return to Reason* (1923) and Fernand Léger's *Mechanical Ballet* (1924), which launched what became known as the Second Avant-Garde.

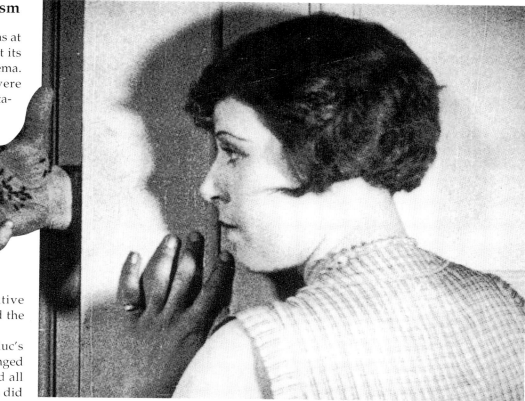

Surrealism also influenced avant-garde cinema. The Surrealists used bizarre and disturbing images to challenge everyday reality. Luis Buñuel and the Surrealist painter Salvador Dalí, for example, made *An Andalusian Dog* (1928), which contained a scene showing an eyeball being sliced with a razor. Buñuel aimed to

△ Ants scurry from a hand trapped in a door in the disturbing, surreal *An Andalusian Dog* (1928), made by Luis Buñuel and Salvador Dalí.

satirize society and shock cinemagoers. René Clair, on the other hand, used Surrealism to amuse his audiences in films like *An Italian Straw Hat*.

◁ René Clair's sparkling comedy *An Italian Straw Hat* (1927) follows a bridegroom as he races around Paris. He cannot get to his wedding until he replaces a hat that has been eaten by his horse.

The French Griffith

Abel Gance was also deeply influenced by the avant-garde. But he earned the nickname 'the French Griffith' for his railroad epic *The Wheel* (1922) and *Napoleon* (1927), which traced the early career of Napoleon Bonaparte. Gance wanted to give audiences a firsthand impression of the fury of battle, so he strapped the camera to a galloping horse's back, to a pendulum and even to a football to suggest the flight of a cannonball. He also pioneered a system, called Polyvision, that used three cameras to record sprawling panoramic views of mountain passes and battlefields. It needed three projectors to cast the images on to a vast screen. Even though it was cut drastically by its producers, *Napoleon* remains one of the finest achievements of the silent era.

Gance combined D. W. Griffith's way of storytelling with the imagery of the Expressionists and the Impressionists. He also made use of a form of editing known as 'montage', that had been developed in the Soviet Union.

Soviet montage

Film had played only a minor role in the lives of most Russians before World War I. But this changed after the Russian

△ The French Army crosses the Alps into Italy at the end of Abel Gance's epic masterpiece *Napoleon* (1927). The scene is shown in Polyvision, which produced a picture three times the standard size.

Revolution of 1917 when Lenin became the leader of the new government. Lenin stated that 'the cinema is for us the most important of the arts'. As a result he sent out film crews on a fleet of trains and boats across the country to shoot, edit and exhibit propaganda pictures which were made to influence people's opinions. These 'agit-prop' films were intended to educate the country's millions of illiterate workers by showing them how the new communist system was going to improve their lives.

The most celebrated 'agit-prop' film-maker was Dziga Vertov, who made newsreels called 'cinematic truth' (*kino-pravda*). In films like *The Man with a Movie Camera* he used dozens of shots that flashed rapidly across the screen to show the energy and enthusiasm of the Revolution itself. Vertov also had to use this busy style because of a shortage of celluloid that limited the amount of footage he could use on any one sequence.

A similar problem faced Lev Kuleshov, a tutor at the newly founded Moscow Film

▽ There were over 100 languages in the Soviet Union, so the new communist government chose silent films to help explain its ideas. In the early 1920s it sent out dozens of 'agit-prop' trains to get its message across to the country's 160 million people.

School. He taught his students how to construct a film by re-editing existing features, like D. W. Griffith's *Intolerance.*

Kuleshov believed that a film's meaning depended totally on the way an audience interpreted the order in which the individual shots were joined together. He proved this by an experiment in which the same image of an actor's face appeared to register hunger when shown next to a shot of a bowl of soup, grief when cross-cut with a picture of a corpse in a coffin, and joy when edited together with a shot of a child playing with a teddy bear. Such linking became known as the 'Kuleshov Effect'. It had a major influence on the editing technique known as 'montage'.

Different film-makers adapted montage to suit their own particular visions. Vsevolod Pudovkin, for example, used the method of linking images in his much-praised film *Mother* (1926). Alexander Dovzhenko, on the other hand, developed a highly poetic style that contrasted beautiful images of the Ukrainian countryside with the harsh realities of life in films like *Earth* (1930).

Sergei Eisenstein

But not all film-makers were convinced that linkage was the best way of constructing a picture. Another Soviet director, Sergei Eisenstein, for example, argued that films would have a much greater impact if the images were edited together with such speed and force that they appeared almost to collide into one another. He put his theories into practice in *Strike* (1924) and *The Battleship Potemkin* (1925, see box above). These films not only abandoned traditional plot development, but also the idea of any single performer

---

THE BATTLESHIP POTEMKIN

(USSR, 1925) Director: Sergei Eisenstein

Set in 1905, this powerful film focuses on a mutiny on board the Russian battleship *Potemkin*, and its consequences for the citizens of the nearby port of Odessa.

Eisenstein's ideas on montage and colliding images were fully explored in this precisely edited picture. Containing 1,346 separate shots (compared with 600 in the average Hollywood feature film of the time), it combined documentary realism with moments of intense personal drama and political propaganda.

The sequence depicting the massacre by armed soldiers of a crowd of innocent bystanders, including women and children, on the harbour steps at Odessa was the outstanding scene of the film. Eisenstein shot footage from different angles and distances. He then rhythmically cut between the shots to draw the audience into the centre of the action. He aimed to make viewers feel like victims of the tragedy, rather than witnesses to it, and so hoped to persuade them to support the workers in their struggle against the old ruling classes of Russia.

---

being the central character. Instead Eisenstein made crowds of people the 'mass hero' of the action. His films were so powerful that many countries who feared Communism banned them.

In 1928 Eisenstein made *October*, about the 1917 Revolution. He wanted to express complex ideas in his images, but his film only confused most audiences. The Soviet government soon turned against any individual approaches to film-making. It imposed a style called 'socialist realism' that stated that a director's main duties were to educate the masses and celebrate the achievements of the Communist Party. This code limited creative freedom in film-making and ended an inspired phase of Soviet cinema.

The end of silence

In just over 30 years international film-makers from Méliès and Porter to Griffith and Eisenstein had developed the motion picture from a novelty into a complex artform. Yet by 1927 audiences, particularly in America, were beginning to grow bored with the visual style and the story-line of the average movie, as well as with the captions containing plot details and dialogue that interrupted the action. The movie moguls were soon forced to turn to Talkies to fill their theatres. As Hollywood dominated international cinema, silent production virtually ceased in the western world within three years. An age of bold artistic experiment was over.

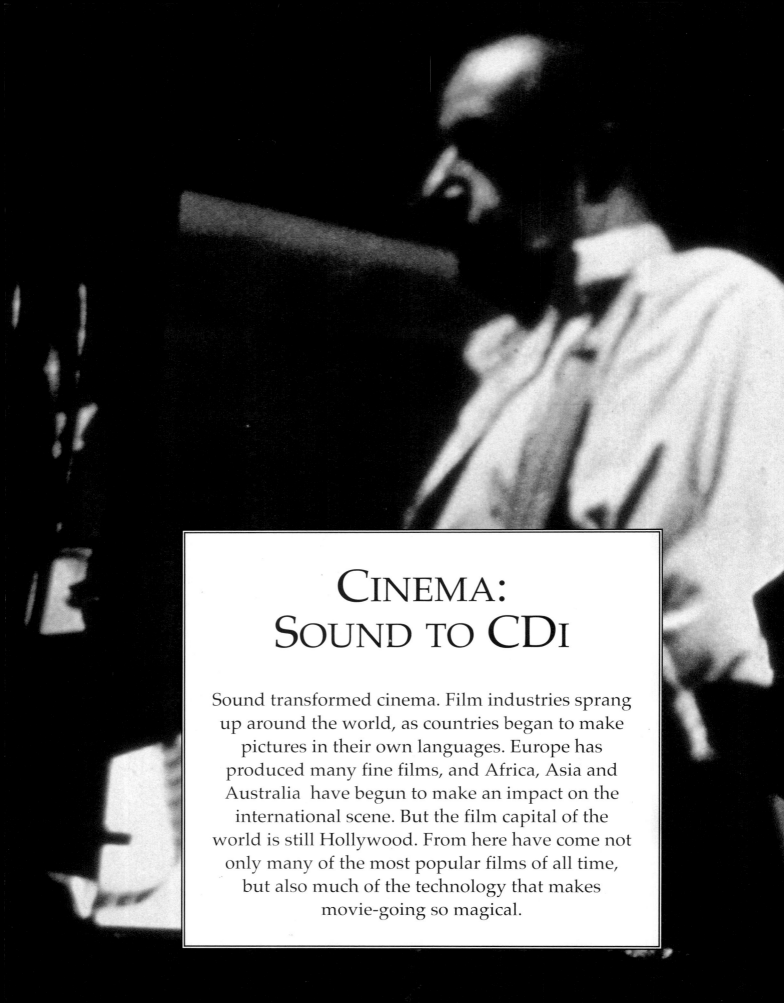

CINEMA:
SOUND TO CDI

Sound transformed cinema. Film industries sprang
up around the world, as countries began to make
pictures in their own languages. Europe has
produced many fine films, and Africa, Asia and
Australia have begun to make an impact on the
international scene. But the film capital of the
world is still Hollywood. From here have come not
only many of the most popular films of all time,
but also much of the technology that makes
movie-going so magical.

THE GOLDEN AGE OF HOLLYWOOD

The coming of sound transformed motion pictures. The movie moguls introduced 'Talkies' to lure back audiences tired of captions and silent film formulas. But they proved so successful that Hollywood was able to enter the most productive period in its history, when its expertly made movies helped audiences worldwide forget the troubled times in which they lived.

Silent movies had never really been truly silent. Even the first film shows had a pianist playing along with the action. By 1920 many movie palaces had their own Wurlitzer organs, sound-effects machines and even their own orchestras.

◁ Greta Garbo in Rouben Mamoulian's *Queen Christina* (1933). The Swedish-born actress was perfect for the part of the 17th-century queen who was forced to give up the throne of Sweden and live abroad.

Sound-on-disc

Cinema's pioneers never intended their films to be silent. William Dickson, for example, had tried to combine the Kinetoscope (see page 17) with the Phonograph (a kind of record player). Several other inventors also experimented with systems that stored sound on gramophone records. Among them was Cecil Hepworth, whose Vivaphone films were quite successful in Britain in the early 1900s. But sound-on-disc was very unreliable because cracks in the record or tears in the celluloid could throw the sound out of time with the image (or 'out of sync'), and the discs had to be changed in mid-film.

Making the sound loud enough for everyone in a theatre to hear it was also a problem, until the American inventor Lee De Forest perfected a way of amplifying sound in 1922. This made it possible for speakers to produce sound that could fill even the largest picture palaces. He also produced a system called Phonofilm, which made it possible to store sound on the film strip itself. Between 1923 and 1927 De Forest made over 1,000 short sound films featuring many famous celebrities.

Over 80 theatres worldwide screened Phonofilms, but Hollywood was still not convinced that the future for the cinema lay with sound. The movie moguls were not keen to spend huge sums of money converting their studios and theatres for sound, in case talking pictures proved to be only a passing novelty. They were also nervous that if Talkies succeeded they would be left with a vast number of silent films that nobody wanted to see. Also audiences in non-English-speaking countries would probably only want to see films in their own languages. The moguls also knew that Hollywood movie stars were trained in mime and might have problems with dialogue. Performers with thick foreign accents like Emil Jannings and Pola Negri or those, such as John Gilbert and Clara Bow, whose voices did not match their screen image, saw their careers suddenly come to an end.

Talking pictures

By the mid 1920s, however, Warner Brothers desperately needed to attract big audiences to stay in business, so Sam

was not the first person to speak or sing on film, but the fact that a fictional character was talking thrilled audiences who were used only to seeing emotions expressed through silent gestures. Jolson's voicing of these completely unrehearsed lines gave viewers the impression of overhearing a real conversation and involved them more closely in the action. The studio originally wanted the lines cut, but Sam Warner insisted that they were left in and the film was a turning point in cinema history.

Learning to talk

Several sound systems were developed, but as the moguls did not want another Patents War (see page 23) they agreed on a single sound-on-film system – the Photophone – that could be used in all their studios and theatres. But even though sound helped the studios overcome their financial worries, it still brought them some artistic and technical problems – for as soon as films began to talk they ceased to move.

The earliest microphones were fixed in one position and their range was so limited that performers had to say their words directly into them, so they could not move around the set while talking. The camera also had to be kept stationary inside a soundproofed booth called an 'ice box', to prevent the microphones from picking up the whirr of its motor. The new sound film strip was also difficult to edit, as the sound signals on the film strip ran ahead of the visual images they were supposed to match up with.

Warner decided to take a risk with sound. In 1926 his studio made *Don Juan*, which was a silent costume drama that included sound effects and orchestral music on a sound-on-disc system called Vitaphone. The film was a success, but the rest of Hollywood was still unsure about sound. Proof that the silent era was really over finally came in October 1927 with the release of *The Jazz Singer*, starring Al Jolson.

Although it contained several songs, the story, about a man who would rather sing on a stage than in a synagogue, was nothing special. But just after finishing one number Jolson suddenly turned to the camera and said: 'Wait a minute...Wait a minute. You ain't heard nothing yet!' He

△ A poster for *The Jazz Singer*, showing Al Jolson in the blackface make-up of a vaudeville minstrel.

▷ A cameraman inside a soundproofed booth used in early sound filming. The lens of the camera poked through the hole in the door. It was very hot and uncomfortable inside these booths, which were jokingly known as 'ice boxes'.

COLOUR

Colour, unlike sound, did not immediately become an essential part of international film-making, and many films continued to be made in black-and-white, or monochrome (as it is also known) up to the 1970s. One reason for this was that most directors preferred the more subtle and atmospheric images they could achieve with monochrome. Colour was also expensive. However, even by the late 1920s a large number of American films used some form of colouring process.

The earliest colour was applied by hand to each frame. Each colour had its own meaning: red for battle or firelight; blue for sadness or moonlight; green for the countryside and sepia (a yellow brown) for building interiors. Sound brought such toning or tinting to an end, because the dye used to colour the film strip spoiled the soundtrack, which ran down the outer edge. Film-makers turned instead to processes in which coloured filters were placed in front of the camera lens.

TECHNICOLOR

The colours obtained with filters were not always true to life and often blurred on screen. In 1917 Herbert T. Kalmus introduced a colour process called Technicolor, in which black-and-white prints were dyed red and green and then cemented together into a single strip to produce a range of colours. This method was used on many silent classics, including *The Black Pirate* (1926). But Kalmus was still unhappy with the quality of the colour and so he developed a new

△ *The Black Pirate*, starring Douglas Fairbanks, was one of the first features made in Hollywood to be shot entirely in colour.

process in which the red and green dyes were transferred to a third print which now contained all the colour and visual information necessary to reproduce the original scenes. Disney's cartoon *Flowers and Trees* (1932) was the first film shot in this new form of 'three-colour' Technicolor, with *Becky Sharp* being the first live-action feature to use the process three years later.

Technicolor, however, not only used three times more film stock than a standard black-and-white film, it also required a specially converted camera, which was only available from Kalmus's own company. So only films with the most expensive budgets, like *The Wizard of Oz* and *Gone With The Wind*, were shot in Technicolor during the 1930s and 1940s.

In the early 1940s a new form of Technicolor called the 'tri-pack' combined the three colour strips into a single layer that could be used in an ordinary movie camera. Within a decade other companies were producing cheaper versions of this multi-layered system and Technicolor lost its hold over Hollywood colour production. The tri-packs in use today are far more light-sensitive and offer sharper, brighter colour pictures than ever before.

◁ The opening scenes of *The Wizard of Oz* were shot in black-and-white to make the brilliant colours of the land of Oz seem even more fantastic.

If films had little movement, they had plenty of talk, as America's top stage performers were brought to Hollywood to deliver lines written by the country's leading playwrights. The studios, however, insisted on so much dialogue that films like *Lights of New York*, which was the first '100% all-talkie', were labelled 'illustrated radio'. Many early Talkies also contained songs to exploit the novelty of sound. But audiences soon tired of this formula and even 'all-talking, all-singing, all-dancing' musicals soon began to fail at the box office. Viewers turned instead to other genres, including the crime film. Sound added to the excitement of pictures like *Little Caesar* (1930) and *Public Enemy* (1931), which were now packed with gunshots, screeching tyres and tough talk. (The impact of sound on the genres is explored in more detail in *Section 3: Subjects and Stories*.)

Sound experiments

Some European directors, like René Clair and Sergei Eisenstein, and a number of Hollywood directors were searching for more inventive ways of using sound. Ernst Lubitsch, King Vidor and Lewis Milestone were among the first in Hollywood to shoot the action silently with a moving camera and then to add the dialogue and soundtrack after filming by means of a process called 'dubbing'. Rouben Mamoulian was even more innovative. He used overlapping dialogue, voices off-screen and non-realistic sound in pictures like *Applause* (1929) and *City Lights* (1931). The introduction of a simple device called a 'blimp' to muffle the noise of the camera, improved microphones, and a new editing machine called a Moviola helped to bring back the action to motion pictures in the early 1930s.

Censorship

Converting to sound was so expensive that Hollywood was forced to turn to banks and other businesses to help finance it. In return, some of these companies, with the support of a number of religious organizations, said that the studios must avoid

▽ Fredric March in *Dr Jekyll and Mr Hyde* (1932). Each time Jekyll turned into Hyde, director Rouben Mamoulian used an ingenious sound effect made up from echoing bells, distorted music and the sound of his own heartbeat.

controversial topics. As a result, in 1934 Hollywood was forced to accept a set of rules known as the Production Code, which was placed under the control of Joseph Breen.

Under this code Hollywood films were not allowed to criticize any religious beliefs or show surgical operations, drug addiction, drunkenness or cruelty to children or animals. Bad language was also forbidden – even words like 'cripes', 'guts' and 'nuts'. Details of robberies and acts of violence were banned, to discourage law breaking, and villains were forbidden to kill cops, although they could be killed themselves. The strictest rules applied to sex. Nudity, romances between people of the same sex or different races and even passionate kissing were all forbidden.

Family films and child stars

In the days before television, moviegoing was a family entertainment, and so films were made to appeal to audiences of all ages. But some types of film were made expressly for younger viewers. The most popular of these were the B picture and the serial. These became an essential part of the Saturday afternoon (or 'matinee') shows, where the audience was made up mostly of children.

But even adults enjoyed films featuring child stars. By far the most famous was Shirley Temple. She made her debut aged four in 1932, and starred in 31 films over the next ten years, including sentimental comedies like *Curly Top* (1935) and *Dimples* (1936). She was so popular that a range of Shirley Temple dolls, dresses and colouring books went on sale.

Child stars were at the peak of their popularity in the 1930s. Some like Freddie Bartholemew, Jackie Cooper, Peggy Ann Garner and Margaret O'Brien appeared in melodramas, but many more appeared in musicals and comedies. Mickey Rooney, for example, played the lead in the Andy Hardy series, as well as starring opposite Judy Garland in musicals like *Babes in Arms* (1939). Classical singer Deanna Durbin was equally popular as a teenage 'Little Miss Fixit'. The success of her films like *That Certain Age* (1938) saved Universal Studios from bankruptcy.

Child stars had to work extremely hard despite the glamour of their lives. Young actors and actresses at MGM, for example, spent the morning at the studio school before starting the day's filming, often only finishing their scenes after midnight. Many children were given pills to keep them awake or to control their weight. Some, like Judy Garland, became dependent on these drugs. Only a handful of child stars remained popular once they had grown up and several found themselves with nothing to live on because their parents had spent all their money. In 1939 child star Jackie Coogan took his mother to court to recover some of his earnings. This resulted in the passing of the Coogan Act, which stated that half of a child's wages had to be saved for them for later years.

◁ A poster for the Shirley Temple film *The Littlest Rebel* (1935). Set during the American Civil War, it was a typical Temple picture in which she brightened up the lives of the troubled adults around her.

The Golden Age

Once Hollywood had mastered how to make Talkies, it returned to producing the kind of high-quality pictures that had made it the world's film capital in the silent era. Hollywood enjoyed a golden age between 1930 and 1945 when the studios produced 7,500 feature films. Most of these were shot in black-and-white, but from 1935 a growing number used Technicolor (see page 38).

The studio system remained largely unchanged as only one major company, RKO, was founded after the coming of sound. Although they had much in common, each studio had its own style.

The studios

The biggest studio was MGM, which claimed to have 'more stars than there are in heaven'. It specialized in glamorous, cheerful family entertainment. Paramount's pictures were very much influenced by European cinema styles. Many dealt with topics like wealth, power and passion. United Artists made no films of its own, but distributed the pictures made by independent producers like Samuel Goldwyn and David O. Selznick.

Warner Brothers was never a rich studio, but it still produced a number of popular gangster films, social 'message' pictures, and musicals. Twentieth Century-Fox also made its musicals, Westerns and costume dramas on very tight budgets. Universal had been one of the biggest names of the silent era, but it was forced to shoot low-budget features after the coming of sound. Its speciality was horror. Columbia was so poor that it survived only by borrowing stars and directors from other studios for its most important pictures.

The stars were the focus of every film, although a good deal of attention was also given to the quality of a picture's script and to its costumes, sets and lighting. Yet the stars no longer received the incredible sums of money they had been paid in the past, and were now tied to a particular studio by very firm contracts. If they refused to accept roles they faced suspension or loan to another company.

In the late 1930s times grew hard for ordinary people. Even the largest studios struggled to attract audiences during the Great Depression. One way to give customers better value was the 'double bill'. The 'A' or main feature would now be supported by a cheaply-made second or 'B' feature. Many B pictures were made by smaller companies known collectively as 'Poverty Row' or the 'B-Hive'. The most

△ A poster for *Gone with the Wind* (1939). One of the most popular films ever made in Hollywood, it topped the box-office charts for 25 years. Behind Clark Gable and Vivien Leigh, the city of Atlanta burns during the American Civil War.

successful were Republic and Monogram, which made on average over 40 pictures a year. Many of these were Westerns, action films and thrillers.

ANIMATION

The animated film, or cartoon, is the oldest form of moving image, dating back to the optical toys of the 19th century. The first cartoon film to enjoy widespread success was J. Stuart Blackton's *Humorous Phases of Funny Faces* (1906), a series of simple line drawings that showed a number of comic expressions. Over the next few years the first cartoon characters like Émile Cohl's accident-prone Fantoche and Winsor McCay's Gertie the Dinosaur became as popular as real performers.

△ Although she was very simply drawn, Gertie the Dinosaur was a big star in the 1910s.

If you think how many drawings it takes to achieve movement for a flick book (see page 15) then imagine how much more demanding movie animation must be, because every second of action requires 24 separate drawings. A ten-minute story needed some 14,400 individual images, so a cartoon took a lot of time and effort to make, especially as the backgrounds had to be reproduced exactly the same for each shot. This technique was greatly simplified by the invention of 'cels'. These are transparent celluloid sheets on which the sequence of pictures required for any one particular movement, expression or gesture are drawn. Each cel is then laid over the background illustration to produce a combined image which is

△ Tom and Jerry fought in over 160 cartoon shorts and won 7 Oscars. They also starred in their own feature, *Tom and Jerry – The Movie* in 1993.

then photographed on to a single frame of film. Until the recent development of computer animation, almost all cartoons used the cel animation method.

Dave and Max Fleischer were among the first animators to use cels. They made series featuring some of the most popular cartoon characters of the 1920s, including Koko the Clown (who began his adventures by climbing out of an inkwell), Betty Boop (an animated woman who was banned by the Hays Office in 1935 for being too sexy) and Popeye the Sailor. George Herriman's Krazy Kat was another favourite, although he lost his place in audience affections to Pat Sullivan's Felix the Cat. Felix remained the most popular of all animated animals until the creation of Mickey Mouse.

◁ The cheeky Felix the Cat was one of the top cartoon stars between 1914 and 1930. He has often appeared on TV since the 1950s, but the film in which he starred in 1989 was a flop.

Each major studio soon had its own animation department making short cartoons, which were shown before the main feature. Walter Lantz created Woody Woodpecker for Universal, while Tex Avery, Chuck Jones and Friz Freleng at Warner Brothers specialized in frenzied, knockabout cartoons (nicknamed 'socko') featuring the likes of Bugs Bunny, Sylvester and Tweety Pie, Daffy Duck, Porky Pig, and Wile E. Coyote and the Roadrunner. MGM's leading animated stars were Tom and Jerry, developed by William Hanna and Joseph Barbera. Hanna-Barbera was later responsible for such television characters as Huckleberry Hound, Yogi Bear, the Flintstones and Top Cat.

Puppet animation was often used to create special effects. The master of the monster model was Willis O'Brien, who designed the dinosaurs for the silent adventure *The Lost World* (1925) and the giant gorilla for *King Kong* (1933). Several of the great names in puppet animation have come from Eastern Europe, among them Wladislaw Starewicz, George Pal, Jirí Trnka and Jan Svankmajer.

△ Bugs Bunny was named after the artist who first drew him, Bugs Hardaway. The rabbit's famous catchphrase 'What's up, doc?' was spoken by Mel Blanc, who also voiced Porky Pig, Daffy Duck, Sylvester and Woody Woodpecker.

WALT DISNEY

Walt Disney started out in animation with a series of short films called *Laugh-O-Grams*, made with his longtime collaborator, Ub Iwerks. In 1923 they moved from Kansas to Hollywood where they produced the *Alice in Cartoonland* and *Oswald the Rabbit* series, but it was their next creation that was to make them famous. This was a black-and-white mouse called Mortimer, who had large round ears and a mischievous personality. By the time he made his first appearance in *Plane Crazy* (1928), Mortimer had been renamed Mickey Mouse. He quickly became a hit with audiences of all ages. He found his voice in *Steamboat Willie* and was soon joined by such familiar characters as Pluto, Goofy, Minnie Mouse and Donald Duck.

Encouraged by this success, Disney began to experiment with animated stories inspired by well-known pieces of music. Among the most ambitious of these *Silly Symphonies* were *Flowers and Trees* (1932) and *The Three Little Pigs* (1933), which were also the first cartoons to be made in Technicolor (see page 38).

As early as 1934 Disney began thinking beyond these short eight-minute films and put his team to work on a full-length cartoon feature. The result was the 80-minute *Snow White and the Seven Dwarfs* (1937). However, in spite of the success of films like *Fantasia* and *Dumbo*, some of the studio's animators were unhappy with Disney's methods. In 1941 a number of artists left to form their own company, United Productions of America (UPA). Introducing such characters as Mr Magoo and Gerald McBoing Boing, UPA's films relied on a simpler drawing style and were often more inventive.

The Disney studio took some time to recover from this loss. It branched out into the production of live-action features such as *Treasure Island* (1950) and 'True-Life Adventure' documentaries like *The Living Desert* (1953). In 1954 it launched the weekly TV series *The Wonderful World of Disney*.

Walt Disney died in 1966, but some 30 years later the empire that bears his name is bigger than ever. In recent years *Beauty and the Beast* (1991), *Aladdin* (1992) and *The Lion King* (1994) have all in turn been the most profitable animated film ever made.

▷ Costing $1.5 million, *Snow White and the Seven Dwarfs* was known as 'Disney's Folly' because so few in Hollywood believed it would do well at the box office. However, the blend of romance, comedy, music and terror was so perfect that almost 60 years after its release it remains among the most popular of all Disney animated films.

THE RISE OF NATIONAL CINEMAS

Talkies threatened to loosen America's hold over world cinema. They gave non-English speaking countries the chance to build up film industries that could make pictures in their own languages. In an age of fierce national pride, cinema soon became an important way of reflecting and controlling public opinion.

European directors adapted to sound more quickly than directors in Hollywood. American producers believed that audiences could only understand a sound if they actually saw its source on the screen. But film-makers in Europe like Eisenstein and Clair believed they could explore the artistic possibilities of sound, just as they had experimented with images in the silent era. Clair, for example, made clever use of off-screen dialogue, songs and sound effects to heighten the on-screen action in such sparkling comedies as *Under the Roofs of Paris* (1929). Other talented directors were also soon making inventive use of sound, including Alfred Hitchcock in *Blackmail* (1929), Josef von Sternberg in *The Blue Angel* (1930) and Fritz Lang in *M* (1931).

At first, Hollywood managed to recover its world dominance by remaking its most important films with foreign actors. It soon found that it was cheaper simply to add, or 'dub', the dialogue into the appropriate language, or to print subtitles on to the film itself. Yet in spite of the competition from Hollywood, many other film industries began to develop distinctive national styles.

French film: poetry and realism

French cinema was the most individual. As directors were not restricted by studio or government policies they could continue to experiment with the bold blend of the real and the surreal, the poetic

and the shocking that had been a feature of the work of French art cinema in the late 1920s. Among the best films were Jean Vigo's surreal story of schoolboy revolt, *Zero for Conduct* (1933) and *L'Atalante* (1934), a romance set on a river barge that was an inspired mix of fantasy and reality.

Vigo's work influenced the style that was to dominate French film-making for the rest of the decade. The style was called poetic realism because directors showed that there was as much poetry and drama in the everyday lives of ordinary people as there was in glamorous Hollywood pictures. France also had a new government which promised reforms to improve people's living standards. Pictures like Jacques Feyder's *Carnival in Flanders* and Marcel Pagnol's 'Marius' trilogy reflected the nation's optimism and confidence in the early 1930s.

But as World War II loomed France became more pessimistic, and its films showed this mood. One of these so-called 'fatalistic' films was Julien Duvivier's *Pépé le Moko* (1937), starring Jean Gabin. This popular actor was to became a symbol of French gloominess for the rest of the 1930s. He also starred in Marcel Carné's *Port of Shadows* (1938) and *Daybreak* (1939). These sombre films traced the final hours of ordinary, decent people who were powerless to prevent their fate. They were later blamed for convincing the French nation that it was doomed to defeat by the Nazis long before World War II actually began.

◁ Marlene Dietrich as Lola, the nightclub singer who ruins the life of a schoolteacher (Emil Jannings), in Josef von Sternberg's *The Blue Angel* (1930). Later that year Dietrich went to Hollywood where she became one of the most glamorous stars of the Golden Age.

◁ Jean Gabin in *Daybreak* (1939), co-written by Marcel Carné and the poet Jacques Prévert. Gabin plays a worker who hides from the police in an attic and recalls the events that led him to become a killer.

The finest French pictures of the time were directed by Jean Renoir, the son of the Impressionist painter Auguste Renoir. He started his career in the late silent era and through films like *Boudu Saved from Drowning* (1932), *Toni* (1934) and *The Human Beast* (1938) became one of France's most versatile film-makers.

His greatest achievements were *Grand Illusion* (1937, see page 120) and *The Rules of the Game* (1938), which tried to show that

European civilization was on the verge of collapse. In making these films Renoir perfected a technique known as *mise-en-scène*. He placed the viewer at the heart of the action by recording scenes in long takes using deep-focus photography which kept all parts of the shot in sharp focus. This method was to have a dramatic effect on world cinema (see page 58).

A brief British boom

For a brief period in the middle of the 1930s Hollywood's most serious competition came from its biggest customer – Britain. But most British movies were cheaply and quickly made, produced only to fulfil the terms of the Quota Act, which stated that 20 per cent of all British screen time had to be filled with British pictures.

Michael Balcon, the head of Gainsborough Pictures, saw that these 'quota quickies' were highly suitable for tackling local themes. As a result he produced a popular series of films featuring such entertainers as Gracie Fields and Jessie Matthews, and music-hall comics like George Formby and Will Hay. He used the profits from these pictures to finance the more sophisticated projects of directors Carol Reed and Michael Powell, who remained major

British film figures for another 30 years. But Balcon's most important director was undoubtedly Alfred Hitchcock.

Hitchcock began his career directing silent thrillers like *The Lodger* (1926). He made his name with the first British Talkie, *Blackmail*, in 1929. This film explored his favourite theme – fear in everyday life. It also introduced the Hitchcock trademark of a famous landmark being used as the location for a film's climax.

Hitchcock was a superb stylist who was deeply influenced by German Expressionism (see page 30). He planned each scene with great precision so that the décor, props, performers and camera angles, as well as the music and sound effects, all added to the tension of the plot. He so effortlessly blended thrills, comedy and romance in pictures like *The 39 Steps* (1935) and *The Lady Vanishes* (1938) that by the time he moved to Hollywood he was known as the 'Master of Suspense'. His first American film was the tense melodrama *Rebecca*, which won the Oscar for Best Picture of 1940 (see page 92).

Alexander Korda, a Hungarian-born director-producer who was based in Britain, was also anxious to achieve American success. He was convinced that if Britain made use of its history and literature, and its wealth of acting talent, it

▷ Alfred Hitchcock (leaning forward) directs Robert Donat and Madeleine Carroll in the spy thriller *The 39 Steps* (1935). Hitchcock hired 62 sheep to make this scene on the Scottish moors more realistic. But they caused chaos and ate part of the studio set.

could make pictures to rival Hollywood. Inspired by the international acclaim for his film *The Private Life of Henry VIII* (1933), he began to expand his studios and invited directors like René Clair and Josef von Sternberg to work there. However, his adaptations of H. G. Wells's sci-fi stories including *Things to Come* (1936), and his imperial adventures like *The Four Feathers* (1939) failed at the box office. By 1938 Korda was almost bankrupt and the British film industry was deep in recession. Only British documentaries continued to prosper.

Documentaries and propaganda

There had been many impressive documentaries (films which show real events or situations) in the silent era. But sound gave the genre a new power. One of the first documentary Talkies made in Britain was *Drifters* (1929), directed by John Grierson. He was the head of several government-sponsored film groups during the 1930's, and he urged directors to try out different documentary techniques. Basil Wright, for example, used a poetic style for *Song of Ceylon* (1934) and *Night Mail* (1936), while Paul Rotha, Arthur Elton and Edgar Anstey experimented with melo-drama and film journalism to draw public

attention to the nation's poor living and working conditions.

In stark contrast were the documentaries made in Adolf Hitler's Germany. Leni Riefenstahl's *Triumph of the Will* (1935), for example, was a skilful piece of propaganda intended to show the power of the Nazi Party. She had been personally selected by Hitler to record the Party's 1934 rally at Nuremburg. She used 30 cameras to capture the various ceremonies and speeches that had been carefully designed to show Hitler as the saviour of the nation. *Olympia* (1938), her account of the 1936 Olympic Games in Berlin, was also attacked for promoting Nazi ideas. But Riefenstahl claimed that her films were works of art, not of political persuasion, or propaganda.

The Nazis also ordered that some fictional films, like *S. A. Mann Brandt* and *Hitler Youth Quex* (both 1933), should contain elements of propaganda. Feature films were also made in the Soviet Union to justify the policies of Joseph Stalin's government and to praise real and imagined communist heroes. But strict censorship prevented film-makers like Eisenstein from tackling such themes in an imaginative way.

▷ An example of Nazi propaganda – the finale of Hans Steinhoff's *Hitler Youth Quex*, in which a boy in the Hitler Youth Movement is killed by communists.

FILM IN ASIA

The wide variety of local languages made life difficult for film-makers in large countries like China and India in the early sound era. Indian cinema soon began to expand, however. Most of the pictures produced were melodramatic musicals called *masalas*. They were based on local legends and the subcontinent's complex customs, and were popular throughout southeast Asia.

Japanese cinema had been among the most adventurous since the silent era. Its studios encouraged their directors to experiment and many developed highly individual styles. Kenji Mizoguchi became known for his long takes and deep-focus photography. He concentrated on the clash between the traditional and the modern, and on the role of women in society in such films as *Osaka Elegy* (1936). Yasujiro Ozu specialized in melodramas like *I Was Born, But...* (1932) that were notable for their realism and low camera angles. In spite of the quality of Japanese films, few were known outside the country. They only gained an international reputation in the 1950s.

depicted the harsh realities of the conflict in the Pacific. Even cartoon characters did their bit for the war effort, among them Donald Duck in *Der Fuehrer's Face* (1943), Tom and Jerry in *The Yankee Doodle Mouse* (1943), and Bugs Bunny in *Hare Force* (1944) and *Herr Meets Hare* (1945).

Many celebrities volunteered to fight, including Clark Gable, James Stewart and David Niven. Distinguished directors like John Ford, William Wyler and John Huston also risked their lives to make combat documentaries. Stars like Bob Hope performed for the Allied troops, and others helped to raise funds for the war.

Many served the customers and performed on the nightclub stage of the Hollywood Canteen, which was opened by Bette Davis and John Garfield. This gave the forces the chance to meet their favourite stars.

German cinema produced some notoriously anti-Jewish films, the most vicious of which was Veit Harlan's *Jew Süss* (1940). Italy also produced some fascist propaganda and entertainment pictures. But in contrast was Luchino Visconti's *Ossessione* (*Obsession*). This started the movement that had a huge impact on international cinema: neo-realism, or new realism.

▷ Soviet director Sergei Eisenstein originally planned to make *Ivan the Terrible* (1944-1946), his life of Tsar Ivan IV, in three parts. But Stalin so disapproved of Part II that it was banned and the unfinished Part III was destroyed. Part II was finally released in 1958.

The world at war

During World War II (1939-1945) films had to provide both information and entertainment. British pictures like *Went the Day Well?* (see page 121) were almost as realistic as documentaries. French cinema was firmly under Nazi control. Nevertheless, Marcel Carné still managed to disguise anti-Nazi feelings in films like *The Children of Paradise* (1945).

Among the best Hollywood war films were *Lifeboat* (1944), Alfred Hitchcock's study of the Nazi menace, and Tay Garnett's *Bataan* (1943), which

▷ A poster for Marcel Carné's *The Children of Paradise* (Les Enfants du paradis), an epic tale of theatre and romance set in Paris during the mid-19th century. Filming was often held up as members of the cast were arrested by the Nazis or joined the French Resistance Movement.

NEW REALITIES AND TRADITIONAL QUALITIES

Cinema was transformed in the period after World War II. A growing number of directors began to make films showing the world around them in a more realistic way. The spread of international film festivals also introduced audiences worldwide to a new generation of film-makers.

'The ideal film would be 90 minutes in the life of a man to whom nothing happens.' This bold statement was made by Cesare Zavattini, a leading Italian scriptwriter and critic. He was one of the architects of an influential style of film-making in the 1940s known as neo-realism, or new realism.

Italy's new realism

Zavattini encouraged directors to abandon melodramatic storylines, and concentrate on the energy and drama that existed in the daily lives of ordinary people. He actively urged them to cast non-professional performers in leading roles and to shoot the action in the streets and houses of the working classes. Finally, to capture the right atmosphere of poverty and pessimism he suggested filming in natural light rather than studio lighting that was carefully designed to glamorize both stars and sets.

The first neo-realist feature to come to international attention was Roberto Rossellini's *Rome, Open City* (1945), which told of the brutal Nazi response to an Italian resistance operation in 1944. Rossellini was forced to shoot on the streets of Rome because the Cinecittà studios had been damaged in the war. He also had to use low quality film bought from stills photographers and spliced (or joined together) on to movie reels, because of the shortage of celluloid. The result was

a film that had the visual texture of a newsreel and the kind of raw power and realism that Zavattini had recommended. Rossellini confirmed his mastery of neo-realism with *Paisà* ('peasant') (1946) and *Germany, Year Zero* (1947), the last of his hugely influential 'war trilogy'.

Following the success of Rossellini's work and Vittorio De Sica's *Bicycle Thieves* (see box above) many other directors began to experiment with their own variations of neo-realism. But by the late 1940s Italy's economic situation had improved and the government declared that neorealist features were bad for the country's reputation abroad. In 1949 a law was passed which effectively prevented such

films from being made. Neo-realism only flourished in Italy for a few years, but it proved to the world's smaller film industries that powerful pictures could be made quite cheaply using local stories, characters and scenery.

∇ A woman (Anna Magnani) is murdered by the Nazis in *Rome, Open City* (1945).

BICYCLE THIEVES

(Italy, 1948) Director: Vittorio De Sica

Written by Cesare Zavattini, *Bicycle Thieves* follows Antonio through the poverty-stricken streets of postwar Rome. He is searching for the stolen bicycle he needs to keep his new job. With him is his son Bruno, who begins to lose faith in his father after he fails to recover the cycle from the thief and his tough friends. Finally, in a moment of desperation, Antonio tries to steal a cycle himself only to be caught. His shame and depression are lifted briefly, however, as Bruno reassures him that the family will survive if it pulls together.

Despite the gloomy nature of its story, De Sica gave *Bicycle Thieves* a poetic feel. He treated the camera as an unseen character which roamed freely about the various locations, adding to the realism of the picture by picking up even the smallest details and gestures in each scene.

△ Soumitra Chatterjee as the adult Apu in *The World of Apu* (1950), the final part of Satyajit Ray's 'Apu' trilogy that began with *Pather Panchali* (1955) and *The Unvanquished* (1956).

Three film artists

Kurosawa was one of four film-makers to bring something new and individual to international cinema at this time.

The Indian director Satyajit Ray was inspired to make films after seeing *Bicycle Thieves*. His much-admired 'Apu' trilogy traced the life of a poor Bengali boy, named Apu, through to adulthood. These films were typical examples of how neo-realism could be used to look at local issues.

The emergence of Japan

Japanese cinema had been producing extraordinary films since the silent era (see page 47). But few people outside southeast Asia were aware of their quality. This changed dramatically when Akira Kurosawa's costume drama *Rashomon* won the Golden Lion award at the Venice Film Festival in 1951.

Set in medieval times, *Rashomon* presents four different accounts of the same encounter in a forest between a married couple and a bandit, which results in the husband's death. Kurosawa skilfully made each storyteller's version seem equally believable by using a mixture of deep-focus photography, flowing camera movements and precise editing. By constantly making the viewers doubt what they had just seen, Kurosawa proved that the camera could lie and showed the power a film-maker had over an audience's imagination. The film was declared a masterpiece, and established Kurosawa as one of cinema's most important artists.

Kurosawa went on to make many impressive features about Japanese warriors, including *Seven Samurai* (1954). He also made imaginative versions of literary classics. *Throne of Blood* (1957) was based on *Macbeth*, while *Ran* ('chaos') (1985) was inspired by another Shakespeare play, *King Lear*. Kurosawa's success helped bring the work of older directors such as Mizoguchi and Ozu, as well as newcomers like Teinosuke Kinugasa and Kon Ichikawa, to wider attention.

▷ A poster for Akira Kurosawa's *Rashomon* (1950), featuring Toshiro Mifune as the bandit and Machiko Kyo as the wife who accuses him of murdering her husband.

△ A medieval knight (Max von Sydow) plays chess with Death (Bengt Ekerot) to spare a family from the plague in Ingmar Bergman's *The Seventh Seal* (1956). This scene was reused for a comic episode in *Bill & Ted's Bogus Adventure* (1991), when Death is challenged to play the party game Twister.

As well as pictures dealing with Indian politics, customs and city life, Ray also made a number of charming children's films. In *The Adventures of Goopy and Bagha* (1968), for example, two wandering musicians were given three wishes and a pair of magic slippers by the King of Ghosts.

The earliest films of Sweden's Ingmar Bergman also used neo-realism to show the difficulties of young lovers in his country after World War II. However, Bergman was the son of the chaplain to the Swedish royal family and was also interested in religious faith, suffering and death. He tackled these themes in an optimistic way in films like *The Seventh Seal* (1956) and *Wild Strawberries* (1957), but later pictures like *Through A Glass Darkly* (1961) were much gloomier in tone.

Bergman later made more experimental films like *Persona* (1966) and *Cries and Whispers* (1972), which focused mainly on women and their personal relationships. Always a gifted storyteller, he touched on almost all his main themes in *Fanny and Alexander* (1982). This film was partly autobiographical (taken from his own life), and provided a magical, if occasionally disturbing, view of the adult world as seen through the eyes of two children growing up in a university town at the turn of the 20th century.

Since the 1920s, Spanish-born Luis Buñuel had delighted in shocking audiences (see page 31). *The Young and the Damned* (1950) brought him back to international attention after a long break from film-making. This powerful film told of the violence and brutality confronting street children in the slums of Mexico City. Buñuel continued to pack his pictures with unexpected and often bizarre visual images. He was an outspoken opponent of the Catholic Church and of the values of the middle classes, which he ridiculed in films like *Viridiana* (1961) and *The Discreet Charm of the Bourgeoisie* (1973).

France: visual quality

France took some time to recover from World War II. As a result, French filmmakers were reluctant to make pictures about the events and the consequences of the Nazi Occupation. Instead they concentrated on highly polished costume dramas and films based on classic books. These pictures placed too much emphasis on lavish sets and sophisticated dialogue, and not enough on visual imagery. The film critic François Truffaut attacked the pictures and claimed they belonged to what he called a 'tradition of quality' as they looked too much like filmed plays. He

▷ Jean Marais and Jouette Day in Jean Cocteau's version of the fairytale *Beauty and the Beast* (1946). The story of a girl whose love releases a handsome prince from a wicked spell was retold by Disney in 1991.

◁ A poster for Jacques Tati's *Mr Hulot's Holiday*. This hilarious comedy helped transform the cinema by ignoring the cross-cutting techniques that had been used in most films since the 1910s.

Tati was influenced by the silent comics Max Linder, Charlie Chaplin and Buster Keaton. He blended slapstick, satire and character comedy in hilarious features like *Jour de fête* ('holiday') (1949) and *My Uncle* (1958). His finest achievement was *Mr Hulot's Holiday* (1953), in which he played the well-meaning eccentric Mr Hulot, whose very presence in a scene almost guaranteed comic chaos. Tati shot the action in long takes from a distance, to allow the people in the audience to discover the jokes for themselves. He also broke with the traditional method of screen storytelling, by building up the film from loosely linked episodes.

British quality

Britain also made highly polished pictures during this period. They were mainly costume melodramas, heroic war films and pictures known as 'Ealing comedies' that gently poked fun at the British character (see page 85). But producers like Alexander Korda and J. Arthur Rank were not content with only pleasing British audiences. They also wanted to succeed in America. They co-produced films like Carol Reed's thriller *The Third Man* (1949) with Hollywood money and stars like Orson Welles and Joseph Cotton. For other films they drew on Britain's colourful history and proud literary heritage. David Lean's version of Dickens's *Great Expectations* (1946) and Laurence Olivier's adaptation of Shakespeare's *Hamlet* (1948) were much admired. But British cinema did not have enough money to challenge Hollywood seriously, even though Hollywood was itself deep in a crisis that threatened its very survival.

called for a more imaginative approach to film-making in which the personality of the director could be clearly seen.

Jean Cocteau and Max Ophüls showed that it was possible to combine personal visions with 'quality'. For his enchanting version of the fairytale *Beauty and the Beast* (1946), Cocteau borrowed from the special effects techniques of Georges Méliès (see page 20) to conjure up the magical atmosphere of the Beast's castle. *Orpheus* (1950), his poetic updated version of the myth of Orpheus in the Underworld, used similar trickery and is generally thought to be his finest picture. Ophüls specialized in witty melodramas like *La Ronde* ('the circle') (1950). These films were good examples of the technique *mise-en-scène* (see page 45).

Two other directors with highly personal but contrasting styles were Robert Bresson and Jacques Tati. Bresson's early work was very much in the style of 'tradition of quality' pictures. But after the war he began to use non-professional performers, and he kept dialogue and props to a bare minimum in features like *The Diary of a Country Priest* (1950).

▷ In Michael Powell and Emeric Pressburger's *A Matter of Life and Death* (1946), a dying RAF pilot (David Niven) appeals to a heavenly court of historical characters to let the surgeons save his life.

WITCH-HUNTS AND WIDESCREENS

1946 was the most successful year ever in American box-office history. But within months Hollywood was plunged deep into crisis by the need to reorganize its studio system, by a change in American viewing habits and by a government investigation into politics in cinema, which became known as the 'Hollywood witch-hunt'.

The cinema had been an American pastime for 30 years. In 1946 alone, approximately 100 million people went to the cinema each week, buying a record $1.7 billion's worth of tickets during the year. Yet shortly afterwards cinema found itself having to compete with several rival forms of entertainment.

Hollywood in crisis

After World War II many Americans left the city centres to settle in the suburbs. While it had once been easy to drop into a downtown cinema, it was now just as convenient to travel to floodlit football or baseball games or to bowling alleys. The money people used to spend on cinema tickets now often went on record albums, electrical gadgets for the home, cars or family holidays. A growing number preferred simply to stay at home and spend the evening in front of Hollywood's most serious rival – the television. By 1954 there were over 30 million television sets in America.

As audiences declined, the studios were also hit by rising production costs and a court ruling that prevented them from operating their own cinema chains. This meant they now had no guaranteed outlet for their pictures, and were forced to compete with each other for screen time. As a result, many expensive movies lost heavily at the box office, and the studio bosses had to cut budgets and sack performers and technicians to save money.

Problem pictures

Many film-makers refused to work under these conditions and left the studios to go independent. Many directors, especially

◁ James Stewart and Donna Reed in Frank Capra's *It's a Wonderful Life* (1946), in which an angel (Henry Travers) prevents a small-town savings banker (Stewart) from taking his own life at Christmas. This sentimental melodrama was the best of the 'feel good' movies that Hollywood produced immediately after World War II. These optimistic entertainments were soon replaced by realistic 'problem pictures'.

△ Juano Hernandez experiences racial prejudice in Clarence Brown's *Intruder in the Dust* (1949).

▷ Ray Milland as the alcoholic author in Billy Wilder's *The Lost Weekend* (1945). The American liquor industry tried to stop the film, because of its anti-drink message.

those who had shot wartime documentaries, no longer wanted to produce purely escapist entertainment. Instead they began to look at problems within American society. These 'problem pictures' were remarkable for the frankness with which they examined such subjects as alcoholism (*The Lost Weekend*, 1945), anti-semitism (*Crossfire*, 1947), and racism (*Intruder in the Dust*, 1949). This cold, cruel side of American society was also investigated in 'true story' crime pictures like *Boomerang!* (1947) and *The Naked City* (1948).

In order to increase the realism of their films, American directors approached their subjects in much the same way as the Italian neo-realists had done. They abandoned artificial studio sets and shot the action on location, often casting less well-known performers in the leading roles rather than big stars. However, even the problem pictures that were most critical of society usually concluded that things would improve if everyone lived according to traditional American values. This idealism was totally absent from a brutal, pessimistic kind of feature film known as *film noir*.

Film noir

John Huston's *The Maltese Falcon* (1941) was the first *film noir* (meaning 'black' or 'dark film'). It introduced a sinister world ruled by greed, treachery, lust and fear. Packed with petty crooks, desperate war veterans, dangerous women (called *femmes fatales*), corrupt politicians and cynical detectives, this world was a place where there was no guarantee that good would triumph in the last reel.

The *film noir* style was best suited to crime stories set in the big city, in which decent people were led astray by the promise of love or money. Many of these stories were told in flashbacks that were linked together by the off-screen voice of one of the main characters. The mood of menace was conveyed by exaggerated camera angles, heavy shadows and contrasts of light and shade that made even the most familiar places seem very threatening.

▽ An example of the shadowy look of *film noir* – Alan Ladd and Veronica Lake in *The Blue Dahlia* (1946).

This visual style was similar to the 'shadow films' (see page 30) made in Germany in the 1920s. Indeed, many of the finest examples of *film noir* were made by film-makers who had come to Hollywood to escape Nazism, such as Billy Wilder's *Double Indemnity* (1944) and Fritz Lang's *The Woman in the Window* (1945). However, there were also many classics directed by Americans, including Edward Dmytryk's *Farewell, My Lovely* (1945) and Orson Welles's *The Lady from Shanghai* (1948).

The Hollywood witch-hunt

Both 'problem pictures' and *film noir* were popular with most audiences and critics. But right-wing politicians were upset by them because they felt they too often glorified the ordinary worker while criticizing big business for being corrupt and uncaring. They also believed that some directors were 'un-American', since they had produced propaganda supporting the Soviet Union during World War II.

As a result, in September 1947 a government body called the House Committee on Un-American Activities (HUAC) came to Hollywood to investigate 'Communism in motion pictures'. Over 40 leading personalities were questioned about people the HUAC suspected of being communists. Among these 'friendly witnesses' were movie mogul Louis B. Mayer, producer Walt Disney and performers Ronald Reagan and Gary Cooper.

Ten screenwriters and directors refused to cooperate and were jailed. Several leading film stars, including Humphrey Bogart, Lauren Bacall and Gene Kelly, campaigned for the release of the 'Hollywood Ten'. However, they decided to back down when the studios threatened to put communists and their supporters on a 'blacklist'. This would prevent them from working within the American film industry.

Anti-communist feeling was stirred up once again in 1951 by Senator Joseph McCarthy. During a second HUAC inquiry witnesses were forced to 'name names', that is betray colleagues whom they thought might have left-wing sympathies. By the end of 1952 the inquiry had blacklisted 324 film artists and technicians, including directors Joseph Losey and Jules Dassin, writer Dorothy Parker and popular stars Paul Muni and John Garfield.

The blacklist resulted in the ruin of many talented individuals, and the 'witch-hunt' created deep divisions within Hollywood. It also severely drained the American film industry of the confidence and creative energy that it badly needed as it searched for ways to meet the challenge of television.

Widescreen technology

In the 1950s television could only provide black-and-white entertainment on a small screen. So the studio bosses decided that the best way to lure audiences back into movie theatres was to offer them lavish widescreen productions in brilliant colour and with stereophonic sound.

The technique of widescreen projection had been pioneered in the 1920s. Among the first systems was Polyvision, developed by Abel Gance (see page 32). But the first widescreen process to appear in the 1950s was Cinerama. This had originally been invented to help train air force gunners during World War II.

Cinerama created a wider screen image by shooting a scene from three different angles with a trio of cameras. These were arranged in an arc and carefully synchronized to begin filming together. The three film strips were then projected from three projectors on to a vast semicircular screen, to produce images six times the standard size. Audiences watching films like *This is Cinerama* (1952) were not only placed at the heart of the action, but also felt as if they were experiencing the same sensations of movement as the people on the screen (see diagram on page 55).

Cinerama was popular with audiences, but it was too expensive and time-consuming to be widely used. The studios

◁ Humphrey Bogart and Lauren Bacall leading a group of film stars, directors and scriptwriters protesting against the investigation into Communism in Hollywood in 1947.

△ This diagram shows how three projectors were used to fill the vast curved Cinerama screen with images up to six times the standard size. The outlined box shows the standard screen size.

next experimented, unsuccessfully, with 3-D (see box on page 56). They then turned to the CinemaScope process, which produced pictures twice the traditional width and also offered stereo sound. It was another product originally developed for war, for use in tank periscopes. CinemaScope 'squeezed' the extra wide image into a standard 35mm frame. The projector was then fitted with a special lens which 'unsqueezed' the image when casting it on to a curved screen.

The first film to use it was Henry Koster's ancient Roman epic *The Robe* (1953). It enjoyed such universal success that within two years the majority of the western world's cinemas had been converted to widescreen. A range of different systems soon became available. Independent producer Mike Todd, for example, introduced the Todd-AO system with the musical *Oklahoma!* (1955). This used wide-angle lenses and 70mm-wide film stock. By the 1960s, however, all the studios had switched to the Panavision system, which gave the sharpest and brightest of all widescreen pictures.

△ The Crucifixion scene from *The Robe*, the first film to be shot in CinemaScope.

3-D

NOTHING IN ENTERTAINMENT HISTORY LIKE WARNER BROS.' AMAZING NATURAL VISION

PUBLICITY ADVERTISING EXPLOITATION

Every amazing scene comes off the screen right at you!

3 DIMENSION HOUSE OF WAX WARNERCOLOR

VINCENT PRICE · FRANK LOVEJOY · PHYLLIS KIRK CAROLYN JONES PAUL PICERNI CRANE WILBUR · ANDRÉ DeTOTH · BRYAN FOY

FLASH! IF YOU ARE EQUIPPED FOR "WARNERPHONIC" SOUND SEE PAGES 6 & 7 FOR THE SPECIAL "WARNERPHONIC" AD. SECTION

△ Vincent Price starred as the mad sculptor in the 3-D horror picture *House of Wax* (1953).

Even early film pioneers like William Friese-Greene and the Lumière brothers had experimented with stereoscopic or three-dimensional moving images. They invented systems in which film strips, tinted red and blue-green, were projected together for viewing through spectacles with similarly coloured lenses.

The first 3-D feature film, *The Power of Love*, was made in black-and-white and released in 1922. In the 1930s polarized filters were introduced, which enabled film-makers to control the amount of light reaching the celluloid. These made possible the experiments with 3-D colour that began in Germany and Italy at the same time.

But only Hollywood made regular use of 3-D in its search for novelty to keep audiences in the 1950s. Arch Oboler's *Bwana Devil* was the first of over 40 features using 3-D produced by the major studios between 1952 and 1954. Most of these were action pictures that startled audiences by creating the illusion that objects such as flaming arrows, pouncing animals, runaway trains and bouncing boulders were coming straight at them through the screen. Unfortunately, viewers disliked the special glasses needed to watch 3-D films, and so attendances dropped. The most recent attempt to revive the process was in 1995 when the action-adventure film *Wings of Courage* was shown in 120 3-D cinemas worldwide.

Widescreen epics

Hollywood believed that widescreen epics were the way to win the war with television. Beginning with King Vidor's *War and Peace* (1956), directors produced a series of 'blockbusters' packed with expensive sets, lavish costumes, all-star casts and often thousands of extras. Films in all genres were made in the widescreen format. But the studios were especially proud of melodramas set in biblical or classical times. They were convinced these would prove the superiority of big screen entertainment over television. At first the formula caught the public imagination, particularly after

William Wyler's *Ben-Hur* (1959) won 11 Oscars. But within three years such spectaculars were abandoned after Joseph L. Mankiewicz's *Cleopatra* – at $43 million then the most expensive picture ever made – flopped dramatically at the box office.

Directors as authors

Film-makers soon discovered that the wider screen gave them the space to combine characters with their surroundings in a single shot. By using deep-focus photography they were able to film scenes in longer takes. Some film critics believed that this made the action more realistic.

Chief among them was the Frenchman André Bazin, who called this new technique 'widescreen *mise-en-scène*'.

Bazin's fellow critic, François Truffaut, was particularly impressed with the way Hollywood directors like Vincente Minnelli, Nicholas Ray and Douglas Sirk made use of this method of film-making. Truffaut had been influenced by the idea that directors should use the camera as a writer would use a pen, to explore their key themes in the most personal way.

Among the film-makers that Truffaut felt were the authors, or *auteurs* (as they were known) of their work in this way were Jean Vigo, Fritz Lang, Jean Renoir, Roberto Rossellini and Howard Hawks.

His favourite *auteur*, however, was Alfred Hitchcock. By always appearing

---

'THE KING OF THE GIMMICKS'

Numerous novelties were introduced in a desperate attempt to make going to the movies a truly unique experience. Among them were a couple of experiments in scented cinema. *Behind the Wall* (1959) was made in 'Aromarama', which used a cinema's air-conditioning system to fill the auditorium with smells linked to the action on the screen. The following year *Scent of Mystery* was released in 'Smell-o-Vision', which produced its aromas by means of pumps positioned between the seats. A more recent example was John Waters's 1981 film *Polyester*, during which audiences could experience various smells thanks to scratch-and-sniff 'Odorama' cards.

But the 'King of the Gimmicks' was director William Castle. He specialized in spoof cinematic processes like 'Emergo', in which a series of wires were used to pass a huge plastic skeleton over the heads of audiences watching *The House on Haunted Hill* (1959). Later that year he launched 'Percepto', which used buzzers fitted beneath the seats to give viewers electric shocks at regular intervals throughout *The Tingler*. Joe Dante recalled Castle's gimmicks and distinctive style of showmanship in the 1993 feature *Matinee*.

◁ Cary Grant tries to escape from the plane that is shooting at him in Alfred Hitchcock's classic spy thriller *North by Northwest* (1959).

The end of an era

Hollywood had changed a lot by the end of the 1950s. The movie moguls had been replaced by the executives of big business corporations. Over the next 30 years every Hollywood studio lost its independence and became part of a multinational, multi-media organization. As a result, box-office success came to count for more than creative film-making. Hollywood remained the film capital of the world, but the boldest and most imaginative pictures were now being made in Europe.

◁ James Dean in Nicholas Ray's *Rebel without a Cause* (1955). Dean's famous jacket was not just fashionable. It also had a symbolic meaning – red for danger.

briefly in his pictures, Hitchcock put his 'signature' on his work. But in features like *Rear Window* (1954), *Vertigo* (1958) and *Psycho* (1960) he also created a film world that was very much his own. Here fear could arise in the most ordinary places and innocent people could become entangled in murder and mystery.

A new method of acting

Many screen stars of the Golden Age remained popular after World War II, along with later Hollywood performers such as Ingrid Bergman, Elizabeth Taylor, Grace Kelly, Marilyn Monroe, Kirk Douglas, Gregory Peck, Charlton Heston and Burt Lancaster. Their looks and glamorous lifestyles were given as much publicity as their ability to act.

The style of screen acting had not changed much since the coming of sound. But, in the late 1950s a new technique known as 'method acting' became popular with young actors like Marlon Brando, James Dean and Paul Newman. They believed that their performances would be more lifelike if they studied the background to their characters for many months before filming started. The result was a depth and realism that had not been seen on screen before.

New World Visions

The 1960s was a decade of enormous change. Exciting new attitudes to sex, fashion and politics were reflected in films, books, music and art. Film-makers everywhere began to reject the basic storytelling methods that had been used for over half a century.

French film-makers, in particular, led the rebellion against the predictable storylines, slick star performances and glossy images found in most mainstream pictures.

The French New Wave

During the 1950s, a number of young French cinema enthusiasts had grown tired of the polished entertainments that were shown at most cinemas around the world. They thought that this style of movie-making lacked energy and imagination and called it *cinéma du papa* ('old man's cinema').

By the end of the decade, a group of critics including François Truffaut, Jean-Luc Godard, Claude Chabrol and Eric Rohmer had begun to make films of their own which proved that motion pictures could still challenge and stimulate as well as entertain an audience. Features like *The 400 Blows* (see below), *Breathless* and *Hiroshima, Mon Amour* (which means 'Hiroshima my love') were all released in 1959. They launched what became known as the 'French New Wave'.

The New Wave directors were inspired by the work of such earlier *auteurs* (see page 56) as Jean Renoir, Roberto Rossellini and Alfred Hitchcock. Many of the new techniques they used, such as shaky footage shot with hand-held cameras, changes in running speed and references to key films in cinema history, replaced outdated film-making methods. Their most distinctive invention was the 'jump' cut. This was an abrupt cut in a scene that disrupted the smooth flow of the action and reminded the audience that it was watching a feature film and not real life.

François Truffaut's *The 400 Blows* (1959) was one of the first New Wave films to attract widespread attention. This realistic account of troubled adolescence was based on Truffaut's own experiences. It was acclaimed for its bold use of long takes and sweeping camera movements. The final shot, in which the action was frozen on the face of his hunted hero, was particularly admired. In *Shoot the Piano Player* (1960) and *Jules and Jim* (1961), Truffaut showed that it was possible to bring polished scripts to life with imaginative visual imagery. His pictures were usually packed with references or 'homages' to his favourite films. Truffaut was so obsessed with cinema that he later revealed many of the secrets of film-making in the comedy *Day for Night* (1973).

Jean-Luc Godard believed that 'a film should have a beginning, a middle and an end, but not necessarily in that order'. He fully captured the rebellious spirit of the New Wave in films like *Breathless* (1959), which broke virtually every rule of screen storytelling. It took themes and styles from the Hollywood B movie and *film noir*. But as the 1960s passed, Godard concentrated less on plots and more on experimenting with ways in which films could make political statements. To achieve this, he developed a new film language. Features like *Weekend* (1967) were filled with interviews, slogans and captions, speeches direct to the camera and shots of the crew actually recording the action. Godard was later one of the first mainstream directors to experiment with videotape.

Many other talented film-makers emerged during the French New Wave. Each developed a highly individual style (except for Louis Malle who tried many different styles). Alain Resnais used elaborate camera movements and extreme close-ups to explore time and memory in *Hiroshima, Mon Amour* (1959) and *Last Year at Marienbad* (1961). Claude Chabrol specialized in sinister Hitchcock-type

◁ Jean-Pierre Léaud as the troubled teenager Antoine Doinel caught stealing a typewriter in *The 400 Blows*. He played Antoine in four more films set at different stages of his life.

▷ A poster for Jean-Luc Godard's *Breathless*, in which Jean Seberg plays an American student who betrays a car thief (Jean-Paul Belmondo) to the police after the thief kills a cop. Cinematographer Raoul Coutard used a handheld camera and was pushed round in a wheelchair in order to shoot some of the location scenes.

thrillers, while Eric Rohmer preferred intimate portraits of personal relationships. Agnès Varda made films from a feminist viewpoint, and the films of her husband, Jacques Demy, paid tribute to the Hollywood musical. Chris Marker used New Wave techniques to make documentaries in a style known as *cinéma-vérité*, or 'cinematic truth'.

The French New Wave ceased to exist as a movement after 1963. But it inspired new waves in film industries across the world. You can still see the influence of many New Wave techniques today in advertisements and pop videos, as well as in mainstream feature films.

Realism and escapism in Britain

British cinema was also transformed during the 1950s and 1960s. This started in 1954 when Karel Reisz and Lindsay Anderson founded the Free Cinema Movement. They produced documentary-like pictures, such as *We Are the Lambeth*

Boys (1958) and *Every Day Except Christmas* (1959), which presented daily life in a lively and realistic way.

British film was also influenced by the 'kitchen sink' stage plays of the late 1950s. These dramas were usually set in the industrial north and dealt with the

▷ Nothing is what it seems in Alain Resnais's *Last Year at Marienbad* (1961). Even the shadows in this shot were painted on the ground. The film is like a riddle without an answer, as we never discover whether the central male and female characters ever met 'last year at Marienbad'.

everyday lives of 'angry young men' who were dissatisfied with their place in society. Some of these plays were adapted for the screen. Many were shot on location to add to their realism. Features like Reisz's *Saturday Night, Sunday Morning* (1960), Tony Richardson's *A Taste of Honey*

△ Just some of the characters that day-dreamer Billy Fisher (Tom Courtenay) imagines himself to be, in the working-class comedy *Billy Liar* (1963).

(1961) and John Schlesinger's *Billy Liar* (1963) blended the best aspects of Free Cinema, kitchen sink drama and the French New Wave. But they soon went out of fashion, to be replaced by features like *A Hard Day's Night* (1964, see page 108), *Alfie* (1966), and the James Bond series (see page 77) which reflected the music, fashions and free-spirited ideas of the 'swinging Sixties'.

Britain at this time attracted several American directors who made important films. Joseph Losey worked with playwright Harold Pinter on some intense dramas, including *The Servant* (1963). A more ambitious director was Stanley Kubrick, who spent his career challenging the conventions of the Hollywood genres. Two of his most acclaimed films were *2001: A Space Odyssey* (1968, see page 114) and *A Clockwork Orange* (1971). The successes of the early 1960s persuaded Hollywood to invest money in British films. But after several expensive flops the studios pulled out leaving British cinema heavily in debt.

Hollywood's new outlook

Hollywood had problems of its own in the 1960s. Shooting in Hollywood itself became so expensive that many American features were made in Europe, where it was cheaper (they were nicknamed

NEW ITALIAN CINEMA

Italian cinema had its own new wave in the 1950s and 1960s, which was labelled the 'second film Renaissance'. Its leading figures were Federico Fellini and Michelangelo Antonioni.

Many of Fellini's earliest films, like *La Strada* (1954), which means 'the road', were influenced by the neo-realist films of the 1940s (see page 48). He became better known, however, for his flamboyant use of imagery in such pictures as *La Dolce Vita* (which means 'the good life') and *8 ¹/₂*. *La Dolce Vita* (1960) was a satire on wealth and religion, and *8 ¹/₂* (1963) was a dazzling fantasy on the problems of film-making. But his next features, *Juliet of the Spirits* (1965) and *Fellini Satyricon* (1969), were attacked for being too extravagant. His later films remained distinctive, but were rather more restrained. Several drew on his past, including *Amarcord* (1973), which recalled his childhood in Rimini.

Antonioni was a master of the technique known as widescreen *mise-en-scène* (see page 56). For example in *L'avventura* (1959), which means 'the adventure', he used details in the landscape of a volcanic island to reveal the emotions of the characters as they search for a rich woman who has mysteriously disappeared. He also developed these themes of loneliness and the miseries of modern life in *The Night* (1960) and *The Eclipse* (1962). In *The Red Desert* (1963) he had whole sections of the town of Ravenna painted red to suggest this sense of hopeless isolation.

Other key film-makers to emerge in this period were Pier Paolo Pasolini and Bernardo Bertolucci. Pasolini made both hard-hitting attacks on society and colourful adaptations of classical and medieval literature. His best-remembered film, however, is a haunting version of *The Gospel According to St Matthew* (1964). Bertolucci began his career by looking at the impact of Fascism on Italian life. But he has since become better known for lavish epics like the Oscar-winning *The Last Emperor* (1987).

◁ Marcello Mastroianni plays a journalist in search of sensational stories among Rome's idle rich in *La Dolce Vita* (1960), directed by Federico Fellini. Mastroianni is one of Italy's leading actors. He also starred in Fellini's *8 ¹/₂* (1963) and *Ginger and Fred* (1986).

▷ Peter Fonda and Dennis Hopper as bikers who 'drop out' of society to find individual freedom in Hopper's *Easy Rider* (1969). The film was a huge hit with teenage audiences. It also made a star of Jack Nicholson, whose performance as a drunken lawyer earned him an Oscar nomination.

◁ Dustin Hoffman as *The Graduate*. In Mike Nichol's daring comedy he plays a young man who falls in love first with an older woman (Anne Bancroft) and then with her daughter (Katherine Ross).

'runaways'). More pictures than ever were based on 'pre-sold' (that is, already popular) sources like best-selling books and hit plays. But even this could not always guarantee box-office success. Many expensive epics like *Mutiny on the Bounty* (1962) lost vast sums of money.

This was because teenage American filmgoers were no longer interested in Hollywood's usual output of family entertainment. They wanted to see something different and producers at smaller studios like American International Pictures (AIP) and Allied Artists (AA) understood this. From the late 1950s they had begun to churn out low-budget science-fiction and horror movies to 'cash in' on, or exploit, youth demand. The king of these 'exploitation' pictures was Roger Corman, who made such films as *Attack of the Crab Monsters* (1956) and *A Bucket of Blood*

(1959). AIP and AA also released dozens of 'teenpics' about high-school life, beach parties and rock'n'roll music.

But still the main Hollywood studios ignored these films and their audiences. They also usually avoided using directors like Sidney Lumet and Sam Peckinpah who had begun to experiment with New Wave techniques. The studio bosses were afraid that audiences would not understand the New Wave's brash new style and would not like the rough quality of its images.

Then, in 1967, a New American Cinema was born with the release of one film – *Bonny and Clyde*. This followed the adventures of two 1930s hoodlums, played by Faye Dunaway and Warren Beatty. The film was packed with effects borrowed from the French New Wave, like changes in running speed and fast, complex cross-

cutting. With brutal scenes like the couple's machine-gun murder, director Arthur Penn introduced a new level of violence to American cinema. The success of *Bonny and Clyde* encouraged other directors to bear in mind the new, more open attitudes to sex and violence. This resulted in pictures like *The Graduate* (1967) and *The Wild Bunch* (1969).

Waves of protest

New Wave techniques were used to increase the impact of films with a political message in many parts of the world. This was especially so in Latin America. In communist Cuba, the country's film institute sponsored a variety of pro-communist pictures, for example Tomás Alea's witty satire *Death of a Bureaucrat* (1966), Santiago Alvarez's powerful documentary about Vietnam *LBJ* (1968) and Humberto Solás's historical epic *Lucia* (1969).

Non-communist countries like Argentina also had lively cinemas of political protest. At its forefront was the Cinema Liberation group. One of its most forceful features was *The Hour of the Furnaces* (1968), which directors Fernando Solanas and Octavio Getino hoped would

make people more aware of the need for left-wing reform throughout South America. The Brazilian New Cinema (*cinema novo*) had similar aims. Its leading figure, Glauber Rocha, combined left-wing ideas, tribal legend and a variety of cinematic styles in features like *Antonio das Mortes* (1969). He influenced other film-makers in the region, including Jorge Sanjinés from Bolivia and Miguel Littin from Chile.

While Communism was associated with freedom in Latin America, it was seen as a force of repression in Eastern Europe. Film-makers were still supposed to work within the guidelines of Soviet 'socialist realism' (see page 33). Yet some of them refused. One of the most important Soviet film-makers was Sergei Paradjanov, who made stunning use of cross-cutting, colour, ingenious camera movements and stylized acting in *Shadows of Our Forgotten Ancestors* (1964) and *The Colour of Pomegranates* (1974). But the Soviet censors decided that his films were politically dangerous and he was jailed. Andrei Tarkovsky and Andrei Konchalovsky also displeased the authorities, but they were allowed to work abroad.

Several young Polish directors, such as Roman Polanski, also chose to go abroad to work so that they could express their ideas freely. But Miklós Jancsó and Dusan Makavejev were allowed to develop their own distinctive styles in Hungary and Yugoslavia respectively.

△ A brutal scene from Glauber Rocha's *Antonio das Mortes* (1969). Set in the Brazil of the 1940s, this powerful film tells the story of a soldier who disobeys his superiors to fight for the poor peasants. Rocha hoped that the Brazilians in the 1960s would also turn against their military government.

▽ Sergei Paradjanov's *Shadows of Our Forgotten Ancestors* (1964) tells a simple story of lovers forced to part because of a family feud. But Paradjanov transformed it into a masterpiece, thanks to his imaginative use of camera movement, colour, editing and music.

New German Cinema

German cinema had produced few films of any quality since World War II. In 1962 Alexander Kluge founded the Young German Cinema movement to encourage more inventive film-making. Many members of this group became important figures in the New German Cinema that emerged in the late 1960s.

Volker Schlöndorff and Margarethe von Trotta were among the first directors whose films attracted attention outside Germany. They later collaborated on political pictures like *The Lost Honour of Katharina Blum* (1975). Schlondörff went on to specialize in adapting novels like *The Tin Drum* (1979), while Von Trotta focused on feminist issues in such films as *The German Sisters* (1981).

The most versatile and controversial film-maker of the period was Rainer Werner Fassbinder. His earliest films like *Why Does Herr R. Run Amok?* (1970), in which a quiet man suddenly kills his family, used very simple visual images. But within two years he was making glossy melodramas that used bright colours and sets full of shiny surfaces to explore the empty lives of the rich and famous. He also made several films on the pressures that arise in relationships, particularly those between people of the same sex or different races. In *Fear Eats The*

Soul (1974), for example, an Arab falls in love with an elderly German woman. Later pictures, like *The Marriage of Maria Braun* (1978), looked at the impact of World War II on German society.

In stark contrast were the haunting, unhurried films of Werner Herzog. Features like *Aguirre, Wrath of God* (1972), *Heart of Glass* (1977) and *Fitzcarraldo* (1982) often dealt with characters at the mercy of overpowering obsessions. The films displayed a fine sense of atmosphere, and were shot in such hostile environments as untamed jungles and barren wildernesses.

The characters in the films of Wim Wenders, on the other hand, seemed to be searching for a purpose in life. Wenders has been very much influenced by Hollywood and has had more box-office success worldwide than any other New German director. Features like *Alice in the Cities* (1974) and *Kings of the Road* (1975), for example, were based on the popular

△ An enthusiastic crowd welcome the Nazis to the city of Danzig in the Oscar-winning *The Tin Drum* (1979).

THE CZECH FILM MIRACLE

Czechoslovakia was a communist country from 1947, and most Czech films had to obey the code of socialist realism. But between 1965 and 1967 its government had a more relaxed approach to cinema. During this brief period Czech New Wave film-makers made some of the most imaginative pictures anywhere in the world. Vera Chytilová's *Daisies* (1966) was a satire on the dullness of Czech society. She used coloured tints, different running speeds and rapid cutting to add to the surrealism of the film.

In his pictures Milos Forman used a mixture of slapstick comedy, gritty realism and the techniques of the French New Wave to attack communist rule. A successful example was the satire *The Fireman's Ball* (1967), in which a small-town beauty contest goes horribly wrong. Forman later moved to Hollywood where he won Oscars for *One Flew Over The Cuckoo's Nest* (1975) and *Amadeus* (1983), his film about the life of the Austrian composer Wolfgang Amadeus Mozart.

Other films like Ján Kadár and Elmar Klos's *The Shop on the High Street* (1965) and Jiri Menzel's *Closely Watched Trains* (1966) poked fun at the subjects and styles allowed under socialist realism. But the New Wave did not last long and Eastern European cinema was back under strict communist control by the late 1960s.

American 'road movie' in which the performers discuss the meaning of life while travelling on long journeys. *Wings of Desire* (1987), a fantasy about two angels watching over Berlin, was extremely successful and greatly increased Wenders's popularity.

Waves around the world

The new waves of the 1960s taught both directors and audiences that motion pictures did not need to have a story to entertain, inform or provoke. They showed that films did not always require clever dialogue, polished performances or high-quality décor to leave a lasting impression on the viewer's mind.

The spread of New Wave ideas was helped by the growing number of 'art-house' cinemas. These were small cinemas that did not usually belong to the major cinema chains. They gave audiences the chance to see the work of independent and foreign-language film-makers. At the same time international film festivals, like Venice, Cannes and Berlin, with their prestigious awards, began to draw attention to the achievements of national cinemas from all corners of the globe.

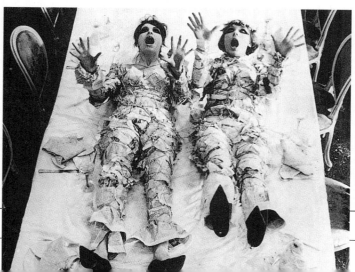

▷ In Vera Chytilová's *Daisies* (1966), two girls named Marie (Jitka Cerhovà and Ivana Karbanavá) decide to play outrageous jokes on the people they blame for making Czech society so boring.

CINEMA WITHOUT FRONTIERS

Hollywood and European films continue to dominate at the box office worldwide. But since the 1970s many other national cinemas have begun to flourish in places like Latin America, Africa, Asia and Australia.

The features produced by these film industries have only recently begun to reach a wide international audience. Film festivals and art cinemas, as well as television and video, have given more people than ever before the chance to see the best of world cinema.

Africa emerges

Films had been produced in Africa since the late 1890s. Egypt's film industry was the busiest on the continent. In the 1920s it was known as 'Hollywood on the Nile'. But the European states that ruled much of the African continent were not keen to support local film-making, so most of the pictures shown in African cinemas were brought in from America, France, India and Hong Kong.

Even after the African countries began to gain their independence in the 1960s, only a handful could afford to support a national cinema. Once again, Egypt led the way. Features like Youssef Chahine's *Cairo Station* (1958) and Shadi Abdel-Salam's *The Night of Counting the Years* (1969) were well regarded for their realistic studies of urban and rural poverty. They encouraged film-makers with similar social or political ideas in other north African Arab states like Algeria, Tunisia and Morocco.

Films made in states south of the Sahara Desert were more popular with international critics and audiences. The driving force behind this sub-Saharan cinema was Ousmane Sembene, from Senegal. His 1962 short, *Borom Sarret*, was the first black African picture to be made on the continent. He developed a thoughtful style that made use of natural locations and non-professional performers. In features like *The Black Girl* (1966) and *Xala* (1974), which means 'the curse', he examined life both before and after Senegal's independence from France.

Sembene's other major theme was the clash between traditional customs and modern values. This subject has also been explored by many other black African film-makers. Among them are Souleymane Cissé from Mali, Med Hondo from Mauritania, Idrissa Ouedraogo from Burkino Faso and Safi Faye from Senegal (the first sub-Saharan woman director). Their pictures have been acclaimed around the world. But they have not always been popular with local audiences, most of whom still prefer escapist adventure films from abroad.

◁ *Brightness* (1987) tells the story of a boy who learns the magic of the Bambara people when his father threatens to kill him. The film was made in Mali by Souleymane Cissé. It is filled with details about tribal customs and magic rituals.

Meeting Hollywood's challenge

Australia had produced the first ever feature-length film, *The Story of the Kelly Gang*, in 1906. But with Hollywood and British pictures filling its local cinemas, there was little demand for Australian-made movies. Between 1932 and 1956 there was only one studio on the entire continent. But in 1970 the government set up the Australian Film Commission to improve the quality of national film-making. Over the next 15 years Australia produced about 400 films, and many of them became hits worldwide.

The finest pictures of this Australian New Wave were set in the early 1900s and used historical settings to examine issues that concern us today. Among them were Peter Weir's *Picnic at Hanging Rock* (1975) based on the true story of the disappearance of some schoolgirls, and Gillian Armstrong's *My Brilliant Career* (1978). The success of these and films like *Mad Max* (1979) and *Crocodile Dundee* (1986) led to many top directors and performers going to Hollywood.

Australia still produces distinctive and imaginative films, like *Strictly Ballroom* (1992). Film-making in New Zealand is also flourishing thanks to the work of Vincent Ward, Peter Jackson and Jane Campion, whose costume drama *The Piano* (1993) was a hit worldwide.

Canadian cinema has also suffered from many of its talented directors and performers going to Hollywood. The English-speaking industry has had only limited success apart from the horror films of David Cronenberg and the satires of Atom Egoyan. French-Canadian cinema, on the other hand, has continued to build on the reputation established by films like Claude Jutra's *My Uncle Antoine* (1971). Denys Arcand's studies of modern life, including *Jesus of Montreal* (1989), have attracted the widest attention.

The view from Asia

India has the biggest film industry in the world. It produces over 900 features each year, compared to Hollywood's average of about 270. Dramas with social messages have been made by directors like Shyam Benegal and Mrinal Sen and have done well at festivals worldwide since the mid-1970s. But Indian audiences still prefer the traditional 'masala musicals' (see page 47), made by the studios of Bombay known collectively as Bollywood.

△ Set in Tokyo in 2019, the Japanese animated film *Akira* (1988) follows a biker with exceptional mental powers as he tries to save the world from destruction.

Audiences in southeast Asia enjoy Indian movies as well. But in recent years many of the region's own film industries have developed, becoming some of the most popular and prolific in the world. Hong Kong specializes in fast-paced martial arts or swordplay pictures, known jokingly as 'chop-socky'. The films of Bruce Lee and King Hu have made kung-fu particularly fashionable. Modern features like John Woo's *Hard-Boiled* (1991) have given the genre a more violent edge. They have also turned Jackie Chan, Chow Yun Fat and Maggie Cheung into super-stars whose popularity rivals that of any leading Hollywood performer.

But not all Asian films are escapist adventures. Directors in Hong Kong and Taiwan have made many pictures with a powerful social content. Among the most impressive are Hou Hsaio-hsien's family drama *City of Sadness* (1990) and Ang Lee's bittersweet comedy of food and family life *Eat Drink Man Woman* (1994).

Chinese cinema revived dramatically in the early 1980s after many years of strict political control. The most influential film-makers were Zhang Yimou and Chen Kaige, who had trained at the Beijing Film Academy. They experimented with colour, the natural landscape and sweeping camera movements to explore China's troubled communist past. They also challenged long-accepted social and cultural ideas. Zhang has concentrated on the role of women in a male-dominated society, as

in *Raise the Red Lantern* (1991). Chen, on the other hand, has focused on the effects of Communism on individuals, such as the opera singer in the prize winning *Farewell, My Concubine* (1993).

▷ Gong Li in *Raise the Red Lantern* (1991), the story of the rivalry between the four wives of a Chinese nobleman. It was directed by Zhang Yimou. Gong Li also starred in Zhang's *Red Sorghum* (1987) and *Ju Dou* (1990).

The European film community

European cinema has produced many noteworthy films and film-makers since 1970. An increasing number of features are co-productions – films made with money and performers from more than one country. Some of the earliest attempts had very dull stories. They were attacked by the critics and flopped at the box office. But award-winning films like Giuseppe Tornatore's *Cinema Paradiso* (Italy/France) and Krzysztof Kieslowski's trilogy *Three Colours: Blue, White, Red* (France/Switzerland/Poland) have shown that co-productions can be successful.

Yet the idea of a thriving national film industry is still as appealing as ever in Europe. French and Italian features remain the most popular films with audiences around the world. But even these countries have rarely made anything to match the achievements of the new waves of the 1960s. Film-making in Denmark and Sweden also still lives in the shadow of the past. Other European countries produce far fewer films, but they have begun to make quite an impact on the world scene.

Eastern European cinema is at a cross-roads. After World War II it was supported

CHINA. 1920. ONE MASTER. FOUR WIVES.

RAISE THE RED LANTERN

A FILM BY ZHANG YIMOU

BRITAIN'S FILM CRISIS?

British cinema has lived in the shadow of Hollywood for most of its history. So even though it has produced a wealth of talent and many fine films, it has always seemed to be deep in crisis. But thanks to the efforts of companies like Goldcrest, HandMade Films and Palace Pictures, and TV stations like Channel 4 and BBC2, the British film industry is, in many ways, better off than it has been for decades.

Many Oscar-winning hits have been British. Some were lavish historical tales like Richard Attenborough's *Gandhi* (1982) or costume dramas adapted from novels such as Merchant Ivory's *Howards End* (1991). Others showed life in modern Britain, like *My Beautiful Laundrette* (1985), *The Crying Game* (1992) and *Four Weddings and a Funeral*, which in 1994 became the most successful British picture of all time.

British performers have done consistently well at the Oscars. Michael Caine, Sean Connery, Ben Kingsley, Daniel Day-Lewis, Jeremy Irons, Anthony Hopkins and Emma Thompson have all won acting awards in recent years. Several British directors have also made a name for themselves in Hollywood, among them Alan Parker, Nicolas Roeg, Adrian Lyne and the brothers Ridley and Tony Scott.

Films which focus on social issues or have distinctive artistic styles have also been successful. Derek Jarman, Peter Greenaway, Mike Leigh and Ken Loach have all directed award-winning work. More features than ever before are also being made in Scotland, Wales and Ireland. And British special effects technicians are regarded as some of the best in the world.

The future of British cinema could look brighter still if it abandoned its dream of competing with America.

◁ *My Beautiful Laundrette* (1985) was a clever mix of comedy and social message. It dealt with racial and sexual prejudice in a run-down part of London.

▽ In this sparkling comedy a tongue-tied Englishman (Hugh Grant) romances a confident American woman (Andie MacDowell) at *Four Weddings and a Funeral*.

by the state, which also protected it from Hollywood competition. Yet film played a key role in the final years of Communism in the 1980s. The films made by Krzysztof Zanussi, Agnieszka Holland and Andrzej Wajda did much to support the Polish trade union Solidarity during the unrest in that country in 1980-81. Since the collapse of Communism at the end of the 1980s, the reorganized film industries of Eastern Europe have suffered from a lack of money.

◁ A talentless rock group tour America and Mexico in Finnish director Aki Kaurismäki's zany comedy *Leningrad Cowboys Go America* (1989).

Crossing the language barrier

The pictures produced by the world's film industries now have a wider audience than at any other time in cinema history. More and more international features are available on video and are shown on TV.

Unfortunately a lot of people are still reluctant to sit through films whose dialogue has either been dubbed or translated into subtitles. They think of these as purely 'art' pictures which could never provide the same entertainment as a big-budget Hollywood movie. As a result many viewers never see films they might really enjoy. As we have seen, pictures made in places as different as Hollywood and Hong Kong, Bollywood and Burkino Faso share many common themes, subjects and stories. Films made in a foreign language do demand a little more concentration, but they very often repay the effort.

KIDPIX AND BLOCKBUSTERS

Since 1970 a new generation of film-makers, nicknamed the 'movie brats', has dominated Hollywood. Their big-budget blockbusters appeal to younger audiences. Action-packed entertainments are released worldwide, with advertising and publicity campaigns to ensure that they succeed at the box office.

Francis Ford Coppola, George Lucas, Martin Scorsese and Steven Spielberg were the best known of this new generation. They were called the 'movie brats' because they had been trained at film schools, where they developed their wide knowledge of cinema history, which influenced their individual styles of directing. Coppola's *The Godfather* (1972, see 'Crime', page 97) and Spielberg's *Jaws* (1975) began a new era of blockbusters.

'Fast-food movies'

Among the most successful were Lucas's Star Wars series (see page 115) and Spielberg's Indiana Jones trilogy. These escapist adventures were known as 'kidpix'. Yet for all their technical wizardry, many of these features were little more than reworked versions of the film serials of the 1930s and 1940s. They rarely challenged viewers to think for themselves, as the two-dimensional characters passed from one spectacular set-piece to another. Even Spielberg himself questioned the quality of such 'fast-food movies'.

Science fiction provided many of the biggest hits, including *E.T. The Extra-Terrestrial* (1982), which remained the all-time box-office No.1 until it was replaced by Spielberg's dinosaur blockbuster, *Jurassic Park*, in 1993. These movies often earned even more money when they were released on video.

△ The poster for *The Godfather* (1972). This was the first box-office blockbuster to be directed by a 'movie brat', Francis Ford Coppola. It was adapted from Mario Puzo's best-selling novel.

New directions

Hollywood directors are now better known to cinemagoers than ever before. Oliver Stone, Jonathan Demme, John Hughes, Ivan Reitman and Robert Zemeckis have all produced popular hits. But they have yet to achieve the 'star' status of Steven Spielberg. He has since been succeeded as the 'wonder kid' of American cinema by Quentin Tarantino. His crime thrillers *Reservoir Dogs* (1992) and *Pulp Fiction* (1994) attracted a lot of media attention for their violence and snappy dialogue.

Some of the most inventive pictures of recent years have been made by independent directors, who prefer to work outside the Hollywood system. Among the best known are Woody Allen, Martin Scorsese, John Cassavetes, Jim Jarmusch, John Sayles and the Coen Brothers (see box on page 69). Independent production has also given more women the chance to direct (see box on page 69).

Megastars

The price of making motion pictures continues to rise. James Cameron's *True Lies* (1994) was reported to have cost about $100 million and was advertised as the most expensive film ever. As a result, producers are willing to pay stars huge fees in order to increase a movie's chances at the box office. By the 1990s Arnold Schwarzenegger was earning $15 million per picture, and even 12 year-old Macaulay Culkin scooped over $5 million for *Home Alone 2: Lost in New York* (1992).

Escapist adventures offer more leading roles to actors than to actresses. Among the stars to have emerged as a result are action-men like Clint Eastwood, Arnold Schwarzenegger, Sylvester Stallone, Harrison Ford and Mel Gibson. There are also many respected character actors including Robert De Niro, Al Pacino, Michael Douglas, Jack Nicholson, Tom Hanks, Kevin Costner and Tom Cruise. Only Julia Roberts, Sharon Stone and Demi Moore have equal box-office appeal. But Hollywood can call on many fine actresses, including Jodie Foster, Michelle Pfeiffer, Meryl Streep, Jessica Lange, Winona Ryder, Geena Davis and Susan Sarandon.

THE SECOND GOLDEN AGE

American self-confidence was very low in the mid-1970s, following its defeat in the Vietnam War and the resignation of President Nixon after the Watergate bugging scandal. America's gloom was reflected in a number of powerful films. Francis Ford Coppola's *The Conversation* (1974), Roman Polanski's *Chinatown* (1974), Milos Forman's *One Flew Over the Cuckoo's Nest* (1975) and Scorsese's *Taxi Driver* (1976) formed part of a Second Golden Age in Hollywood history.

A key director in this period was Robert Altman. He re-worked several film genres, such as the war movie (*M*A*S*H*, 1970), the Western (*McCabe and Mrs Miller*, 1971), the detective thriller (*The Long Goodbye*, 1973) and the musical (*Nashville*, 1975) to challenge the glamorous image of America usually presented by Hollywood. He even poked fun at the movie business itself in *The Player* (1992).

△ Tim Robbins played an arrogant studio executive in *The Player* (1992). The film took a sly behind-the-scenes look at Hollywood, and was packed with top stars playing minor parts.

◁ Robert De Niro as Travis Bickle in *Taxi Driver* (1976), directed by Martin Scorsese. In this powerful picture of life on the streets of New York, Travis goes on a killing spree to protect his only friend, played by Jodie Foster.

◁ Macaulay Culkin as Kevin McCallister, who comes up with several ingenious ways to defend his house against burglars (Joe Pesci and Daniel Stern) when his family fly to France without him by mistake in *Home Alone* (1990). Kevin meets the crooks again when he gets on the wrong flight at the start of another holiday in *Home Alone 2: Lost in New York* (1992).

The 'feel good' factor

The problem facing Hollywood in the 1990s is how to appeal to young audiences while retaining the loyalty of adults who have grown out of 'kidpix' escapism. Studio executives have fallen back on the familiar storylines of the Hollywood genres (see also Section 3: Subjects and Stories) to find a solution.

When complaints were made about the amount of sex and violence in movies, producers began to concentrate more on 'feel good' entertainment. Pictures like *Pretty Woman* (1990) and *Sleepless in Seattle* (1993) marked a return to the romantic comedies of the Golden Age of Hollywood. Similarly, *Honey, I Shrunk the Kids* (1989), *The Secret Garden* and *Mrs Doubtfire* (both 1993) suggested that a growing number of films once more were being produced for family viewing.

DIRECTORS

WOMEN DIRECTORS

Susan Seidelman: *Desperately Seeking Susan* (1985)
Penny Marshall: *Big* (1988)
Amy Heckerling: *Look Who's Talking* (1990)
Kathryn Bigelow: *Point Break* (1991)
Martha Coolidge: *Rambling Rose* (1991)
Barbra Streisand: *The Prince of Tides* (1991)
Penelope Spheeris: *Wayne's World* (1992)
Nora Ephron: *Sleepless in Seattle* (1993)

△ Barbra Streisand directing *Yentl* (1983).

INDEPENDENT DIRECTORS

John Cassavetes: *A Woman Under the Influence* (1974)
Jim Jarmusch: *Down by Law* (1986)
John Sayles: *City of Hope* (1991)
Joel and Ethan Coen: *Raising Arizona* (1987); *Barton Fink* (1991); *The Hudsucker Proxy* (1994)
Hal Hartley: *Simple Men* (1992)
John Dahl: *The Last Seduction* (1994)

△ Arnold Schwarzenegger as the hit man from the future in *Terminator 2: Judgment Day* (1991).

◁ An eccentric medium (Whoopi Goldberg) helps a ghost (Patrick Swayze) to contact his wife (Demi Moore) in *Ghost* (1990).

▽ Fred Flintstone and Barney Rubble in the big screen version of *The Flintstones* (1994).

AFRICAN-AMERICAN CINEMA

In spite of the storm of protest caused by *The Birth of a Nation* in 1915 (see page 22), Hollywood did little over the next 50 years to change its policy of casting black performers as slaves, servants and rogues. But Americans were forced to re-think their attitudes towards race in the 1960s when Martin Luther King and Malcolm X led very different campaigns for black rights. Hollywood responded in 1967 with the release of *In the Heat of the Night* and *Guess Who's Coming to Dinner* (both starring black actor Sidney Poitier), in which various white characters came to see the error of racial prejudice. Despite Poitier's success, African-American performers still find it hard to break into mainstream cinema. The best known black performers in America today are Eddie Murphy, Denzel Washington, Whoopi Goldberg and Wesley Snipes.

African-American directors began to make an impact following Melvin Van Peebles's *Sweet Sweetback's Baadasssss Song* (1971). But the most important development in African-American cinema was the emergence of Spike Lee with *She's Gotta Have It* in 1986. He followed this comedy with *Do the Right Thing* (1989), a controversial study of inner-city racial tension. Here, at long last, was a film that explored the problems of growing up in modern America from a black viewpoint. Lee's work has inspired many young black filmmakers, including John Singleton, Ernest R. Dickerson and Julie Dash.

▽ A poster for *Do the Right Thing*, in which racial rivalry in a pizza parlour results in a riot.

Some blockbusters like *Terminator 2: Judgment Day* (1991) and *Judge Dredd* (1995) still rely heavily on special effects. But others are now spending their budgets on lavish costumes and sets for such swash-buckling historical adventures as *Robin Hood: Prince of Thieves* (1991) and *Braveheart* (1995). Many other period pieces are adapted from novels, like *The Age of Innocence* (1993) and *Interview with the Vampire* (1994).

In the search for a winning box-office formula, Hollywood prefers to 'play safe' by making sequels to successful pictures like *Batman* and *Lethal Weapon*. It has begun to draw more than ever on its glittering past, by re-making such old hits as *Cape Fear* and *Miracle on 34th Street*. In addition, many more pictures like *Three Men and a Baby* (1987) and *Sommersby* (1993) are being adapted from acclaimed foreign-language films. *The Fugitive* (1993) and *The Flintstones* (1994) are among the growing number of features to have been inspired by a TV series.

A big budget is no guarantee that a picture will be popular with audiences. Each year several less publicized pictures capture the public imagination. Among the so-called 'sleepers' to have triumphed in the 1990s are *Ghost*, *Sister Act* and *Speed*.

For future presentation

During the first century of its existence, the cinema has usually managed to find imaginative ways of using the latest technology. Sound, colour and widescreen all eventually became essential elements in film-making, after long periods of trial and error. Perhaps the same will be said one day for 3D, interactive systems such as CD-i and virtual reality.

Digital video (DV) now makes it possible to store moving images on a compact disc. When it is inserted into a CD-Rom system, the disc allows viewers either to watch the action as it unfolds in the normal way or to interact with it. The viewer can influence a film's plot and ending simply by using a joypad. Computer imaging will soon make it possible for viewers not only to alter the storyline of popular pictures like *Gone with the Wind* and *Raiders of the Lost Ark*, but also to star in them themselves! It is

even possible that holographs and virtual reality will be used in film making.

Meanwhile audiences are already experiencing ever-more impressive methods of projection. The Imax system is capable of producing pictures three times the standard widescreen size. A modified version called Omnimax uses special lenses to cast spectacular 180° images on to curved domes above the audience's head. But these expensive processes are only available in a few special cinemas. Current research might lead to the projector itself becoming extinct. Electronic processes such as high-definition video (HDV) will enable cinemas to screen movies passed along fibre optic cable or beamed down via satellite links.

After a century of cinema projection, the 'electronic cinema' may take us through the next 100 years. Whatever happens, it is clear that the moving image will continue to excite, entertain and enthrall audiences of all ages and tastes.

▷ The apartment screen in the CD-i murder mystery *Voyeur* (1993). Players interact with this mix of movie and computer game, by clicking on parts of the room and looking for clues in the scenes that follow. The detective is called when a player knows whodunnit.

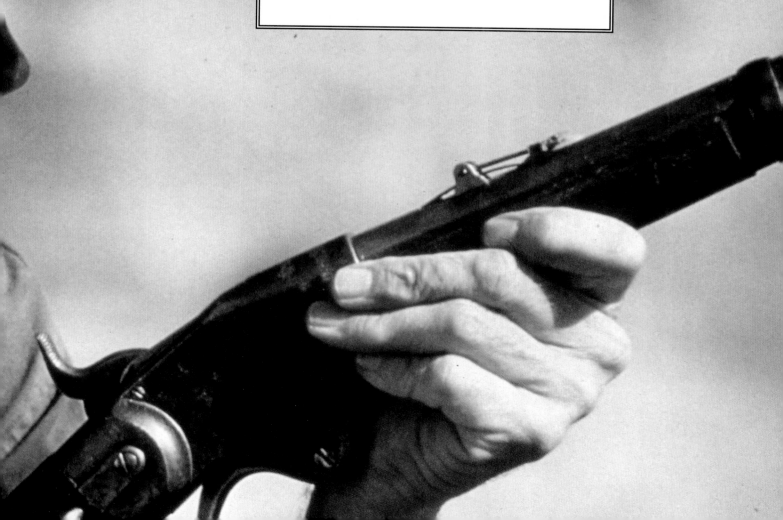

SUBJECTS AND STORIES

During the silent film era, Hollywood studios wanted to attract the widest audiences, so they began to make films within certain subject areas, called genres, which gave audiences familiar plots, characters and settings. The different genres offer exciting adventure, hilarious comedy, unbearable suspense, heart-warming romance and much more.

ACTION AND ADVENTURE

Action and adventure movies are pure escapism. They are usually simple tales of heroes and villains locked in a struggle between good and evil. The pace is fast and furious; the chases, rescues, fights and escapes are spectacular. There is also humour and romance, but they only play supporting roles. The only demand made on the audience is to sit back and enjoy itself.

In all other genres, the action sequences form only part of the story. In adventure films they are everything.

Serials and swashbuckling

The action-adventure film first became widely popular with serials like *The Perils of Pauline* (1914), starring Pearl White. In weekly episodes throughout the silent film era, villains came up with fiendish ways of menacing brave heroines. Similar stories appeared in other serials and B pictures during the sound era.

In the 1920s the all-action film became more sophisticated in the hands of performers like Douglas Fairbanks (see also page 25). Athletic, charming and full of impudent fun, he was ideally suited to the kind of dare-devil costume adventure known as the 'swashbuckler'. Fairbanks became one of the most successful Hollywood actors of his day. He brought a swaggering, acrobatic style to many of the screen's best-loved adventurers, including Robin Hood, D'Artagnan (see opposite), the *Thief of Bagdad* and *The Black Pirate*.

One of his favourite characters was Zorro, a masked avenger who defended the poor of the 1830s against their cruel landowners. *The Mark of Zorro* (1920) and *Don Q, Son of Zorro* (1925) were an all-action blend of the Western and the costume melodrama, with swords replacing pistols. Zorro has since appeared in dozens of Hollywood and European pictures. The most notable was a remake of *The Mark of Zorro* (1940), with Tyrone Power in the lead.

But Fairbanks's true heir in the sound era was Errol Flynn. This dashing Australian starred in historical adventures like *The Charge of the Light Brigade* (1936), as well as in many Westerns and war films. His most famous role, however, was as the outlaw of Sherwood Forest in *The Adventures of Robin Hood* (see box).

Costume adventures

Adventures set in historical times have always been popular with cinemagoers. The costumes, settings and weapons of bygone days add to the glamour of the action and help to draw the audience into

◁ In *The Thief of Bagdad* (1924) Douglas Fairbanks plays the thief who poses as a prince to win the heart of a princess and find a treasure chest that contains the secret of happiness. The film's magical special effects were among the most dazzling of the silent film era.

THE ADVENTURES OF ROBIN HOOD

(USA, 1938) Director: William Keighley & Michael Curtiz

When, in 1192, King Richard the Lionheart is captured on his way back from the Crusades, his brother Prince John (Claude Rains) seizes the throne. He is supported by his ambitious henchmen the Sheriff of Nottingham (Melville Cooper) and Guy of Gisbourne (Basil Rathbone). But one knight opposes his schemes – Robin, Earl of Locksley (Errol Flynn). He gathers a band of Merrie Men and begins stealing from the rich, as they pass through Sherwood Forest, to raise a ransom for Richard's release. When Robin's deeds win the heart of Maid Marian (Olivia De Havilland), who is under royal protection, Prince John sees a chance to lure him into a trap.

So far 58 different performers have played Robin Hood on screen. Errol Flynn's witty man of action is easily the best. His duel with Guy on the winding steps of Nottingham Castle is one of the gems of screen swashbuckling. Indeed, only Alan Rickman's villainous Sheriff in *Robin Hood, Prince of Thieves* (1991) has since improved on any of the performances in this rousing adventure.

▽ ▷ Errol Flynn played Robin Hood with plenty of energy and humour. Kevin Costner gave a more serious performance in *Robin Hood, Prince of Thieves*, concentrating on the emotions of a man seeking revenge rather than on heroic actions.

---

the plot. Many pictures have tried to recreate actual events, including such epics as *El Cid* (1961), with Charlton Heston as the 11th-century Spanish warlord, and Mel Gibson's *Braveheart* (1995) about the 13th-century Scottish rebel, William Wallace. Other features focus on the true-life exploits of intrepid explorers like *Stanley and Livingstone* (1939) and *Scott of the Antarctic* (1948).

But most costume adventures are based on famous novels. Pictures such as *Ivanhoe* (1952), adapted from Sir Walter Scott's book, returned to the days of knights and chivalry. Some told tales of reckless courage that took place on imperial campaigns, including *Lives of a Bengal Lancer* (1935) and *The Four Feathers* (1939). Others, like *Beau Geste* (1939), involved the French Foreign Legion and its struggle with the tribes of the Sahara Desert.

▷ Van Heflin as Athos, Gene Kelly as D'Artagnan, Gig Young as Porthos and Robert Coote as Aramis in George Sidney's *The Three Musketeers* (1948). Packed with action, intrigue, comedy and romance, it is the most thrilling version of Alexandre Dumas's classic novel.

A favourite author with film-makers is the French novelist Alexandre Dumas. Several of his books, including *The Count of Monte Cristo* and *The Man in the Iron Mask*, have been brought to the screen. But his most adapted creations are The Three Musketeers. Generations of moviegoers have become familiar with Athos, Porthos, Aramis and D'Artagnan and their duels with the scheming Cardinal Richelieu and the wicked Milady de Winter. Apart from Douglas Fairbanks's 1921 silent classic, the most enjoyable version was the one made in 1948 with Gene Kelly as an energetic, almost gymnastic D'Artagnan. The director Richard Lester made three light-hearted variations on the story in the 1970s and 1980s. *The Three Musketeers* was made yet again for younger viewers in 1993.

Several other swashbuckling adventures have been set on the high seas. Here again Douglas Fairbanks set the trend in *The Black Pirate* (1926), which was followed by *Captain Blood* (1935) starring Errol Flynn. Later features like *The Black Swan* (1942) and *Anne of the Indies* (1951) drew on the deeds of such real pirates as Sir Henry Morgan and Anne Bonney, who, over 200 years ago, terrorized the part of the Caribbean known as the Spanish Main.

The pirate picture has been out of fashion since the late 1950s, but it enjoyed a brief revival with Steven Spielberg's *Hook* (1991) and *Cutthroat Island (1995)* starring Geena Davis.

Lords of the jungle

Perhaps the most distinctive action hero of all was Tarzan. In 1913, novelist Edgar Rice Burroughs created the English noble who was raised by apes in the African jungle. Tarzan arrived on screen five years later, played by Elmo Lincoln. A total of 98 Tarzan pictures have been made to date, with 16 different actors starring in the lead role. Johnny Weismuller, a former Olympic swimmer, was easily the most famous Tarzan. He played the Lord of the Apes a dozen times.

Most of Tarzan's adventures involved white hunters or treasure seekers who were threatened by wild animals or hostile local tribes. But few of these expeditions stumbled across anything as remarkable as the giant gorilla in *King Kong* (1933). Inspired by profit rather than by scientific curiosity, Carl Denham (Robert Armstrong) removes Kong from the island which is inhabited by prehistoric monsters and where he is worshipped as a god. He brings Kong to New York, to exhibit him as a freak of nature. But, unable to bear the humiliation of his captivity, Kong escapes and searches Manhattan for Ann Darrow (Fay Wray), the only person who has shown him any kindness. The scene in which Kong is attacked by aeroplanes as he sits on top of the Empire State Building brilliantly arouses excitement and pity in the viewer. It is among the most memorable moments in cinema history.

Secret agents

Spy stories are another favourite theme for action films. Greta Garbo starred as a German agent during World War I in *Mata Hari* (1931), and several later pictures dealt with spies in the war against Hitler. In the 1950s, when relations between America and the Soviet Union cooled rapidly, films like *My Son John* (1952) reflected the anti-communist hysteria in America at that time. But other spy films added humour to the formula. Among them was Alfred Hitchcock's *North by Northwest* (1959), in which a businessman (Cary Grant) becomes the target of a gang of traitors led by an enemy agent (James Mason).

The mock-serious approach has also been used for the long-running series featuring the most resourceful of all screen spies – James Bond. These thrilling pictures, loosely based on the novels of Ian Fleming, pitted Bond, or 007 to give him his code name, against a variety of Soviet KGB agents and eccentric criminals determined to take over the world. Bond always entered the fray armed with ingenious gadgets designed to get him out of the tightest corner. Shot in exotic locations all over the world and packed with spectacular action sequences, the 19 Bond movies from *Dr No* (1962) to *Goldeneye* (1995) have proved popular with audiences of all ages and tastes (see box on page 77).

THE AFRICAN QUEEN

(UK / USA, 1951) Director: John Huston

The African Queen is not a typical adventure picture, but it has plenty of exciting action. The story involves Rose Sayer (Katharine Hepburn) and her brother Samuel (Robert Morley), who are Christian missionaries in the African jungle on the eve of World War I. When Samuel is killed by German soldiers, Rose accepts a lift to the coast from Charlie Allnut (Humphrey Bogart), the captain of a small boat called *The African Queen*. At first the prim, religious Rose and the drunken, cynical Charlie do not get along. But their dangerous river journey leads to romance.

The film concentrates on Rose and Charlie's relationship as their adventures unfold. Bogart and Hepburn are magnificent in the leading roles. Both were nominated for Oscars, with Bogart winning one for the only time in his career.

SEAN CONNERY	ROGER MOORE
Dr No (1962)	*Live and Let Die* (1973)
From Russia With Love (1963)	*The Man with the Golden Gun* (1974)
Goldfinger (1964)	*The Spy Who Loved Me* (1977)
Thunderball (1965)	*Moonraker* (1979)
You Only Live Twice (1967)	*For Your Eyes Only* (1981)
Diamonds are Forever (1971)	*Octopussy* (1983)
Never Say Never Again (1983)	*A View to a Kill* (1985)

DAVID NIVEN	TIMOTHY DALTON
Casino Royale (1967)	*The Living Daylights* (1987)
	Licence to Kill (1989)

GEORGE LAZENBY	PIERCE BROSNAN
On Her Majesty's Secret Service (1969)	*Goldeneye* (1995)

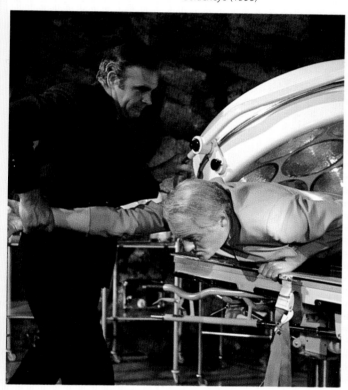

△ Sean Connery as James Bond battles for his life with Charles Gray who plays arch villain Blofeld in *Diamonds are Forever* (1971). Connery claimed he would never play Agent 007 again, but he returned to the role in *Never Say Never Again* (1983).

RAIDERS OF THE LOST ARK

(USA, 1981) Director: Steven Spielberg

Set in 1936, *Raiders of the Lost Ark* follows professor of archaeology Indiana Jones (Harrison Ford) and his former lover Marion Ravenswood (Karen Allen) in their attempt to beat a band of Nazi agents to the sacred Ark of the Covenant, which contains the Ten Commandments.

The film was inspired by the adventure serials of the 1930s. But Indiana Jones himself is also remarkably similar to the title character in the little-known British picture, *Pimpernel Smith* (1941), which starred Leslie Howard. Spielberg was offered the chance to direct the film after he told producer George Lucas about his ambition to make a James Bond movie. He certainly puts the Bond blend of witty dialogue and spectacular action to good use.

At the centre of this comic-book quest is Harrison Ford, who plays 'Indie' as a mix of Errol Flynn and Humphrey Bogart. He returned to the role for the less impressive *Indiana Jones and the Temple of Doom* (1984) and *Indiana Jones and the Last Crusade* (1989).

Disaster movies

A new style of action adventure helped launch the blockbuster era in the early 1970s. The disaster movie relied on an all-star cast being caught in a sudden emergency. One of the first starred Gene Hackman, who led the survivors of a shipwreck to safety in *The Poseidon Adventure* (1972). But the best of them all was *The Towering Inferno* (1974), in which an architect (Paul Newman) and a fireman (Steve McQueen) try to evacuate a blazing skyscraper. A gruesome, nerve-racking variation on the same theme was Steven Spielberg's *Jaws* (1975), in which a tourist beach is menaced by a Great White Shark.

Action man

But the younger audiences of the 'kidpix' era (see page 68) soon tired of the disaster formula. They demanded a faster-moving, more vigorous sort of entertainment, full of breakneck stunts and breathtaking special effects. Many of the most successful pictures of this period were made in the science-fiction genre (see page 112). But some were in the true tradition of the action-adventure. Chief among them was Spielberg's *Raiders* trilogy, starring Harrison Ford as that most unlikely hero, Indiana Jones (see box above).

◁ Arnold Schwarzenegger in spectacular action in *Total Recall* (1990). The Austrian-born actor entered films after winning many body-building contests. He became one of Hollywood's biggest stars in adventures like *Conan the Barbarian* (1982), *Commando* (1985), *Predator* (1987) and the *Terminator* films.

◁ Nicknamed 'the muscles from Brussels', Jean-Claude Van Damme escapes from a burning truck in *Hard Target* (1993), directed by martial arts specialist, John Woo.

These action movies were clearly influenced by the serials and B pictures of Hollywood's past. But the exploits of action men like Sylvester Stallone, Arnold Schwarzenegger, Bruce Willis, Steven Seagal and Jean-Claude Van Damme were a far cry from the graceful swashbuckling of the classic adventure style. In their movies, raw power now mattered more than speed of thought or reaction. The old-fashioned fist fight was replaced by kung-fu. Instead of skilful swordplay there was calculated slaughter with a pump-action shotgun, and in place of witty dialogue came the punchy one-liner.

But, Hollywood's musclebound stars are getting older and their big-budget movies are no longer sure-fire winners at the box office. Recent pictures like *Speed* (1994), with Keanu Reeves, and *Mission Impossible* (1995), starring Tom Cruise, suggest that a new breed of action hero, who relies more on his wits and less on physical strength, has already arrived.

Screen sport

Sports are a popular topic with action film-makers. Surprisingly few pictures of any quality have been made about the world's number one sport, soccer. But other sports with an international appeal have inspired fine films, including boxing – *Rocky* (1976) and *Raging Bull* (1980), horse racing – *Broadway Bill* (1934) and *Phar Lap* (1983), and motor sports – *The Crowd Roars* (1938) and *Days of Thunder* (1990). In addition to documentaries like *Olympia* (1938), there have also been several features set at the Olympic Games. One of the most successful was *Chariots of Fire* (1981) about British runners at the 1924 Olympics.

△ Cop Keanu Reeves urges emergency driver Sandra Bullock to keep the bus above 50 miles per hour, to prevent a bomb from exploding in *Speed* (1994).

▽ Robert De Niro in *Raging Bull* (1980). In the fight scenes, director Martin Scorsese used close-ups, dramatic angles and slow-motion to show the power and the pain of the punches.

As Hollywood dominates world cinema, America's favourite sports such as baseball, basketball, American football and ice hockey have often been the subject of action films. Baseball has inspired the most enjoyable American sports movies. Several of these have even been popular with audiences in other parts of the world, even though they do not know the rules of the game. *Eight Men Out* (1988), for example, tells the story of the legendary Chicago White Sox team, who were involved in a bribes scandal during the 1919 World Series. In *Field of Dreams* (1989), Ray Liotta plays the ghost of one of that team, 'Shoeless' Joe Jackson, who persuades a farmer (Kevin Costner) to prepare a baseball field on his land.

FILMS TO WATCH

Films are made in the US unless otherwise stated

HISTORICAL ADVENTURE

The Charge of the Light Brigade (1936)
Kidnapped (1938)
The Adventures of Robin Hood (1938)
Robin Hood, Prince of Thieves (1991)
Braveheart (1995)
Rob Roy (1995)
First Knight (1995)

IMPERIAL CAMPAIGNS

Lives of a Bengal Lancer (1934)
Beau Geste (1939)
The Four Feathers (UK, 1939)
Khartoum (UK, 1966)
Young Winston (UK, 1972)
The Man Who Would Be King (1975)

EXPLORERS

The Adventures of Marco Polo (1938)
Stanley and Livingstone (1939)
Hudson's Bay (1940)
Scott of the Antarctic (UK, 1948)
King Solomon's Mines (1950)
Mountains of the Moon (1989)

SWASHBUCKLERS

The Count of Monte Cristo (1934)
The Scarlet Pimpernel (UK, 1934)
The Prisoner of Zenda (1937)
The Man in the Iron Mask (1939)
The Mark of Zorro (1940)
The Three Musketeers (1948, 1973, 1993)

PIRATES

Treasure Island (1934, 1950)
The Sea Hawk (1940)
The Black Swan (1942)
Anne of the Indies (1951)
Hook (1991)
Cutthroat Island (1995)

ALL AT SEA

Mutiny on the Bounty (1935, 1962)
Moby Dick (1956)
HMS Defiant (UK, 1962)
Jaws (1975)
The Abyss (1989)
The Hunt for Red October (1990)
Crimson Tide (1995)

ABOVE THE CLOUDS

Only Angels Have Wings (1939)
No Highway (UK, 1951)
The Spirit of St Louis (1957)
The Flight of the Phoenix (1965)
Top Gun (1986)
Point Break (1991)
Drop Zone (1994)

JUNGLES

Tarzan the Ape Man (1932)
King Kong (1933, 1976)
Tarzan and His Mate (1934)
Mogambo (UK, 1953)
Hatari! (1962)
The Emerald Forest (UK, 1985)
White Hunter, Black Heart (1990)

THE GREAT OUTDOORS

The Call of the Wild (1935)
The Treasure of the Sierra Madre (1948)
The Wages of Fear (France, 1953)
The Incredible Journey (1963)
Deliverance (1972)
Stand By Me (1986)
K2 (1991)
Cliffhanger (1993)
The River Wild (1994)
Far From Home: The Adventures of Yellow Dog (1994)

ON SECRET SERVICE

Confessions of a Nazi Spy (1939)
The House on 92nd Street (1945)
North by Northwest (1959)
The Manchurian Candidate (1962)
The Ipcress File (1965)
True Lies (1994)
Mission Impossible (1995)

DISASTERS

San Francisco (1936)
The Rains Came (1939)
Airport (1970)
The Poseidon Adventure (1972)
The Towering Inferno (1974)
Earthquake (1974)
The Hindenberg (1975)
Jaws (1976)

ACTION MEN

Enter the Dragon (1973)
Predator (1987)
Die Hard & 2, & 3 (1988, 1990, 1995)
Under Siege (1992)
Demolition Man (1993)
Hard Target (1993)
The Fugitive (1993)

UNLIKELY HEROES

Raiders of the Lost Ark (1981)
Romancing the Stone (1984)
The Jewel of the Nile (1985)
Danny the Champion of the World (UK, 1989)
The Last Action Hero (1993)
The Mask (1994)

COMEDY

If you have ever told a favourite joke, only to find no one laughing, you will know that a sense of humour is quite unpredictable. Comedy is a hit-and-miss affair and an audience will not laugh unless it 'gets' the joke. Yet even then, an inspired piece of clowning or witty dialogue will not appeal to everyone. This unpredictability makes comedy the most difficult film style to do consistently well.

Comedy is the oldest form of film fiction. The very first cinema show given by the Lumière brothers in 1895 included a comic short film – *L'Arroseur arrosé* (*The Sprinkler Sprinkled*) – in which a small boy tricked a gardener into soaking himself with his own hose.

Although the English film comic Pimple, and the Italian clown Cretinetti, were popular in their own countries, the best early screen comedy came from France. Georges Méliès produced many amusing pictures, but it was his great rival Ferdinand Zecca who had a better understanding of comic timing. In addition to perfecting the ever-popular comic chase, he also produced the films starring Max Linder, whose accident-prone man-about-town was a huge hit worldwide from the early 1910s. Linder was a major influence on Charlie Chaplin, whose famous Tramp was in many ways a shabby version of Max's 'Gentleman of Paris'.

Slapstick

Almost without exception, the first screen comics learned their skills while performing in the circus, pantomime, burlesque or vaudeville (also known as music-hall). As silent film prevented them from actually telling jokes, they borrowed elements from the other stage traditions in order to make moviegoers laugh. They created a form of purely visual comedy that presented the world as a crazy place in which people had little or no control over their lives. This style was named 'slapstick', after the wooden sticks that clowns used to slap together to encourage the audience to applaud.

Sennett: 'The King of Comedy'

Mack Sennett combined the pace of Ferdinand Zecca with the precision editing of D. W. Griffith. He had just two film-making rules: that movies moved, and that no joke should last longer than 100 seconds. He was the undoubted 'king' of slapstick and produced hundreds of frantic comedies for his own Keystone company, many of which starred the incompetent Keystone Kops.

Most of Sennett's films were knock-about comedies (although some used camera trickery to add to the fun). Performers were treated like unbreakable objects as they either tripped, crashed, fought or plunged through a series of perfectly timed gags or fell victim to props as varied as runaway vehicles, collapsing house fronts and flying custard pies.

Sennett also had an eye for talent. Roscoe 'Fatty' Arbuckle, Mabel Normand, Ben Turpin, Harry Langdon, Carole Lombard and Charley Chase were all stars who began their careers at Keystone. His most important discovery, however, was undoubtedly Charlie Chaplin.

Chaplin

Charlie Chaplin was raised in poverty in London, and he followed his mother and brother on to the stage in 1897. While on a vaudeville tour of America in 1912, he was offered his first film chance by Mack Sennett. In just his second picture, *Kid Auto Races at Venice* (1914), he invented the character of the Tramp that he was to play in most of his pictures. A romantic, a rascal and an outsider who always backed the underdog, the 'little fellow' with his bowler hat, baggy trousers, walking stick, outsize shoes and funny walk made Charlie Chaplin both a millionaire and the

◁ Crazy, clumsy and incompetent, the Keystone Kops were the comic invention of director Mack Sennett in 1912. They were rivalled in popularity only by his other famous creation, the Bathing Beauties.

◁ Charlie Chaplin was the most famous film star of his day. In Europe he was known as 'Charlot' and huge crowds came to see him when he toured there in 1921. Rival studios even made films featuring Chaplin imitators. He also starred in his own cartoon. A variety of Chaplin toys went on sale, including clockwork dolls and painted statuettes. There was even a hit song called 'The Moon Shines Bright on Charlie Chaplin'.

The Golden Age of Comedy

Silent comedy reached its peak in the 1920s, with Chaplin universally acclaimed as the finest comedian of his day. However, many modern critics think that Buster Keaton was an even better director and performer.

Among the period's other leading figures was Harold Lloyd, who made his name playing Willie Work and Lonesome Luke in over 100 films for producer Hal Roach, who was later responsible for creating the team of Laurel and Hardy. Lloyd is probably best remembered for his 'comedy of thrills', in which his eager boy-next-door character always found himself in perilous predicaments. The stunts performed in features like *Safety Last* (1923) are all the more remarkable because Lloyd had lost part of his right hand in an accident during the filming of *Haunted Spooks* in 1920.

In great contrast to the confident Lloyd was the timid Harry Langdon, who came to fame briefly through subtle comedies like *Long Pants* (1927). Although his popularity faded with the coming of sound, his baby-faced hero was the model for

cinema's first international superstar.

Chaplin soon began to direct the films in which he starred, slowing down the pace so that he could combine his graceful clowning with comedy based on the Tramp's personality and a social message. His short films drew on his own experiences and the events of daily life, and so appealed to audiences of widely differing backgrounds. So too did his classic feature films *The Kid*, *The Gold Rush*, *City Lights* and *Modern Times*.

Chaplin was convinced that screen comedy should be silent and he resisted the Talkies until *The Great Dictator* in 1940. He was never at ease with sound and much of his later work was over sentimental and pretentious. In 1952 he released *Limelight*, which included a hilarious routine with another great silent comic, Buster Keaton. Shortly afterwards Chaplin left America in protest at having his political views criticized, and he refused to allow his pictures to be shown there for many years. He returned in 1971 to receive a special Oscar in recognition of his contribution to film art.

BUSTER KEATON

Born in 1895 into a showbusiness family, Keaton was given his nickname by the famous escape artist Harry Houdini after a fall (or 'buster') down some steps. After many years on the stage, he starred in a series of films with Roscoe 'Fatty' Arbuckle that were so successful that he was able to start his own production company in 1919.

Keaton's comedies were enjoyed for the pace and precision of their gags, in which the actor was placed at the mercy of a range of giant props, including a train, a boat, a waterfall, bouncing boulders and a falling house-front. His comic trademark was his 'stone face' expression, which rarely altered no matter what his predicament. Keaton continued to perform until the 1960s, but he never recaptured the glories of his silent career.

▷ Keaton's finest film is undoubtedly *The General* (1927). Set during the American Civil War, it was a fast-paced comedy-adventure in which Buster tried to foil a gang of enemy train-nappers.

countless simple-minded characters who unsuspectingly disrupted the world around them. A recent example of such an 'innocent abroad' is *Forrest Gump* (1994).

Although slapstick belongs mainly to the silent era, many later comedies have included knockabout routines. A highly popular example in the 1960s and 1970s was Blake Edwards's *Pink Panther* series, starring Peter Sellers as the bungling Inspector Clouseau. More recently Jim Carrey has continued the slapstick tradition in such features as *Ace Ventura, Pet Detective* (1993) and *The Mask* (1994). Slapstick's true heir, however, has been the fast-paced 'socko' cartoon, in which humans are replaced by animals like Tom & Jerry, Sylvester and Wile E. Coyote, who always emerge unharmed from the severest of poundings.

▷ Harold Lloyd usually played an optimistic Everyman, who nearly always found himself in perilous situations like this one in *Safety Last* (1923).

LAUREL AND HARDY

Laurel and Hardy were already established solo comedians before they were first brought together for *Slipping Wives* in 1926. Over the next quarter-century they made a further 99 films and became the finest comedy team in movie history. Although they made many popular features, their style was best suited to the comic short.

Both were rarely without their famous bowler hats, and the pompous, boastful, bullying Ollie and the childlike, spiteful Stan inevitably brought chaos and destruction to the most harmless situations. Although their pictures had verbal wit, the comedy also made use of their contrasting physical appearances and the props which they used to throw, trip over, smash or simply hit each other with.

FILMS TO WATCH

CHARLIE CHAPLIN

SHORT FILMS
The Tramp (1915)
The Pawnshop (1916)
The Rink (1916)
The Cure (1917)
Easy Street (1917)
The Immigrant (1917)
FEATURE FILMS
The Kid (1921)
The Gold Rush (1925)
City Lights (1931)
Modern Times (1936)
The Great Dictator (1940)
Limelight (1952)

BUSTER KEATON

SHORT FILMS
One Week (1920)
Playhouse (1921)
The Balloonatic (1923)
Sherlock Jr. (1924)
FEATURE FILMS
Our Hospitality (1923)
The Navigator (1924)
The General (1927)
Steamboat Bill Jr. (1928)

LAUREL AND HARDY

SHORT FILMS
The Battle of the Century (1927)
Big Business (1929)
Hog Wild (1930)
Come Clean (1931)
Helpmates (1931)
The Music Box (1932)
Towed in the Hole (1932)
Busy Bodies (1933)
FEATURE FILMS
Sons of the Desert (1933)
Our Relations (1936)
Way Out West (1937)
A Chump at Oxford (1940)

HAROLD LLOYD

Grandma's Boy (1922)
Safety Last (1923)
Girl Shy (1924)
The Freshman (1925)

HARRY LANGDON

The Strong Man (1926)
Long Pants (1927)

Comedy talks!

Sound transformed the comic film. As the public demanded more Talkies, producers abandoned visual comedy and concentrated instead on dialogue films sprinkled with verbal humour.

Several styles already successful in the theatre were adapted for the screen. One of these was farce, in which ordinary situations were reduced to near chaos by a series of coincidences and misunderstandings. A common variation on this was the comedy of errors, in which characters became caught up in cases of mistaken identity.

Equally popular was the comedy of manners, which poked fun at the attitudes and actions of a particular social class. The master of this form was Ernst Lubitsch, who directed a number of sparkling comedies set among the idle rich, including *Trouble in Paradise* (1932).

Although these polished pictures were much admired, most audiences preferred the crazier comedy of W. C. Fields, Mae West and the Marx Brothers.

Wisecrack comedy

Permanently irritable and in need of alcohol, W. C. Fields spent his pictures complaining comically about his life and cursing everything from small children to animals. Mae West was another wise-cracking performer who, like Fields, wrote her own scripts. As well as mocking the glamour of Hollywood's leading ladies, she loved to shock delicate audiences with songs and dialogue loaded with sugges-tive double meanings. The censors thought her dialogue so vulgar that by the mid-1930s they had ordered her to tone down the sexual content of her material.

Even more distinctive were the zany antics of the Marx Brothers. While Harpo refined the mime of the silent clowns, Groucho and Chico perfected a blend of puns, nonsense and insults that was a verbal equivalent of slapstick. A fourth brother, Zeppo, played romantic roles before he left the group in 1933. But even the crazy style of the Marx Brothers was tamed after they changed studios from Paramount to MGM, in the mid-1930s. With his cigar, painted moustache and loping walk, Groucho usually stole the show with his hilarious lines:

'One morning I shot an elephant in my pyjamas. How he got into my pyjamas I'll never know.' (Animal Crackers)

'You've got the brain of a four-year-old child, and I bet he was glad to get rid of it.' (Horse Feathers)

'Either he's dead or my watch has stopped.' (A Day at the Races)

FILMS TO WATCH

W. C. FIELDS

It's a Gift (1934)
You Can't Cheat an Honest Man (1939)
The Bank Dick (1940)
Never Give a Sucker an Even Break (1941)

MAE WEST

She Done Him Wrong (1933)
I'm No Angel (1933)
Belle of the Nineties (1934)
Klondike Annie (1936)

THE MARX BROTHERS

Animal Crackers (1930)
Monkey Business (1931)
Horse Feathers (1932)
Duck Soup (1933)
A Night at the Opera (1935)
A Day at the Races (1937)

Screwball comedy

While Mae West and the Marx Brothers were being toned down, a new brand of hectic, wisecracking film was beginning to emerge – the screwball comedy. The key feature of screwball was the disruption of a dull male's ordered existence by a forceful female with whom he eventually fell in love, after many comic misadventures.

In two of the best examples of this type of comedy, *It Happened One Night* (1934) and *Bringing Up Baby* (1938), the madcap or screwball figure was a bored heiress. But she was just as likely to be an ambi-tious career woman out to prove herself the equal of her male colleagues, as in such 'battles of the sexes' as the hilarious news-paper comedy *His Girl Friday* (1940).

▽ Clark Gable and Claudette Colbert starred in Frank Capra's *It Happened One Night* (1934), which became the first film to win the 'Big Four' Oscars — Best Picture, Best Director, Best Actor and Best Actress.

◁ Chico, Zeppo, Groucho and Harpo. Originally a top vaudeville act, the Marx Brothers were at their best in zany, fast-talking pictures like *Duck Soup* (1933).

Frank Capra established himself as the leading screwball director by adding small-town common sense and satire to the formula. Satire is the use of humour to expose society's worst faults. Capra's work inspired hundreds of romantic comedies and was the forerunner of the 'feel good' movies of the 1990s. Joel and Ethan Coen's 1994 picture *The Hudsucker Proxy* was a tribute to Capra's genius.

Writer-director Preston Sturges was influenced by screwball. He sharpened its satire and also dared to ridicule such topics as sex, politics, war and death. His style influenced not only such adult comedies as Billy Wilder's *Some Like It Hot* (1959), but also 'black' comedies which found humour in serious subjects. One example of 'black' humour was Stanley Kubrick's farce about the outbreak of nuclear war, *Dr Strangelove* (1963).

△ Starring Joel McCrea and Veronica Lake, *Sullivan's Travels* follows a Hollywood comedy director on his search for the realistic subject that will establish him as a serious artist.

△ Breezy heiress Katharine Hepburn and her pets – a dog and a leopard – bring dinosaur expert Cary Grant's routine crashing down around him in *Bringing Up Baby* (1938). The director was Howard Hawks, who made the other classic screwballs *Twentieth Century* (1934) and *His Girl Friday* (1940).

▽ In Billy Wilder's daring comedy *Some Like It Hot*, Tony Curtis and Jack Lemmon join a women's dance band to hide from murderous gangsters. Curtis's life becomes even more complicated when he falls in love with the band's singer, Marilyn Monroe.

FILMS TO WATCH

FRANK CAPRA

It Happened One Night (1934)
Mr Deeds Goes to Town (1936)
You Can't Take It With You (1938)
Mr Smith Goes to Washington (1939)
Meet John Doe (1941)
Arsenic and Old Lace (1944)

PRESTON STURGES

Sullivan's Travels (1941)
The Lady Eve (1941)
The Palm Beach Story (1942)
The Miracle of Morgan's Creek (1943)
Hail the Conquering Hero (1944)

BRITISH COMEDY

Britain has a long and proud tradition of literary and theatrical comedy. Two of the great silent clowns – Charlie Chaplin and Stan Laurel – were English. Yet, curiously, British film comedy has had little international impact. Although former music-hall performers like Gracie Fields, George Formby and Will Hay were big stars at home during the 1930s, they were virtually unknown abroad.

Intelligent comedies produced by Ealing Studios after World War II earned much wider recognition. Two of the best were *Kind Hearts and Coronets* (1949) and *The Lavender Hill Mob* (1951). Such films were called 'Ealing comedies' and poked gentle fun at the British character. They were also particularly admired in America. Another British hit in the mid-1950s was *Genevieve*, which followed the relationships between two couples during a veteran car rally.

The 'Carry On' series of work comedies and saucy parodies was very popular in the 1960s and 1970s. In the following decade the Monty Python team enjoyed international TV and film success with their blend of absurd humour and satire.

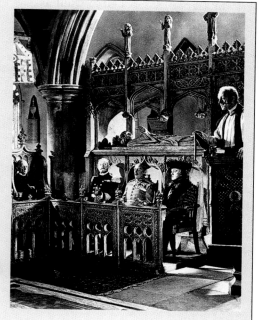

△ Alec Guinness played all eight members of the D'Ascoyne family in the 1949 Ealing comedy *Kind Hearts and Coronets*. The largest number of parts played by a single performer in one film is 27, by Rolf Leslie in the 1913 picture *Sixty Years a Queen*.

FILMS TO WATCH		
GRACIE FIELDS	**WILL HAY**	**EALING COMEDIES**
Sally in Our Alley (1931)	*Good Morning Boys* (1937)	*Hue and Cry* (1947)
Sing as We Go (1934)	*Oh Mr Porter* (1938)	*Whisky Galore* (1949)
GEORGE FORMBY	*The Ghost of St Michael's* (1941)	*Kind Hearts and Coronets* (1949)
	The Goose Steps Out (1942)	*The Lavender Hill Mob* (1951)
Come On, George (1939)		*The Man in the White Suit* (1951)
Let George Do It (1940)		*The Ladykillers* (1955)

The joke wears thin...

Many film genres have continued to discover fresh ways of exploring their themes, but the Hollywood comedy has stood surprisingly still since World War II. The most innovative humour has been produced instead in Britain and Europe.

Although comedy double-acts like Bob Hope and Bing Crosby, Bud Abbott and Lou Costello, and Dean Martin and Jerry Lewis were very successful, they did little to develop the conventions established long before by Laurel and Hardy. Similarly, romantic comedies like *Pillow Talk* (1959), starring Doris Day and Rock Hudson, lacked the vigour of screwball comedy and the many spoofs (or parodies) that have been released since the 1970s, like the *Naked Gun* films, have done no more than update a trend that was begun by Mack Sennett in the 1910s.

◁ The self-important, impatient Bud Abbott partnered the podgy, cowardly Lou Costello in over 30 slapstick comedies between 1940 and 1956. Among the best was *Abbott and Costello Meet Frankenstein* (1948). They later starred in a long-running TV series.

One of the reasons for this long decline has been the rise of television comedy. Widescreen technology (see page 54) filled the screen with spectacular action but it was totally unsuitable for the more intimate form of comedy, which was much more suited to being shown on TV. As a result, top comic scriptwriters, performers and directors began to concentrate on making 30-minute situation comedies ('sit-coms' for short), or shows made up of stand-up routines and wacky or satirical sketches.

Actor-directors like Woody Allen and Mel Brooks began their careers writing for TV in the 1960s, and many of today's top comic stars, including Eddie Murphy, made their names on programmes like *Saturday Night Live*. Cinema's debt to TV comedy has become even more evident in the 1990s with a growing number of blockbusters like *Wayne's World* , *The Addams Family* and *The Flintstones* being adapted from small-screen originals.

Hollywood today seems to be content to make what are in effect feature-length TV episodes and pale imitations of its own comic classics. If this pattern continues, it would appear that film comedy's best days might already be over.

▷ Stylishly shot in black and white, *Manhattan* (1979) is both a witty adult comedy and a song of praise to Woody Allen's home city, New York.

WOODY ALLEN'S
MANHATTAN

▽ Mike Myers as Wayne and Dana Carvey as Garth whose excellent homemade TV series *Wayne's World* is in danger of a takeover by a major network – Not!

FILMS TO WATCH

ABBOTT AND COSTELLO

Hold That Ghost (1941)
In Society (1944)
Abbott and Costello Meet
  Frankenstein (1948)

BOB HOPE

The Cat and the Canary (1939)
My Favourite Blonde (1942)
Road to Morocco (1942)
The Paleface (1948)

JERRY LEWIS

Artists and Models (1955)
The Bellboy (1960)
The Nutty Professor (1963)
The Disorderly Orderly (1964)

MEL BROOKS

The Producers (1968)

Blazing Saddles (1974)
Young Frankenstein (1974)
Silent Movie (1976)
High Anxiety (1978)
Space Balls (1987)

WOODY ALLEN

Play It Again Sam (1972)
Sleeper (1973)
Love and Death (1975)
Annie Hall (1977)
Manhattan (1979)
Zelig (1983)
Broadway Danny Rose (1984)
The Purple Rose of Cairo (1984)
Hannah and Her Sisters (1986)
Crimes and Misdemeanours (1989)
Husbands and Wives (1992)
Manhattan Murder Mystery (1993)
Bullets over Broadway (1994)

A WORLD OF COMEDY

While many countries have produced popular comedians, their films are often so suited to domestic audiences that they are hardly ever seen abroad. American comedy, however, has dominated the world market since the slapstick era, and the stars and directors from other countries who have established international reputations have usually worked within the broad comic styles popularized by Hollywood.

The Danish comedians Harald Madsen and Carl Schenstrøm, for example, were a slapstick double act much like Laurel and Hardy. In the 1920s and 1930s René Clair followed in the footsteps of Ernst Lubitsch and the Swedish director Mauritz Stiller to perfect the sophisticated comedy of manners. The Frenchman Fernandel specialized in farce in the 1950s, while fellow countryman Jacques Tati was the undoubted master of mime. More recently Japanese film-maker Yoji Yamada has produced nearly 50 feature films following the misadventures of the unsuspecting innocent Tora-san.

Satire has never done well at the American box office, but European directors of the quality of Luis Buñuel, Federico Fellini and Jean-Luc Godard have been attracted by its aggressive, intellectual style. It has also been a popular comic outlet for directors working in countries with strict political systems, as in Eastern Europe and Latin America in the 1960s (see page 44).

Two highly original film-makers emerged in Europe in the 1980s. The Spaniard Pedro Almodóvar mocked modern culture in extravagant films like *Women on the Verge of a Nervous Breakdown* (1988). Finnish director Aki Kaurismäki used more subtle humour in comedies like *Leningrad Cowboys Go America* (1989). Also blending the offbeat and the outrageous, Australian comedy has become more widely known over the last decade thanks to films like *Crocodile Dundee* (1986) and *Strictly Ballroom* (1992).

△ Paul Hogan and friend in *Crocodile Dundee* (1986). It traces the adventures of an Australian bushman in New York, and is still the most successful non-Hollywood film of all time.

FILMS TO WATCH

Films are made in the US unless otherwise stated

COMEDY OF MANNERS

Trouble in Paradise (1932)
Adam's Rib (1949)
Born Yesterday (1950)
Four Weddings and a Funeral (UK, 1994)

FARCE

An Italian Straw Hat (France, 1927)
What's New Pussycat? (1965)
Clockwise (UK, 1986)
Sister Act (1992)

COMEDY OF ERRORS

My Man Godfrey (1936)
Tootsie (1982)
Trading Places (1983)
After Hours (1987)
Dave (1993)

SCREWBALL

Twentieth Century (1934)
Nothing Sacred (1937)
Bringing up Baby (1938)
The Philadelphia Story (1940)
His Girl Friday (1940)
What's Up, Doc? (1972)
A Touch of Class (UK, 1973)
Arthur (1981)
A Fish Called Wanda (UK, 1988)

SATIRE

The Apartment (1960)
Billy Liar (1963)
Being There (1979)
Barton Fink (1991)
Strictly Ballroom (Australia 1992)

BLACK COMEDY

To Be Or Not To Be (1942)
Throw Momma from a Train (1987)
Heathers (1989)
Delicatessen (France, 1990)
Death Becomes Her (1992)
Serial Mom (1994)

ROMANTIC COMEDY

The Shop Around the Corner (1940)
Barefoot in the Park (1967)
When Harry Met Sally... (1989)
Green Card (1990)
Groundhog Day (1993)
Sleepless in Seattle (1993)

KID COMEDY

The Happiest Days of Your Life (UK, 1950)
The Belles of St Trinian's (UK, 1954)

Breaking Away (1979)
Gregory's Girl (UK, 1982)
Big (1988)
Honey, I Shrunk the Kids (1989)
Look Who's Talking (1989)
Uncle Buck (1989)
Home Alone & 2 (1990, 1992)
Dazed and Confused (1994)

FAMILY COMEDY

Life with Father (1947)
Father of the Bride (1950, 1991)
Raising Arizona (1987)
Three Men and a Baby (1987)
Parenthood (1989)
Mrs Doubtfire (1993)

INNOCENTS ABROAD

The Secret Life of Walter Mitty (1947)
Harvey (1950)
Mr Hulot's Holiday (France, 1953)
Crocodile Dundee (Australia 1986)
The Fisher King (1991)
Dumber and Dumber (1995)

ODD COUPLES

The Odd Couple (1968)
The Blues Brothers (1980)
Planes, Trains & Automobiles (1987)
Twins (1988)
Junior (1994)

WORK COMEDIES

The Front Page (1931)
Carry on Nurse (UK, 1959)
I'm All Right Jack (UK, 1959)
Working Girl (1988)
How to Get Ahead in Advertising (UK, 1989)
Ace Ventura, Pet Detective (1993)

PARODY

Carry on Cleo (1964)
Kentucky Fried Movie (1977)
Airplane I & II (1980, 1982)
Dead Men Don't Wear Plaid (1982)
The Naked Gun & 2 1/2 & 33 1/3 (1988, 1991, 1994)
Hot Shots! (1991)

TV SPIN-OFFS

Monty Python's Life of Brian (UK, 1979)
Pee-Wee's Big Adventure (1985)
The Addams Family (1991)
Wayne's World & 2 (1992, 1993)
The Flintstones (1994)

COSTUME AND MELODRAMA

Everybody likes to lose themselves in a good story. Films about other people's lives help us forget our own troubles. Pictures set in the past, known as costume dramas, open up a dream world of romance and heroism. But we also enjoy modern-day melodramas in which ordinary people successfully tackle the problems of daily life.

△ Peter O'Toole as the British soldier who led the Arabs in their revolt against the Turks in David Lean's epic, *Lawrence of Arabia* (1962).

Film-makers have been fascinated by historical subjects since the 1890s. Thomas Edison's company, for example, made *The Execution of Mary, Queen of Scots* in 1895, for watching on a Kinetoscope. Far more sophisticated films were produced in France and Italy in the 1910s (see page 28). But silent cinema's finest 'period pictures' were the witty dramas about life at court in centuries past, which were shot in Germany by Ernst Lubitsch after World War I (see page 30).

Historical dramas

Films based on historical characters and events are known as costume dramas or period pictures because they rely on lavish costumes and detailed sets to transport viewers to settings as different as ancient or biblical times, the Middle Ages or the Victorian era.

Royalty has always been a popular topic. Rulers from all over Europe have been the subjects of dramas like *Ivan the Terrible* (1944–1946) and *Queen Margot* (1994). But not all royal films have focused on glamorous romances or gripping power struggles. *The Madness of King George* (1994), for example, showed that monarchs are human like the rest of us. The lives of many American presidents have also been covered in pictures like *Young Mr Lincoln* (1939). *JFK* (1991), on the other hand, tried to reconstruct the events that led to the assassination of President John F. Kennedy in 1963.

Historical films can be hard to follow as the characters and the times in which they lived are not always familiar. As a result, audiences often prefer period pieces in which the history is simply an exotic background to a swashbuckling adventure or a romance. The classic example of this kind of picture is *Gone with the Wind* (see box).

Features tracing a real person's life story are called 'biopics'. Some, like Tim Burton's *Ed Wood* (1995), about the legendary director of awful B movies, are lively and informative. But they have never been as successful as features like *Citizen Kane* (see box), which turn factual events into a fictional story. These pictures are called *films à clef*.

◁ The Royal Family greets the crowds from the steps of St Paul's Cathedral in *The Madness of King George* (1994). Great care was taken to make the lavish costumes historically accurate.

GONE WITH THE WIND

(USA, 1939) Director: Victor Fleming

On the eve of the American Civil War in 1861, high-spirited Scarlett O'Hara (Vivien Leigh) loses the man of her dreams, Ashley Wilkes (Leslie Howard), to her neighbour, Melanie Hamilton (Olivia De Havilland). Out of spite Scarlett weds Melanie's brother, but when he is killed in action, she marries the charming Rhett Butler (Clark Gable). But their relationship is extremely stormy and finally ends because of a family tragedy and Scarlett's continuing infatuation for Ashley.

Gone with the Wind was adapted from Margaret Mitchell's best-selling novel. It has enthralled audiences ever since its release in 1939. Over 1,500 women applied for the part of Scarlett O'Hara, including such top stars as Bette Davis, Joan Crawford and Katharine Hepburn. The favourite was Paulette Goddard, but the producer, David O. Selznick, finally cast an unknown British actress, Vivien Leigh. Filming began with George Cukor as director, but Gable had him sacked for paying too much attention to the female characters. Sam Wood also shot several sequences, because Victor Fleming was recovering from a nervous breakdown brought on by the pressure of the project.

Gone with the Wind won 10 Oscars and is still regarded as one of the masterpieces of the Golden Age of Hollywood. If the changing value of money is taken into account, it is easily the biggest box-office success in cinema history.

△ Scarlett struggles to hide her jealousy when she hears that Ashley is going to marry Melanie.

CITIZEN KANE

(USA, 1941) Director: Orson Welles

Citizen Kane traces the career of a newspaper tycoon whose dying word, 'Rosebud', remains a mystery until the end of the picture. It was the first film of actor-director Orson Welles, who was best known at the time for his radio version of *War of the Worlds* (1938). This science-fiction radio drama convinced millions of Americans that the country really was being invaded by Martians.

Welles tried to experiment with sound and image in almost every sequence of *Citizen Kane*. In telling his story he used flashbacks, deep-focus photography, expressionist lighting, long takes, symbolic angles, sweeping camera movements, sets with ceilings and overlapping dialogue. What was so remarkable about the film was that Welles took all these techniques and shaped them into a single, orderly style.

But the picture was not very successful when it was first released, because the press baron William Randolph Hearst recognized himself as the model for Kane, and ordered all his newspapers to blacklist the film. But today *Citizen Kane* is regarded by many critics and film-makers as the finest feature of all time.

From page and stage

Thousands of costume dramas and melodramas have been based on best-selling books and hit plays. But 'adapting' or shaping a familiar story for the screen is not always an easy task. Many plays like *Dangerous Liaisons* (1988) and *Shadowlands* (1994) have been transferred to the screen 'literally', that is word for word. But the directors usually develop them by filming the action in a variety of locations, rather than on a theatre stage.

Some film-makers make 'faithful' adaptations of books by using the language of film to capture the spirit of the original material. Two of the best recent examples are Merchant–Ivory's adaptation of E. M. Forster's *Howards End* (1992, see box on page 90) and Gillian Armstrong's version of Louisa May Alcott's *Little Women* (1995), starring Winona Ryder. Other directors 'loosely' base a story of their own on the action of an existing work. Akira Kurosawa, for example, found the inspiration for *Ran* (meaning 'chaos') in Shakespeare's drama, *King Lear*.

△ A poster for the colourful epic *Ran* (1985). Director Akira Kurosawa specialized in costume dramas set in medieval Japan, many of which contained dramatic battles fought by warriors called samurai.

Audiences can find screen versions of dramas very disappointing if the scriptwriter and the director do not show people and places in the way that they had imagined them. Film-makers, therefore, often choose a popular modern story (often called 'pulp fiction') rather than classic novels or plays, as people are usually less attached to the original book.

Melodrama

Drama has been popular with theatre audiences since the time of the ancient Greeks. Film-makers quickly realized the pulling power of pictures packed with moments of high drama. Almost all movies contain conflicts of ideas or emotions, but in films dealing with topics like romance, family life and the problems of growing up these clashes become the centre of attention.

The themes found in drama are exaggerated in melodrama. The term melodrama

HOWARDS END

(UK, 1992) Director: James Ivory

Set in England in about 1910, *Howards End* is a dramatic story about the dangers of class prejudice, good intentions and hidden emotions. Ruth Wilcox (Vanessa Redgrave) rewrites her will so that when she dies her country house, Howards End, will be inherited by her new friend, Margaret Schlegel (Emma Thompson). After Ruth's death, her husband Henry Wilcox (Anthony Hopkins) and his daughter Evie (Jemma Redgrave) decide to destroy the will to prevent Margaret from inheriting the house, but soon afterwards Henry and Margaret marry. Meanwhile Margaret's sister, Helen (Helena Bonham-Carter) has met a poor clerk named Leonard Bast (Samuel West) and their relationship has tragic consequences for the whole family.

Howards End was the third novel by the Edwardian author E. M. Forster to be adapted for the screen by the director–producer team of James Ivory and Ismail Merchant. *Howards End* was an even bigger success than the previous two – *A Room with a View* (1985) and *Maurice* (1987). It was nominated for nine Oscars, and won three, including one for Emma Thompson as Best Actress.

△ Helen Schlegel (Helena Bonham-Carter) is the unhappiest character in *Howards End*. Having been rejected by Henry Wilcox's son, she has a disastrous affair with Leonard Bast.

originally meant 'a play with music'. These stage shows first appeared in the mid-19th century and had a big influence on the earliest films. Melodramas are usually sensational, romantic stories full of simply drawn characters and improbable events. More emphasis is often placed on costumes and sets than on the plot, in which virtue always triumphs and wickedness is always punished. Yet some

of the most popular films ever made have been melodramas.

The master of the silent melodrama was D. W. Griffith (see page 22). In dozens of his films Lillian Gish played the innocent heroine. But, as Griffith's style went out of fashion in the 1920s, she was replaced by more worldly-wise characters played by Clara Bow and Gloria Swanson. The most influential Hollywood melodrama of this

▷ The stunning city set for the classic silent melodrama *Sunrise* (1927).

△ A forgotten star (Gloria Swanson) watches one of her old silent films in *Sunset Boulevard* (1950).

period was F. W. Murnau's *Sunrise* (1927). In this picture a loyal country wife rescues her husband after he has been lured away by an elegant city woman. This beautiful film sweeps the viewer from moonlit marshes to rain-soaked streets. It is a classic example of the most popular of all forms of drama – the romance.

Affairs of the heart

The screen romance had only one golden rule: that true love should never run smoothly. Only when the lovers had overcome all obstacles in their path could they be united in a final kiss. There have been many popular romantic screen couples including Greta Garbo and John Gilbert in the silent film era, Joan Crawford and Clark Gable in the 1930s, Katharine Hepburn and Spencer Tracy in the 1940s, and Elizabeth Taylor and Richard Burton in the 1960s. There have been few romantic teams in recent years as modern stars try to avoid being paired together too often.

A common romantic storyline was one in which the characters were not immediately attracted to each other. Rock Hudson, for example, spent much of *Pillow Talk* (1959) trying to persuade Doris Day that he was her 'Mr Right'. More recently, in *Frankie and Johnny* (1991), Al Pacino as a cook finds himself in a similar situation with a waitress played by Michelle Pfeiffer. Sometimes the stumbling block

REBECCA

(USA, 1940) Director: Alfred Hitchcock

The first film that Alfred Hitchcock made in Hollywood is a remarkable blend of romance and suspense. Maxim De Winter (Laurence Olivier) marries a plain, shy girl (Joan Fontaine) while on holiday. But when they return to his country mansion, Manderley, the new Mrs De Winter encounters the sinister housekeeper, Mrs Danvers (Judith Anderson). She convinces the girl that she can never take the place of the glamorous Rebecca, Maxim's first wife who died in a sailing accident. But the boat at the bottom of the sea hides a secret that will change the lives of all at Manderley.

Based on Daphne Du Maurier's popular novel, *Rebecca* won an Oscar for the Best Picture of 1940. Hitchcock skilfully guides the melodramatic story from its romantic opening, through its menacing middle at Manderley, to a tense courtroom sequence and its fiery finale. Laurence Olivier makes a moody Maxim, and George Sanders is splendid as Rebecca's shady cousin who accuses him of murder. But the best performances come from Joan Fontaine as the timid girl and Judith Anderson as her scheming enemy.

▷ Maxim watches as the new Mrs De Winter is confronted by Mrs Danvers, the housekeeper who was devoted to his first wife, Rebecca.

was that one of the lovers was already married, as in David Lean's *Brief Encounter* (1945). Other lovers, like Laurence Olivier in *Rebecca* (see box) or Juliet Stevenson in *Truly Madly Deeply* (1991), could not easily forget a partner who had recently died. Other problems facing cinema sweethearts have included racial prejudice, in films like *Guess Who's Coming to Dinner?* (1967), and class snobbery, as in *Pretty in Pink* (1986).

In many pictures the lovers were parted forever in sentimental endings that did not leave a dry eye in the cinema. 'Weepies' like *Camille* (1936) and *Love Story* (1970) tugged even more at the heart strings by having one of the partners die just as they had found true love.

The 'woman's picture'

Hollywood producers believed that dramas about love, marriage and relationships were largely of interest to women only. As a result, they created the 'woman's picture' for viewers to escape from their own problems and become involved in the sufferings of women from all times and places. Several films of the early sound era focused on 'fallen women', whose lives had been ruined by dangerous or disastrous relationships.

One of them, *Christopher Strong* (1933), was made by Dorothy Arzner, one of the few women directors in Hollywood during the 1930s. 'Fallen women' were banned by the censors in 1934, but heroines who suffered hardships remained popular with filmgoers. Their favourite actress was Greta Garbo, who brought a unique sense of mystery and tragedy to films like *Queen Christina* (1933) and *Anna Karenina* (1935). Garbo retired while she was still a major star in 1941. She was succeeded by Bette Davis and Joan Crawford, whose characters in films like *Jezebel* (1938) and *Humoresque* (1946) schemed to get their revenge on those who had harmed them.

Women's pictures were popular with audiences, but not with film critics who thought the stories were too melodramatic. In *Stella Dallas* (1937) and *Mildred Pierce* (1945), for example, Barbara Stanwyck and Joan Crawford played unhappy mothers who devote their entire lives to helping their daughters get on in the world. But film critics gradually changed their minds and began to see that these pictures were bold attempts to show independent women succeeding against all the odds.

The problems facing women trying to combine a career with a troubled home life were also dealt with in John M. Stahl's *Imitation of Life* in 1934. Another tale of the conflict between mothers and daughters, it also dealt with racial prejudice. The film was remade in 1959 by Douglas Sirk. He specialized in glossy melodramas that skilfully used bright colours and stylish décor to gently mock the entire genre, as well as to tell the story. Pictures like *Magnificent Obsession* (1953) and *Written on the Wind* (1956) had a huge influence on other major film-makers, for example Rainer Werner Fassbinder (see page 62), as well as on TV soap operas like *Dallas* or *Dynasty*.

▽ Anne Baxter (left) plays a woman who exploits a famous actress (Bette Davis, centre) in her bid for stage stardom, in *All About Eve* (1950).

◁ A rich widow (Jane Wyman) and her gardener (Rock Hudson) find love in spite of her disapproving friends in Douglas Sirk's *All That Heaven Allows* (1955).

◁ Joan Crawford's Oscar-winning performance in Michael Curtiz's *Mildred Pierce* (1945) revived her flagging career. She suffered and schemed in many more melodramas, including *Possessed* (1947) and *Sudden Fear* (1952).

▽ Glenn Close plays a woman desperate for revenge on the married man (Michael Douglas) who broke off their love affair, in the tense melodrama *Fatal Attraction* (1987).

Teenpix

The woman's picture had been aimed at women, who made up the bulk of cinema audiences in the 1930s and 1940s. But from the 1950s most filmgoers were teenagers, and Hollywood producers began to make movies designed to appeal to them by dealing with issues like money, sex, friendship and rebellion from a modern teenage viewpoint.

'Coming of age' films, which dealt with the problems of growing up, and 'rites of passage' pictures, which followed characters through the key turning points of their lives, were popular. For Tom Cruise in *Risky Business* (1983), for example, the dramatic incident that transformed his life was his first sexual experience, while for Keanu Reeves in *My Own Private Idaho* (1991) it was coming into an inheritance.

The very first teenage films like *The Wild One* (1954) and *Rebel without a Cause* (1955) shocked America with scenes showing juvenile violence, and made household names of Marlon Brando and James Dean respectively. Later features, known as 'teenpix', like *The Breakfast Club* (1985) and *Ferris Bueller's Day Off* (1986) focused on school and family life from the adolescent angle. They also made stars of the 'Brat Pack', a group of young performers that included Matthew Broderick, Matt Dillon, Molly Ringwold and Demi Moore.

FILMS TO WATCH

Films are made in the US unless otherwise stated

ROMANCE

Sunrise (1927)
Roman Holiday (1953)
Out of Africa (1985)
Moonstruck (1987)
Green Card (1990)
Indecent Proposal (1993)

DOOMED LOVE

A Farewell to Arms (1932)
Camille (1937)
Gone with the Wind (1939)
Brief Encounter (UK, 1945)
From Here to Eternity (1953)
Love Story (1970)
Shadowlands (UK, 1994)

FAMILIES

This Happy Breed (UK, 1944)
East of Eden (1955)
Cat on a Hot Tin Roof (1958)
Kramer vs Kramer (1979)
Ordinary People (1980)
Rain Man (1988)
Parenthood (1989)

'WOMEN'S PICTURES'

Imitation of Life (1934, 1959)
Stella Dallas (1937)
Magnificent Obsession (1935, 1954)
All That Heaven Allows (1955)
Written on the Wind (1956)
Terms of Endearment (1983)

CHILDHOOD

The Fallen Idol (UK, 1948)
Kes (UK, 1969)
Fanny and Alexander (Sweden, 1982)
My Life as a Dog (Sweden, 1985)
The Long Day Closes (UK, 1992)
The Slingshot (Sweden, 1993)
Free Willy (1994)

SCHOOLDAYS

Goodbye Mr Chips (1939)
The Browning Version (UK, 1950, 1994)
Tom Brown's Schooldays (UK, 1951)
The Prime of Miss Jean Brodie (UK, 1969)
Another Country (UK, 1984)
The Breakfast Club (1985)
Au Revoir les Enfants (France, 1988)
Dead Poets Society (1989)
Dazed and Confused (1994)

TEENAGE

The Wild One (1954)
Rebel without a Cause (1955)
Gregory's Girl (UK, 1980)

Risky Business (1983)
St Elmo's Fire (1985)
Pretty in Pink (1986)
Ferris Bueller's Day Off (1986)
Some Kind of Wonderful (1987)

RITES OF PASSAGE

Greed (1923)
Diner (1982)
The Frog Prince (UK, 1985)
Distant Voices Still Lives (UK, 1988)
Avalon (1990)
My Own Private Idaho (1991)
A River Runs Through It (1993)

ANCIENT WORLD

The Last Days of Pompeii (1935)
Quo Vadis? (1951)
Ben-Hur (1959)
Spartacus (1960)
The Fall of the Roman Empire (1964)

ROYALTY

The Scarlet Empress (1934)
Sixty Glorious Years (UK, 1938)
Ivan the Terrible (USSR, 1944-46)
Henry V (UK, 1944, 1989)
Lady Jane (UK, 1986)
The Madness of King George (1994)

HISTORICAL DRAMA

The Man in Grey (UK, 1943)
Julia (1977)
Ran (Japan, 1986)
Dangerous Liaisons (1988)
Sommersby (1993)
Restoration (1995)

LITERARY ADAPTATIONS

David Copperfield (1935)
Wuthering Heights (1939, 1992)
Pride and Prejudice (1940)
Rebecca (1940)
Jane Eyre (1943, 1995)
Great Expectations (1946)
Tess (France/UK, 1979)
Little Dorrit (UK, 1987)
Howards End (UK, 1992)
Much Ado About Nothing (UK, 1993)
The Remains of the Day (UK, 1993)
Orlando (UK, 1993)
The Age of Innocence (1993)

CHILDREN'S LITERATURE

Little Women (1933, 1949, 1994)
Treasure Island (1934, 1950)
The Adventures of Tom Sawyer (1938)
The Secret Garden (1949, 1993)
The Railway Children (UK, 1970)
Black Beauty (UK, 1995)

CRIME

The crime film presents a very sinister picture of modern city life. Set on crowded, unwelcoming streets, the action is often fast and the talk is always tough. Gangsters, bank robbers and murderers seem to lurk on every corner, while cops, private eyes and special agents search for clues to solve baffling mysteries. In the crime film, city life has become an 'urban nightmare'.

Crime was a popular subject in the silent film era. The earliest screen crooks were usually burglars or melodramatic villains and swindlers. But films like D. W. Griffith's *The Musketeers of Pig Alley* (1912) contained much more menacing thugs who terrorized the poor in the slums of New York.

Gangsters

In *Dr Mabuse, the Gambler* (1922) Fritz Lang introduced a new breed of criminal. The sinister Mabuse was a master of disguise, who employed a gang of rogues to do his dirty work. He also hypnotized bankers, politicians and policemen into following his orders. Gang bosses like Mabuse became familiar figures in American features following Josef von Sternberg's *Underworld* (1926), a brooding crime thriller in which an escaped gangster sacrifices himself to save his girlfriend.

The gangster film was transformed by the coming of sound. The rattle of machine-gun fire, the screams of onlookers and the screeching tyres of getaway cars all added to the excitement and realism of these tough-talking pictures. The hoodlums in the films in the classic gangster era (1930-1933) were often based on real gangsters who operated in American cities like Chicago. Many of the stories in these features were taken directly from true crime reports splashed across the daily newspapers.

Films like *Little Caesar* (1930), *Public Enemy* (1931) and *Scarface* (see box) presented the city as an urban jungle with danger on every street. Much of the action took place at night, to add to the mood of menace. The neon lights reflecting in the rain-soaked pavements also gave the city a cold, unfriendly feel. This hostile setting helped to explain why the gangster had

SCARFACE

(USA, 1932) Director: Howard Hawks

Scarface traces the rise and fall of gangster Tony Camonte (Paul Muni). Camonte calmly kills his way to power. But he is so insanely jealous of his sister (Ann Dvorak) that he fails to notice that his rivals are uniting against him.

Originally entitled *Scarface, Shame of a Nation*, this was the most brutal of Hollywood's 1930s gangster films. It was the first crime picture to show a hoodlum using a machine gun, and it contained 28 deaths in all. In the film Howard Hawks compares Tony to the 16th-century Italian prince Cesare Borgia, who was just as ruthless and was also obsessed with his sister, Lucretia. Yet in spite of the violence and the clever comparisons, Hawks was more interested in showing gangsters as excited children playing deadly games. As a result the film is full of cynical humour. The censors did not see the joke, however, and the feature was only released after some scenes were cut.

Director Brian De Palma remade the film in 1983 with Al Pacino in the title role, Maria Elizabeth Mastrantonio as his sister and Michelle Pfeiffer as his boss's drug-addicted wife. The extreme violence caused much controversy, but the film is packed with exciting action and excellent performances.

◁ Paul Muni as vicious gangster Tony Camonte preparing to fill one of his rivals full of lead.

▷ Mervyn LeRoy's *I am a Fugitive from a Chain Gang* (1932) was a tough look at life in America's jails during the Depression. Paul Muni was nominated for an Oscar for his performance as a decent man whose life is ruined by poverty and prison.

been driven to crime and killing, and it won him the sympathy of the audience. The gangsters were played by top stars like James Cagney, Edward G. Robinson and Humphrey Bogart, which increased their box-office appeal. As they usually died in a hail of bullets, they were admired as 'tragic heroes'.

But powerful people disapproved of the ruthless methods gangsters used to build up their empires. They persuaded the movie moguls to stop making gangster pictures in 1934. The lives of criminals like Al Capone, John Dillinger and Baby Face Nelson were later retold in a series of gangster films in the 1950s. The gangster has since returned to screens around the world. He is particularly popular in Japan, where he is known as a *yakuza*.

The strong arm of the law

Screen tough guys like Cagney next turned to playing government agents working on the side of the law. But they were every bit as cynical, arrogant and violent as the underworld bosses. Pictures like *G-Men* (1935) and *T-Men* (1947) showed that crime did not pay by making sure the villains were always caught. They also revealed the technology involved in modern detection. Collecting and analyzing evidence, fingerprinting, identity parades and checking criminal records were filmed with almost documentary realism. These films were known as 'police procedurals' and were most popular in the late 1940s when 'true-life' crime stories became fashionable (see page 53).

△ Henry Fonda (standing) tries to convince a jury of a man's innocence in the tense courtroom drama, *12 Angry Men* (1957).

Sleuths...

In contrast to the efficiency of the cop and the special agent were the more eccentric methods of the amateur detective or 'sleuth'. The most famous of these was Sherlock Holmes. He made his first screen appearance in 1903 and has since become the most often portrayed character in screen history. Over 70 different actors have played the role. Holmes's screen cases were usually based on the stories of Sir Arthur Conan Doyle and were set amid the bustling, foggy streets of Victorian London. But the most popular pictures starred Basil Rathbone as Holmes and Nigel Bruce as his faithful assistant, Dr Watson. They starred in 14 adventures together, many of which, like *Sherlock Holmes Faces Death* (1943), were set during World War II.

WARREN BEATTY
FAYE DUNAWAY

THEY'RE YOUNG... THEY'RE IN LOVE... AND THEY KILL PEOPLE

BONNIE AND CLYDE

MICHAEL J. POLLARD · GENE HACKMAN · ESTELLE PARSONS
WRITTEN BY
DAVID NEWMAN and ROBERT BENTON · Charles Strouse · WARREN BEATTY · ARTHUR PENN
TECHNICOLOR® FROM WARNER BROS.-SEVEN ARTS · RELEASED THROUGH WARNER-PATHE

◁ Faye Dunaway and Warren Beatty in a poster for the influential crime film *Bonnie and Clyde*. The picture became such a cult hit that fans began to wear 1930s clothes and even stuck fake bullet holes on to the windscreens of their cars.

In the 1930s and 1940s several other sleuths found their way on to the screen from the pages of popular fiction. Among them were Charlie Chan from China and the Japanese detective Mr Moto. Some were wealthy playboys with a nose for danger like The Saint and The Falcon, who were often suspected of the crimes they were trying to solve by plodding police inspectors. The most sophisticated films of this type were the Thin Man series, starring William Powell and Myrna Loy as Nick and Nora Charles. The British author Agatha Christie's best-known character, the Belgian detective Hercule Poirot, has featured in a number of all-star 'whodunnits', including *Murder on the Orient Express* (1974).

◁ Ray Liotta, Robert De Niro, Paul Sorvino and Joe Pesci as the mobsters whose careers of crime are followed between 1955 and 1980 in Martin Scorsese's hard-hitting Mafia picture, *GoodFellas* (1990).

...and private eyes

After World War II the gloomy, threatening atmosphere of *film noir* (see page 53) added a touch of evil to Hollywood crime. *The Maltese Falcon* (1941) launched this shadowy style and introduced a new kind of detective, the private eye, also known as the 'shamus'. He first appeared in the

▽ P. C. George Dixon (Jack Warner) bends down to talk to a small boy in *The Blue Lamp* (1949). Warner later played the friendly copper in the long-running TV series, *Dixon of Dock Green*.

pages of hard-edged thrillers by American writers like Dashiell Hammett and Raymond Chandler. World-weary and charming, the private eye solved baffling mysteries in which there were as many murders as there were twists in the plot.

Humphrey Bogart played Sam Spade in *The Maltese Falcon*, and went on to star as the equally tough Philip Marlowe in *The Big Sleep* (1946, see box). Several other actors have also played the part of Marlowe, including Dick Powell in *Farewell, My Lovely* (1944) and Elliott Gould in *The Long Goodbye* (1973). But the role is usually associated with Bogart. Other private eyes in the same cynical mould include Mike Hammer in the brutal *Kiss Me Deadly* (1955) and J. J. Gittes, played by Jack Nicholson in *Chinatown* (1974) and *The Two Jakes* (1990).

The Mob and the Mafia

The *film noir* era of the late 1940s also saw less of the individual crook and more of the 'Mob'. In the 1950s organized groups, or mobs, had begun to take over much of America's big crime operations, including gambling and drug dealing. Several pictures dealt with the Mob, among them *The Big Heat* (1953), *On the Waterfront* (1954) and *The Big Combo* (1955).

The most feared of these mobs was the Mafia, a group of tightly knit families originally from Sicily. The Mafia had featured in Italian films like *Salvatore Giuliano*, but apart from *New York Confidential* (1954) it had rarely been tackled by Hollywood. Francis Ford Coppola's *The Godfather* (see box) turned the Mafia into a popular box-office topic, with *The Godfather Part II* (1974) becoming the first sequel ever to win the Oscar for Best Picture. Martin Scorsese has also directed a number of fine Mob pictures, among them *GoodFellas* (1990) and *Casino* (1995).

Heists and capers

The carefully planned and carried out robbery has been a popular crime subject since the 1950s. Two of the best of these 'heist' pictures starred Sterling Hayden as the leader of the gang. In John Huston's *The Asphalt Jungle* (1950) he led a raid on a jewellery shop, while in Stanley Kubrick's *The Killing* (1956) he plotted to rob a race-track betting office. However, in each case the precise plan goes wrong and ends in disaster. A recent variation on this theme was Quentin Tarantino's *Reservoir Dogs* (see box on page 98).

Equally ingenious robberies were the subject of films like *Rififi* (1954) and *The Italian Job* (1968). These so-called 'caper movies' included as much knockabout comedy as crime. But their success was only short-lived, as audiences really preferred crime pictures that thrilled rather than amused them.

THE BIG SLEEP

(USA, 1946) Director: Howard Hawks

A retired general hires private eye Philip Marlowe (Humphrey Bogart) to investigate a shady bookseller who is blackmailing him. He also wants to find a missing friend. Marlowe takes the case, only to become caught up in a tangled web of gambling, drugs and murder. Amidst it all he also finds romance with the general's older daughter (Lauren Bacall).

The Big Sleep is both a nail-biting mystery and one of the finest examples of *film noir*. The plot is so complex that not even Raymond Chandler, the author of the original book, was sure who had killed the general's chauffeur. When Howard Hawks phoned to ask him the question he replied: 'How should I know? You figure it out.' Humphrey Bogart is superb as the cynical shamus. In spite of being double-crossed, beaten up and held at gunpoint, he still tracks down the vital clues. But to this day the case of the murdered chauffeur remains unsolved.

▷ Rebellious rich girl Vivian Sternwood (Lauren Bacall) gets private eye Philip Marlowe (Humphrey Bogart) out of a knotty situation in this classic detective thriller.

△ Don Vito Corleone (Marlon Brando) reluctantly hands on the family business to his son Michael (Al Pacino) in *The Godfather*.

THE GODFATHER

(USA, 1972) Director: Francis Ford Coppola

Vito Corleone (Marlon Brando) is the Don, or head, of one of New York's leading Mafia families. While his sons Sonny (James Caan) and Fredo (John Cazale) are also part of the business, his middle son Michael (Al Pacino) has been kept away from crime. But then an attempt is made on the Don's life after he blocks a drugs deal, and a gang war breaks out. When Sonny is murdered, Michael takes charge and masterminds a bloodbath which removes the family's enemies.

Based on Mario Puzo's best-selling Mafia novel, *The Godfather* is a gripping piece of cinema. Superbly acted and directed, it began the wave of blockbusters that revived American cinema in the early 1970s (see page 69).

The Godfather, Part II (1974) was better than the original, proving that sequels are not always a disappointment. Much of the opening action is made up of flashbacks to the early career of Vito Corleone (this time played by Robert De Niro). These scenes show how far Michael has strayed from his father's family values as he ruthlessly builds up a gambling empire in Las Vegas and Cuba. *The Godfather, Part III* (1990) was far less impressive than its predecessors, apart from another elaborately staged massacre at the end.

RESERVOIR DOGS

(USA, 1992) Director: Quentin Tarantino

Joe Cabot (Lawrence Tierney) and his son Nice Guy Eddie (Chris Penn) plan a diamond heist. They hire six strangers for the job and give them the code names Mr White (Harvey Keitel), Mr Orange (Tim Roth), Mr Pink (Steve Buscemi), Mr Blonde (Michael Madsen), Mr Blue (Edward Bunker) and Mr Brown (Quentin Tarantino). But the raid backfires and when the survivors meet back at an empty warehouse they begin to suspect each other of being the traitor who tipped off the police.

Packed with violent incidents and black humour, *Reservoir Dogs* achieved instant cult status. It disproves the proverb that there is honour among thieves. The film bristles with snappy dialogue and is slickly played by an expert cast. In his remarkable debut as writer-director, Quentin Tarantino manages to poke fun at the traditions of the crime film, while at the same time paying them tribute. As with *The Big Sleep* a mystery remains – who hit Nice Guy Eddie in the final shootout?

▷ Mr White (Harvey Keitel) and Mr Pink (Steve Buscemi) both find themselves looking down the barrel of a gun, after a slight difference of opinion in *Reservoir Dogs*.

Thrillers and killers

Nothing can create suspense quite like cinema. The soundtrack can build up the tension as a character goes further into a darkened house or moves closer towards a crazed killer. The camera can allow the viewer to see through the character's eyes or to follow from a safe distance. It can capture objects from disturbing new angles or it can shock with a sudden crosscut that reveals a face emerging from the shadows, a weapon glinting in the dimmed light or a hand reaching out...

Often characters in these suspense thrillers face danger in the line of duty, including the FBI agent played by Jodie Foster in *The Silence of the Lambs* (1990). Some are placed in peril because they have stumbled across a crime, like James Stewart and Grace Kelly in *Rear Window* (1954). But others are innocent bystanders caught up in shady dealings, like the blind woman played by Audrey Hepburn in *Wait Until Dark* (1967).

Alfred Hitchcock (see box on page 99) believed that the strongest sense of suspense is created when the viewer knows what to expect, because waiting for it to happen then becomes almost unbearable.

But he also included sudden surprises in some of his pictures. The most shocking was the brilliantly edited 'shower scene' in *Psycho* (1960). This 45-second sequence shows motel-owner Norman Bates (Anthony Perkins) stabbing an escaping thief (Janet Leigh) in her bathroom. It contains 87 separate shots and is made all the more terrifying by Bernard Herrmann's famous shrieking violin music.

But long before Norman Bates began terrorizing guests at his motel, the screen had seen several other evil killers. One of the most notorious was played by Peter Lorre in *M* (1931), Fritz Lang's chilling tale of child murder.

Crime is often violent and films can reflect this with terrifying realism. Such films are often censored to limit their influence on people, especially younger viewers. A fierce debate about violence in cinema has raged throughout the 1990s. In 1994, for example, *Natural Born Killers* was attacked for showing serial killers obviously taking pleasure in their crimes. Whatever their merits as motion pictures, these films are undoubtedly a sad reflection of the times in which we live.

◁ Fred MacMurray is convinced that he and Barbara Stanwyck have been caught in the act of murdering her husband in *Double Indemnity* (1944), a gripping *film noir* directed by Billy Wilder.

VERTIGO

(USA, 1958) Director: Alfred Hitchcock

Scotty Ferguson (James Stewart) becomes a private eye when his vertigo, a medical term for fear of heights, causes him to retire from the police force. Soon after this a friend hires him to follow his wife Madeleine (Kim Novak), whom he believes is in danger. Scotty falls hopelessly in love with her. But because of his vertigo he is unable to prevent her plunging to her death from a church bell tower. While still deep in shock, he meets a woman called Judy (also played by Kim Novak), who reminds him of Madeleine. He begins to change her appearance so that she comes to look more like the dead Madeleine. But, unknown to him, there is a reason why Madeleine and Judy look alike – murder.

Filmed in a widescreen process called Vista Vision, *Vertigo* is a skilful blend of the ghost story and the thriller. It is both a chilling story and a compelling study of obsession. But it is also a fascinating insight into the cinema's ability to create illusion. With its stunning use of camera movement, colour and visual imagery, many critics believe this complex film is Hitchcock's masterpiece, although it was not a box-office success when it was first released.

△ Unaware that he is being lured into a dangerous game, Scotty Ferguson (James Stewart) catches up with Madeleine (Kim Novak) on the streets of San Francisco.

FILMS TO WATCH

Films are made in the US unless otherwise stated

GANGSTERS

Dead End (1937)
Angels with Dirty Faces (1938)
The Roaring Twenties (1939)
White Heat (1948)
Once Upon a Time in America (1983)

GANGSTER BIOPICS

Al Capone (1958)
Bonnie and Clyde (1967)
Dillinger (1973)
Bugsy (1991)

GANGLAND CRIME

The Enforcer (1951)
The Big Heat (1953)
On the Waterfront (1954)
The Big Combo (1955)
Underworld USA (1960)
Dick Tracy (1990)

THE MOB

The French Connection (1971)
The Godfather I, II & III (1972, 1974, 1990)
Prizzi's Honour (1985)
Things Change (1988)
GoodFellas (1990)
A Bronx Tale (1993)

SPECIAL AGENTS

Bullets or Ballots (1936)
The FBI Story (1951)
The Untouchables (1987)
The Silence of the Lambs (1990)
In the Line of Fire (1993)

COPS

In the Heat of the Night (1967)
Dirty Harry (1972)
48 Hours (1982)
Beverly Hills Cop (1985, 1987, 1994)
Lethal Weapon (1987, 1989, 1992)
Falling Down (1993)

WATCHING THE DETECTIVES

The Thin Man (1934)
Charlie Chan at the Opera (1936)
The Saint Strikes Back (1939)
The Maltese Falcon (1941)
The Falcon Takes Over (1942)
Sherlock Holmes Faces Death (1943)
Farewell, My Lovely (1944, 1975)
The Big Sleep (1946)
Murder on the Orient Express (UK, 1974)

HEISTS & CAPERS

The League of Gentlemen (UK, 1960)
The Heist (1971)
The Hot Rock (1972)

The Getaway (1972, 1994)
Reservoir Dogs (1992)
Sneakers (1992)

BRITISH CROOKS

Brighton Rock (UK, 1948)
The Long Good Friday (UK, 1980)
Mona Lisa (UK, 1986)
The Krays (UK, 1990)
Let Him Have It (UK, 1991)

ASSASSINS

The Samurai (France, 1967)
The Day of the Jackal (UK/France, 1973)
Nikita (France, 1990)
The Assassin (1993)
Pulp Fiction (1994)
Leon (1994)

NATURAL BORN KILLERS

Shadow of a Doubt (1943)
The Night of the Hunter (1955)
Psycho (1960)
Cape Fear (1961, 1991)
Badlands (1973)
Heathers (1989)

PEOPLE IN PERIL

Suspicion (1941)
Sorry, Wrong Number (1948)
Rear Window (1954)
Vertigo (1958)
Misery (1990)
The Hand that Rocks the Cradle (1992)
The Bodyguard (1992)
A Perfect World (1993)

COURTROOM DRAMA

Fury (1936)
The Accused (1988)
In the Name of the Father (1993)
The Firm (1993)

PRISON

The Big House (1930)
Brute Force (1947)
The Defiant Ones (1958)
Bird Man of Alcatraz (1961)
Cool Hand Luke (1967)
The Shawshank Redemption (1994)

MODERN *FILM NOIR*

Body Heat (1981)
House of Games (1987)
Dead Again (1991)
Final Analysis (1992)
The Last Seduction (1994)
Shallow Grave (UK, 1995)

HORROR

Horror plays on all our worst fears. In many films our dreams come true, but in the horror movie it is our nightmares that unfold before us. Eerie shadows, howling winds, creaking doors and screaming victims have been scaring us for decades. Modern horror movies add gruesome special effects, but the most frightening pictures leave the unexplained to our imagination.

Many of the first horror films retold European folk tales about devils and witchcraft. Others dealt with ghosts and ghouls who returned from the grave to haunt the living.

Silent shadows

The pioneer of screen horror was Étienne Robertson, whose *Phantasmagoria* (1798) terrified audiences in Paris during the French Revolution (see page 11). An important influence on the horror movie was *Grand Guignol*. This was a ghoulish form of melodrama in which bloodthirsty killings and sensational changes in appearance took place on stage.

Many early horror film directors were inspired by 'Gothic romances', which also first appeared at the end of the 18th century. These novels were set in ruined castles and gloomy monasteries built in the Gothic style of architecture. Several horror favourites, like Frankenstein's monster, first came to life in these books. Many other familiar terrors, including the Hunchback of Notre Dame, the Phantom of the Opera, and Dr Jekyll and Mr Hyde, also rose from the pages of popular books.

Georges Méliès made the first horror movie, *The Devil's Castle*, in 1896. It was full of demons and skeletons. The genre became more sophisticated in the 1920s. In Hollywood Lon Chaney, nicknamed 'the

Man of a Thousand Faces', created a gallery of ghouls using nothing more than make-up and his own acting genius. At the same time in Germany, Robert Wiene made *The Cabinet of Dr Caligari* (see page 30), the first in a series of 'shadow films'. These created a sinister atmosphere through a clever mix of light, shade and unusual camera angles. Among them was F. W. Murnau's *Nosferatu*, which first brought the vampire to the screen in 1922. Shadow films also introduced such unnatural creatures as the clay giant called the Golem, and the *doppelgänger* (or lookalike).

A gallery of ghouls

Many horror characters like the vampire, the werewolf and the Mummy have appeared in films set in very different times and places. Dracula, for example, has terrified people in 16th-century Transylvania as well as modern-day New

◁ Lon Chaney as the Phantom of the Opera. He was also the most memorable screen Hunchback of Notre Dame. His son, Lon Chaney Jr., also starred in many horror movies.

◁ Max Schreck played the screen's first vampire in *Nosferatu* (1922). The director F. W. Murnau shot the film on location, to make the sinister action seem even more chilling. Another German director, Werner Herzog, remade the picture in 1979 with Klaus Kinski in the title role.

Films about Dr Jekyll and Mr Hyde have also usually stuck closely to the tale first told by Robert Louis Stevenson. Dr Jekyll is a scientist who transforms into an evil monster, named Mr Hyde, after drinking from a steaming chemical potion. When Hyde commits murder, Jekyll realizes that to put an end to his creation he must die himself. *Mary Reilly* (1995) adds a new twist to the plot by telling the story from the viewpoint of Jekyll's housekeeper.

Related to Jekyll and Hyde is the legend of the *doppelgänger*, or lookalike. He first appeared in *The Student of Prague* (1913), featuring the German actor-director Paul Wegener in the leading role. This tells of a

penniless student called Baldwin, who sells his reflection to the shady Dr Scapinelli in return for wealth and a good marriage. But the reflection takes on a life of its own and Baldwin is forced to shoot it, so causing his own death.

Wegener also starred in and directed both versions of *The Golem* (1915 & 1920), which were based on another Central European myth. These films told of a clay giant brought to life by a rabbi in the 16th-century to protect the Jews of Prague from a cruel emperor. When the Golem is discovered in modern times it comes to life again and falls in love with an antique dealer's daughter, who destroys it.

DRACULA

(USA, 1931) Director: Tod Browning

Count Dracula (Bela Lugosi), a 500-year-old vampire, sees a picture of Mina Seward (Helen Chandler) and leaves his Transylvanian castle to make her his bride. Determined to find Mina, he comes to London with his insect-eating servant, Renfield (Dwight Frye). But she is protected by her fiancé Jonathan Harker (David Manners) and expert vampire hunter Professor Van Helsing (Edward Van Sloan).

Dracula was based on a 1920s stage play rather than on the famous 19th-century novel by Bram Stoker. Bela Lugosi's elegant charm and hypnotic eyes made him the perfect vampire, and the scenes in which he conquers his victims are full of evil menace. The film is now beginning to look old-fashioned, but Count Dracula has never been so chilling, even though he has since appeared in over 150 pictures.

York. But in each movie featuring these ghouls certain elements of the plot remain the same, whatever the story. In werewolf pictures, for example, a person bitten by a wolf takes on the shape and nature of the beast at full moon, and can only be stopped by a silver bullet. The vampire has no reflection, hates garlic and crucifixes, and can only be killed by daylight, running water or a stake through the heart.

In some horror classics, however, the plot and the characters never vary – yet the stories are so thrilling that audiences return to them again and again. In *The Hunchback of Notre Dame* the deformed bellringer, Quasimodo, always loses his life protecting Esmeralda, a gypsy girl sheltering inside Paris's medieval cathedral. *The Phantom of the Opera* is another 'beauty and the beast' story: a disfigured composer terrorizes the company of the Paris Opera House so that Christine, the singer he adores, can become a star.

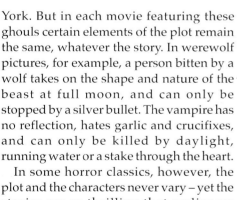

◁ Peter Cushing defends himself against Christopher Lee in the 1959 Hammer horror film, *The Mummy*.

minor classics for the RKO studio. He concentrated on the more neglected areas of horror like the supernatural fantasy, grave robbing and lunatic asylums in pictures like *The Curse of the Cat People* (1944), *The Body Snatcher* (1945) and *Bedlam* (1946). With *I Walked with a Zombie* (1943) he also revived film interest in zombies – dead bodies that are re-awakened during the rituals of a Caribbean religious cult known as voodoo.

Not of this world...

The horror film has always been closely linked to science fiction. Frankenstein and Jekyll were both scientists whose work had horrific consequences. In the 1950s people were worried that experiments with nuclear power would have equally

Talking terror

The shadows of silent films had been spooky enough. But the 'Talkie' era brought chilling sound effects and a new generation of performers, including Bela Lugosi and Boris Karloff, whose eerie voices alone could freeze the blood.

Karloff and Lugosi were key figures in the horror pictures produced in Hollywood by Universal Studios in the early 1930s. Features like *The Old Dark House*, *The Murders in the Rue Morgue* and *The Black Cat* were spine-tingling stories filled with evil characters and menacing, shadowy settings. Universal also started the trend for horror sequels with *Bride of Frankenstein* (1935, see box) and *Dracula's Daughter* (1936). It also introduced several new characters in pictures like *The Invisible Man* (1933). In this classic film, a scientist experimenting with a new drug becomes invisible. But his harmless pranks soon lead to madness and murder. The picture used the latest special effects, and made an overnight star of Claude Rains, even though for much of the action he was either wrapped in bandages or 'invisible'!

Horror was not so popular in the 1940s and became a subject for B movies. Nevertheless, Russian-born producer Val Lewton still managed to make several

BRIDE OF FRANKENSTEIN

(USA, 1935) Director: James Whale

In *Frankenstein* (1931), the German scientist Baron Victor Frankenstein (Colin Clive) had used electricity to bring to life a being (Boris Karloff) constructed entirely from dead body parts. But this monster's brain was so badly damaged that he was unable to control either his strength or his emotions. Having caused a series of deaths in the local village, he is trapped in a blazing windmill.

Bride of Frankenstein continues the story. The monster has survived the fire and wanders through the forest in search of friendship. He is treated kindly by a blind hermit (O. P. Heggie), but soon falls into the hands of Dr Pretorius (Ernest Thesiger), a wicked scientist who has created a family of miniature people. He blackmails Frankenstein into making a companion, or bride, for the monster. But the bride (Elsa Lanchester) finds him repulsive and the heartbroken monster destroys Pretorius, the bride and himself with a surge of electrical power.

James Whale's films are only loosely based on Mary Shelley's novel, but they fully capture the tragedy of the monster whose need for love results only in death. Boris Karloff brings touches of real humanity to the creature's rage and confusion, even though he is barely recognizable beneath Jack Pierce's legendary make-up.

▷ A scene from *Frankenstein* (1931) in which Boris Karloff accidentally drowns a small girl who is kind to him. His search for affection also ended in tragedy in the 1935 sequel, *Bride of Frankenstein*.

▷ In *The Masque of the Red Death*, Vincent Price (right) plays Prince Prospero, the medieval devil worshipper who gives a party for his rich friends while the plague or 'red death' kills off the peasants outside his castle.

disastrous results. This mood of fear was reflected in many sci-fi horror films like *The Thing* (1951) and *Them!* (1953). These films also gave make-up and special effects artists the chance to create new monsters like aliens and giant insects.

Many of these features were aimed at the growing teenage audience. The master of these so-called 'exploitation' films was Roger Corman. His earliest horror films like *The Little Shop of Horrors* (1960) were as much comedies as chillers. But his stylish adaptations of Edgar Allan Poe's Gothic tales were more disturbing. In films such as *The House of Usher* (1960), *The Pit and the Pendulum* (1961), *The Masque of the Red Death* (1964) and *The Tomb of Ligeia* (1965) he made striking use of bright colours, cheap special effects and the acting talents of Vincent Price, who became a major horror star.

Hammer horror

Hammer is one of the great names of the world of horror. This small company gave Britain a reputation for horror films when it began re-making the genre's classic tales in the mid-1950s. Hammer retold the stories of Dracula, Frankenstein, the Mummy, the werewolf and the Phantom of the Opera in ghoulish colour. These pictures had low budgets and tight schedules. But they were internationally

popular and made huge stars of actors like Peter Cushing and Christopher Lee.

Hammer made horror more horrific by using gruesome close-ups. You could see Frankenstein's monster dissolving in an acid bath. You could watch Count Dracula sinking his fangs into a bared neck, his eyes turning red as he drank his fill. You could spot the glistening entrails of the werewolf's latest victim in a pool of moonlight.

Hammer horrors like *The Curse of Frankenstein* (1956) and *Dracula* (1958) stayed close to the familiar story. But later features like *Dr Jekyll and Sister Hyde* (1971) tried to be more original, as the doctor turned into a woman each time he drank his special potion.

▽ Christopher Lee (left) arranges his friends inside a charmed circle to prevent the devil from stealing one of their souls in *The Devil Rides Out* (1968).

ASSOCIATED BRITISH-PATHE LIMITED PRESENTS
A HAMMER FILM PRODUCTION
CHRISTOPHER LEE · CHARLES GRAY
NIKE ARRIGHI · LEON GREENE
in "THE DEVIL RIDES OUT"
also starring PATRICK MOWER · GWEN FFRANGCON-DAVIES
SARAH LAWSON · PAUL EDDINGTON
TECHNICOLOR ®
RELEASED THROUGH WARNER-PATHE DISTRIBUTORS LTD.

◁ A terrifying moment from Alfred Hitchcock's disturbing classic, *The Birds* (1963).

But the makers of these 'teens in peril' pictures were often more interested in gory special effects and ingenious make-up than in imaginative plots. After *Friday the Thirteenth* (1980) horror was dominated by cheaply made 'schlock' or 'splatter' movies, many of which were released directly on to video. In the early 1980s there was a great debate about the effects 'video nasties' like Abel Ferrara's *Driller Killer* could have on young viewers.

The sight of too much blood and guts can revolt rather than scare us.

▽ Brutal murder movies are often deeply disturbing. One of the most shocking is *The Silence of the Lambs*, directed by Jonathan Demme. The film follows FBI agent Clarice Starling (Jodie Foster) as she tries to track down a ruthless serial killer nicknamed 'Buffalo Bill'. Only one man has the expertise to help her solve the case, but Dr. Hannibal Lecter (Anthony Hopkins) is himself a vicious murderer known as 'Hannibal the Cannibal', because of his habit of eating his victims. As Clarice closes in on 'Buffalo Bill', Lecter escapes in order to take his grizzly revenge on a cruel jailer.

Slash and splatter

Corman's movies paved the way for a new type of horror film – the 'American nightmare' in which terrors lurked in isolated little communities throughout America. In Alfred Hitchcock's *The Birds* (1963) and George A. Romero's *Night of the Living Dead* (1968) no matter where you ran, there was no place to hide from savage birds or zombie flesh-eaters. Evil spirits could also take possession of ordinary people, like the 12-year-old girl played by Linda Blair in *The Exorcist* (1973).

The 'American nightmare' also concentrated on crazed killers or 'psycho-slashers'. These maniacs lived only for bloodshed and usually chose teenagers for their victims. They had first appeared in so-called 'yellow horror' films, which were incredibly gory movies made by Italian directors like Mario Bava and Dario Argento. But now, mass murderers like Leatherface in *The Texas Chainsaw Massacre* (1974) and Michael Myers in *Halloween* (1978) were on the loose in America.

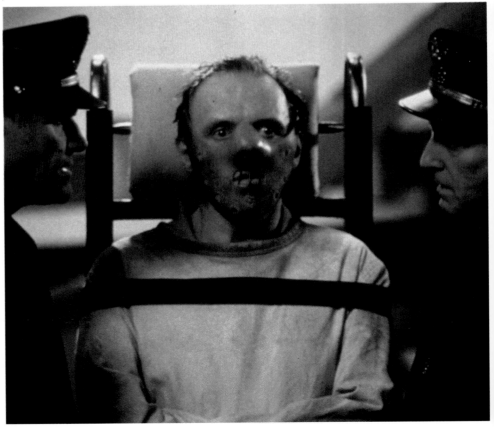

A NIGHTMARE ON ELM STREET

(USA, 1984) Director: Wes Craven

Freddy Kreuger (Robert Englund) is burned alive as a child killer. Years later, he returns to Elm Street to haunt the dreams of the children of the people who put him to death. But when the dreams start to come true, the nightmare begins.

This is an ingenious and unnerving film. Wes Craven keeps the action tense by blurring the line between imagination and reality. As a result, the viewer can never really be sure whether a character is dreaming or awake. With his scarred face, red and green striped pullover and gloves with knives in the fingertips, Freddy Kreuger is one of horror's most terrifying figures. Although *A Nightmare on Elm Street Part VII* (1991) was subtitled *Freddy's Dead*, he returned three years later to scare audiences all over again in *Wes Craven's New Nightmare*.

Nevertheless there were some genuinely heart-stopping horror films made in the 1980s. These included David Cronenberg's *Scanners* (1981), which contains scenes of human heads suddenly bursting open, Tobe Hooper's *Poltergeist* (1982), in which a small girl is threatened by evil spirits, and Wes Craven's *A Nightmare on Elm Street* (1984, see box).

'Body count' movies are still churned out on video. But in the 1990s, Hollywood has returned to the Gothic horror style. Tim Burton gave horror a heart in his modern-day Gothic fantasies *Edward Scissorhands* (1990) and *Tim Burton's The Nightmare Before Christmas* (1993). This approach has also been followed with big-budget versions of classic tales like *Bram Stoker's Dracula* (1992) and *Mary Shelley's Frankenstein* (1994). It would seem that the horror film is anything but dead and buried.

FILMS TO WATCH

Films are made in the US unless otherwise stated

MAN-MADE MONSTERS

The Student of Prague (Germany, 1913, 1926)
The Golem (Germany, 1915, 1920)
Dr Jekyll and Mr Hyde (1931, 1941)
The Murders of the Rue Morgue (1932)
The Invisible Man (1933)
Darkman (1990)
Mary Reilly (1995)

THE CREATURE

Frankenstein (1931)
Bride of Frankenstein (1935)
Son of Frankenstein (1939)
Curse of Frankenstein (UK, 1956)
Mary Shelley's Frankenstein (UK, 1994)

HORROR WITH HEART

The Hunchback of Notre Dame (1923, 1939)
The Phantom of the Opera (1925, 1943)
Man Made Monster (1941)
Curse of the Cat People (1944)
The Elephant Man (1980)
The Fly & II (1986, 1989)
Edward Scissorhands (1990)

VAMPIRES

Nosferatu (Germany, 1922, 1979)
Dracula (1931; UK, 1958)
Dracula's Daughter (1936)
Brides of Dracula (UK, 1960)
Dracula, Prince of Darkness (UK, 1965)
The Lost Boys (1987)
Near Dark (1987)
Bram Stoker's Dracula (1992)
Interview with the Vampire (1994)

WEREWOLVES

The Ghoul (UK, 1933)
Werewolf of London (1935)
The Wolf Man (1941)
Frankenstein Meets the Wolf Man (1943)
House of Frankenstein (1944)
An American Werewolf in London (1981)
Wolf (1994)

RISEN FROM THE GRAVE

The Mummy (1932; UK, 1959)
White Zombie (1932)
The Mummy's Hand (1940)
Night of the Living Dead (1968)
Return of the Living Dead (1985)
Day of the Dead (1985)

DEVIL WORSHIP

Faust (Germany, 1926)
The Black Cat (1934)
Night of the Demon (UK, 1957)
The Masque of the Red Death (1964)
The Devil Rides Out (UK, 1968)
Rosemary's Baby (1968)
The Wicker Man (UK, 1973)
The Omen (1976)

WITCHCRAFT

Witchcraft Through the Ages (Sweden, 1922)
I Married a Witch (1942)
Witchfinder General (UK, 1968)
The Witches of Eastwick (1987)
The Witches (1990)

GHOSTS

The Ghost Goes West (UK, 1935)
Blithe Spirit (UK, 1944)
Dead of Night (UK, 1945)
Kwaidan (Japan, 1964)
Ghostbusters & II (1984, 1989)
Rouge (Hong Kong, 1987)

HAUNTED HOUSES

The Old Dark House (1932)
The Uninvited (1944)
The Innocents (UK, 1961)
The Amityville Horror (1979)
Paperhouse (UK, 1988)
Beetlejuice (1988)

MASS MURDER

The Abominable Dr Phibes (UK, 1971)
Theatre of Blood (UK, 1973)
Suspiria (Italy, 1976)
Halloween (1978)
Friday the Thirteenth (1980)
Nightmare on Elm Street (1984)
The Silence of the Lambs (1990)

THE PARANORMAL

The Exorcist (1973)
Carrie (1976)
The Shining (1980)
Poltergeist & II & III (1982, 1986, 1988)
Angel Heart (1987)
Candyman (1992)

SPINE TINGLERS

Eraserhead (1976)
Gremlins & 2 (1984, 1990)
Hellraiser (1987)
Society (1989)
Tim Burton's The Nightmare Before Christmas (1993)
Cronos (Mexico, 1994)

THE MUSICAL

The musical is perhaps the purest form of film entertainment. Its tunes and dance sequences offer a complete escape from everyday life. We often have a piece of music at the back of our minds that reflects our mood or recalls a memory. The musical takes these and turns them into full-scale song-and-dance numbers.

Audiences had been enjoying stage musicals, operas and vaudeville long before the movies arrived. The coming of Talkies meant, at long last, that these shows could be presented on screen.

Backstage musicals

Following the success of the first Talkie, *The Jazz Singer* (1927), producers slipped songs into virtually every kind of film to exploit the public's fascination with sound. But only a few pictures, like Ernst Lubitsch's *The Love Parade* and Rouben Mamoulian's *Applause*, used music imaginatively as part of the dialogue or to suggest thought and memory.

Lights of New York (1928), advertised as the first '100% talking, 100% singing, 100% dancing' musical, made such films fashionable. Many of these were adapted from recent stage hits. But original screen musicals were soon being produced, with words and music by leading songwriters like Jerome Kern, Irving Berlin, George Gershwin and Cole Porter. Yet, as they were usually filmed with stationary cameras, audiences soon got tired of them.

Broadway Melody (1929) was the first musical to win the Oscar for Best Picture and it gave the genre a new direction. It was set backstage and showed how a theatre company went about putting on a show. The 'backstage musical' followed a familiar storyline. A producer struggles to raise the money to stage what he is certain will be a sure-fire hit. The chorus girls crack jokes throughout rehearsals, while keeping a look-out for unmarried millionaires. The playwright is usually a rich young man in hiding from his disapproving family. He inevitably falls madly in love with one of the chorus girls, who then gets the chance to become a star when the leading lady quits the show on the opening night.

'Backstagers' like *42nd Street*, *Footlight Parade* and *Gold Diggers of 1933* made the names of performers like Dick Powell, Ruby Keeler and Joan Blondell. But the true star of these pictures was the designer of the dance sequences (or choreographer) Busby Berkeley. He transformed song-and-dance routines, known as 'production numbers', into breathtaking extravaganzas. He experimented with kaleidoscopic and zoom lenses, optical effects and rhythmic cutting. But it was his dynamic use of the camera that made his work unique. Berkeley fixed it to swooping cranes, ran it along specially designed rails and placed it in trenches below the soundstage to achieve unusual angles. His most famous invention was the 'top shot', which looked down on the action from a great height to reveal patterns formed by carefully positioned chorus girls.

Ginger and Fred

In contrast to Berkeley's flamboyant style was the graceful elegance of Fred Astaire. He was already a major stage star when in 1933 he formed a screen partnership with Ginger Rogers that remains one of the best-loved in cinema history.

They shared only one dance in their first

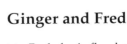

◁ Busby Berkeley's dramatic design for the 'Remember My Forgotten Man' number in *Gold Diggers of 1933*, directed by Mervyn LeRoy.

film together, *Flying Down to Rio* (1933). But it captured the public imagination and they starred in a further nine musicals. Romantic comedies like *Top Hat* (see box) and *Swing Time* (1936) told simple stories, but they became magical when Ginger and Fred began to dance.

Astaire was a perfectionist who planned their dances to the last detail and made Rogers rehearse for long hours. His dance routines were always inventive. He also insisted that each dance formed a part of the plot, unlike in most other musicals where the story stopped until the number

was over. Ginger eventually chose to perform in more dramatic pictures, but Fred remained one of Hollywood's most popular musical stars, in films like *The Band Wagon* (1953).

◁ Jeanette MacDonald and Maurice Chevalier in Ernst Lubitsch's musical comedy *One Hour with You* (1932).

TOP HAT

(USA, 1935) Director: Mark Sandrich

Song-and-dance man Jerry Travers (Fred Astaire) falls head over heels in love with Dale Tremont (Ginger Rogers). But Dale resists him because she mistakes him for Horace Hardwick (Edward Everett Horton), the producer of Jerry's new show and the husband of her best friend Madge (Helen Broderick). Instead she marries her dress designer (Erik Rhodes) only to discover Jerry's true identity. But as the marriage ceremony had only been performed by Jerry's butler (Eric Blore) posing as a clergyman, Jerry and Dale can marry after all and the film ends happily.

Top Hat is without doubt the best of the Ginger and Fred musicals. The simple story of mistaken identity is hugely enjoyable. But, as ever, audiences flocked to see the graceful dance numbers that skilfully show the different stages of the couple's blossoming romance. Irving Berlin's songs, including 'Cheek to Cheek' and 'Top Hat, White Tie and Tails', became popular hits. The film itself became one of the most successful in the RKO studio's history.

△ Ginger Rogers and Fred Astaire trip the light fantastic with the grace and flair that put them among the best-loved musical film stars of all time.

△ Fred Astaire dances with Marjorie Reynolds in *Holiday Inn* (1942), in which he and Bing Crosby open a nightclub that is only open on the 15 holidays celebrated in America each year.

On a different note

Many other musicals in Hollywood's Golden Age featured singing stars, although each had a distinctive style. Jeanette MacDonald and Nelson Eddy appeared in a series of successful light operas including *Rose Marie* (1936). Teenager Deanna Durbin also sang classical songs in lively comedies like *That Certain Age* (1938). Bing Crosby, however, adopted a more relaxed approach to singing, known as 'crooning', in pictures like *Holiday Inn* (1942), in which he first sang 'White Christmas'. Frank Sinatra, who had a more modern singing style, was a great favourite with teenage girls called 'bobbysoxers'. He was nicknamed 'The Voice' for his unique interpretation of songs like 'The Charm of You' in *Anchors Aweigh* (1945) and 'Who Wants to Be a Millionaire?' in *High Society* (1956). Finally, Alice Faye and Betty Grable combined song and dance in glossy productions like *Tin Pan Alley* (1940).

The leading vocalist of the period, however, was Judy Garland. Following the international success of *The Wizard of Oz* (see box), she starred in a number of pictures with Mickey Rooney, including *Babes in Arms* (1939). In these films a group of teenagers overcame all odds to stage a musical. But Garland's best performance came in *Meet Me in St Louis* (1944), directed by Vincente Minnelli. This charming tale of family life at the turn of the 20th century helped to change the face of the musical.

MGM magic

From the mid-1940s, a group of talented film-makers began to find ways of making song-and-dance numbers seem a more natural part of the storyline. Under the guidance of MGM producer Arthur Freed, Vincente Minnelli directed a series of stylish pictures that were a perfect balance of story, décor, song and dance. Among the most popular were *The Pirate* (1947), *The Band Wagon* (1953) and *Gigi* (1958).

He also pioneered the 'dream ballet'. Often lasting up to ten minutes, these routines were a mixture of classical and popular dance. The most ambitious one came at the end of *An American in Paris* (1951) and drew on the work of several

---

THE WIZARD OF OZ

(USA, 1939) Director: Victor Fleming

When a whirlwind sweeps past their farm, Dorothy (Judy Garland) and her dog Toto are carried off to Munchkinland. Here, Glinda the Good Witch (Billie Burke) tells her that only one person can help her get home – the Wizard who rules the city of Oz that lies at the end of the yellow brick road. Wearing the magical ruby slippers given to her by the Good Witch, Dorothy sets off on her journey. She is joined on the way by a Scarecrow who wants a brain (Ray Bolger), a Tin Man who needs a heart (Jack Haley) and a Cowardly Lion who wishes to be brave (Bert Lahr). They also hope the Wizard (Frank Morgan) can grant their wishes, but the Wicked Witch of the West (Margaret Hamilton) is determined to prevent them from reaching Oz.

The Wizard of Oz is a truly magical film. The episodes set in the real world were shot in black-and-white to make the Technicolor land of Oz seem even more fantastic. MGM originally wanted Shirley Temple or Deanna Durbin to play Dorothy. But it is now hard to imagine anyone but Judy Garland singing the classic songs 'Over the Rainbow' and 'We're Off to See the Wizard'. Richard Thorpe, Lewis Milestone, King Vidor and George Cukor all directed various sequences. But the picture was credited solely to Victor Fleming, who also made the other smash hit of 1939, *Gone with the Wind* (see page 41).

French painters for its rhythm and design. The star of this Oscar-winning film was Gene Kelly, whose athleticism and energy were very different from the suave style of his friendly rival Fred Astaire. Many of Kelly's best routines were solos, although he also shared some memorable dances with female partners Judy Garland, Vera-Ellen and Cyd Charisse.

In addition to choreographing many of his own numbers, Kelly also co-directed three pictures with Stanley Donen. They boldly took the musical out of the studio and into the streets of New York for the influential *On the Town* (1949). They also created perhaps the finest musical of all time in *Singin' in the Rain* (see box).

But the rising cost of producing musicals meant that the MGM bosses were less willing to risk their money on original screen musicals. Instead they returned to the old policy of adapting shows that had already been successful on the Broadway stage in New York. Several of these blockbusters were written by Richard Rodgers and Oscar Hammerstein, including *Oklahoma!* (1955), *Carousel* (1956), *The King and I* (1956) and *South Pacific* (1958).

SINGIN' IN THE RAIN

(USA, 1952) Directors: Gene Kelly & Stanley Donen

Don Lockwood (Gene Kelly) and Lina Lamont (Jean Hagen) are Hollywood's leading romantic team of the silent era. But their popularity is threatened when the studio decides to turn their next picture into a musical. This will make Don an even bigger star, as he began his career in vaudeville. But Lina has an awful singing voice and an accent that does not match her elegant screen image. Lina agrees to allow Kathy Selden (Debbie Reynolds) to dub her lines, but she soon becomes jealous of the relationship between her stand-in and her co-star.

Singin' in the Rain is widely regarded as the finest musical of all time. It hilariously captures the chaos caused by the new technology of the Talkies, and is a superb send-up of Hollywood in the early sound era. The dance routines vary from the graceful 'Broadway Melody' ballet to the energetic slapstick 'Make 'Em Laugh' number. But topping them all is Gene Kelly's joyous performance of the title song, in which he celebrates his new-found love for Kathy by dancing happily through the rain-soaked streets in a torrential downpour.

◁ Having passed through the Haunted Wood, Dorothy, the Cowardly Lion, the Tin Man and the Scarecrow come face to face with the soldiers guarding the Wicked Witch's castle.

◁ Gene Kelly was not just the star of *Singin' in the Rain*, he also co-directed the picture and choreographed all the dances, including the one for the famous title song.

Pop goes the musical

The 1960s began well for the traditional musical, with *West Side Story* (1961), which set the tale of Romeo and Juliet in New York's gangland and included such hit songs as 'America' and 'Maria'. Four years later *The Sound of Music*, starring Julie Andrews, became the biggest box-office musical of all time. It included many

△ Julie Andrews in *The Sound of Music*, in which a singing family escapes from the Nazis in the 1930s.

△ A street gang perform an energetic dance routine in *West Side Story* (1961).

memorable songs including the catchy 'Do-Re-Mi' and the ballad 'Edelweiss'.

But musical tastes had been changing since the mid-1950s and rock'n'roll was now Number One with the record-buying public. Many rock and pop stars appeared in pictures aimed specifically at their adoring fans. Although Elvis Presley was known as the 'King of Rock'n'Roll', he had only become a singer in the hope of breaking into movies. He made 33 films in all, but after *Jailhouse Rock* (1957) and *King Creole* (1958) they were usually based on a dreary 'boy-meets-girl' formula and contained few hit songs. Cliff Richard made several similar features in Britain, including *The Young Ones* (1961) and *Summer Holiday* (1963). But the most inventive pop pictures of the period starred the amazingly successful group from Liverpool, The Beatles. In addition to *A Hard Day's Night* (1964, see box) and *Help!* (1965), they also featured in the surreal animated adventure, *Yellow Submarine* (1968).

Another type of rock movie emerged during the 1960s – the concert film, in which top bands were recorded playing live. Among the best was *Woodstock*, which captured the sights and sounds of a famous rock music festival held on a farm in America in 1969, at which the message of love and peace was as important as the music.

Fading to silence?

The genre briefly became popular once more with dance pictures starring John Travolta. In *Saturday Night Fever* (1977) he plays a shop worker who lives only for his nights on the disco floor. He later played opposite Olivia Newton-John in *Grease* (1978). Set in 1950s America, it follows summertime sweethearts back to high

---

A HARD DAY'S NIGHT

(UK, 1964) Director: Richard Lester

A Hard Day's Night tells the story of 36 hours in the lives of The Beatles – John Lennon, Paul McCartney, George Harrison and Ringo Starr. Having escaped from their screaming fans at the railway station, the band head for a TV studio. But during a break in rehearsals Paul's grandfather (Wilfrid Brambell) convinces drummer Ringo that the rest of the group think they could do without him. Ringo goes missing and the other Beatles have to find him before the start of their TV show.

This highly imaginative and often very funny picture was made at the height of 'Beatlemania'. Packed with classic Beatles songs, it captured perfectly the surreal world in which they lived at that time. The Fab Four often improvised their own lines, many of which had a Marx Brothers ring to them. Director Richard Lester gave the action a non-stop energy that recalled the films of Buster Keaton and Federico Fellini. Many of the techniques invented to shoot the songs are still used in pop videos today.

▷ The Beatles singing 'I Should Have Known Better' at the end of the film.

school where their friends nearly drive them apart. The film contained two No. 1 hits, 'You're the One that I Want' and 'Summer Nights'.

Although musicals are still extremely popular in the theatre, they now rarely succeed on the screen. The stage version of *The Rocky Horror Picture Show*, for example, was a long-running cult classic, in which stranded motorists Brad (Barry Bostwick) and Janet (Susan Sarandon) have a close encounter of the weirdest kind with Dr Frank N. Furter (Tim Curry), a cross-dressing alien in his house of horror. But the movie version, made in 1974, was less enjoyable and failed at the box office.

Other inventive original musicals like Alan Parker's *Bugsy Malone* (1976) and *The Commitments* (1991) have been few and far between. The screen musical is so out of fashion that producers are now even removing the songs from films like *I'll Do Anything* (1994), which was originally intended to be a musical. Television and pop videos have largely taken over from the film musical, although Parker returned to the musical in 1995 with an adaptation of Andrew Lloyd-Webber and Tim Rice's smash stage musical *Evita*, starring Madonna.

△ Jodie Foster as the tough-talking Tallulah in the gangster musical spoof, *Bugsy Malone* (1976). Directed by Alan Parker, the musical was unique in having an all-kid cast.

FILMS TO WATCH

Films are made in the US unless otherwise stated

EARLY MUSICALS
The Jazz Singer (1927)
Hallelujah! (1929)
Applause (1929)
Monte Carlo (1930)
One Hour With You (1932)
Love Me Tonight (1932)

BUSBY BERKELEY
Whoopee (1930)
42nd Street (1933)
Gold Diggers of 1933 (1933)
Footlight Parade (1933)
Dames (1934)
Strike Up the Band (1940)
The Gang's All Here (1943)

GINGER AND FRED
Flying Down to Rio (1933)
The Gay Divorcee (1934)
Roberta (1935)
Top Hat (1935)
Swing Time (1936)
Follow the Fleet (1936)
Shall We Dance? (1937)
Carefree (1939)

ASTAIRE SOLO
You'll Never Get Rich (1941)
Holiday Inn (1942)
Yolanda and the Thief (1945)
Blue Skies (1946)
Easter Parade (1948)
Funny Face (1957)

JUDY GARLAND
The Wizard of Oz (1939)
For Me and My Gal (1942)
Meet Me in St Louis (1944)
Ziegfeld Follies (1945)
The Pirate (1947)

VINCENTE MINNELLI
Cabin in the Sky (1942)
The Band Wagon (1953)
Brigadoon (1954)
Kismet (1955)
Gigi (1958)
A Star Is Born (1959)

GENE KELLY
For Me and My Gal (1942)
Cover Girl (1944)
Anchors Aweigh (1945)
Take Me Out to the Ball Game (1949)
On the Town (1949)
An American in Paris (1951)
Singin' in the Rain (1952)
It's Always Fair Weather (1955)
Invitation to the Dance (1956)

FOX MUSICALS
Rose of Washington Square (1939)
Down Argentine Way (1940)
Tin Pan Alley (1940)
Move Over Miami (1941)
Coney Island (1943)
How to Marry a Millionaire (1953)

COMPOSER BIOPICS
Alexander's Ragtime Band (1938)
Rhapsody in Blue (1945)
Night and Day (1946)
Till Clouds Roll By (1946)
Words and Music (1948)
The Glenn Miller Story (1953)

BROADWAY BLOCKBUSTERS
Show Boat (1951)
Kiss Me Kate (1953)
Seven Brides for Seven Brothers (1954)
Oklahoma! (1956)
Carousel (1956)
The King and I (1956)
South Pacific (1958)
West Side Story (1961)
My Fair Lady (1964)
The Sound of Music (1965)

MODERN MUSICALS
Oliver! (UK, 1968)
Sweet Charity (1968)
Cabaret (1972)
Saturday Night Fever (1977)
Grease (1978)
All That Jazz (1979)
Fame (1980)
Flashdance (1983)
A Chorus Line (1985)
The Commitments (Ireland, 1991)

CHILDREN'S MUSICALS
Mary Poppins (1964)
Chitty Chitty Bang Bang (1968)
Bedknobs and Broomsticks (1971)
Bugsy Malone (UK, 1976)
Annie (1982)

POP AND ROCK FILMS
Jailhouse Rock (1957)
The Young Ones (UK, 1961)
A Hard Day's Night (UK, 1964)
Woodstock (1978)
The Last Waltz (1978)
Stop Making Sense (1984)
This is Spinal Tap (1984)
Under the Cherry Moon (1986)
La Bamba (1987)
Rattle and Hum (1988)
Great Balls of Fire (1989)

SCIENCE FICTION

Science-fiction films have been made since the early 20th century. Many of the first pictures were set in the future or on distant planets, and included experiments with camera tricks, special effects, costumes and make-up. It is thanks to science fiction that many devices and processes were invented that have since become common in films of all kinds.

Four of the ten most successful films of all time are science fiction (sci-fi for short). Today we think of science-fiction movies like *Star Wars* (see box on page 115) as big-budget epics packed with fantastic spaceships, eerie aliens and spectacular effects. But science fiction has not always been popular. There were few directors in the first 60 years of cinema history with the imagination to take the subject beyond the comic strip adventures of superheroes like Flash Gordon.

It was not until the Cold War era of the 1950s, when invasion and nuclear holocaust seemed very real threats, that more serious themes were tackled. Even then, sci-fi films did not have big budgets or big stars, so the special effects – and the acting – were usually both second rate. Although it was unfashionable again during the 1960s, sci-fi returned with a bang in the late-1970s and remained a firm box-office favourite throughout the 1980s.

Rockets and spaceships

A Trip to the Moon (1902) is the first true science-fiction film. It was directed by Georges Méliès, who drew on all his genius as a magician and trick photographer (see page 20) to

◁ Flash Gordon was played in 40 'Sensational Sense Staggering Episodes' by Larry 'Buster' Crabbe.

bring both the simple tale and the obviously homemade scenery to life. Méliès's astronauts may have been old men in top hats, but at least they travelled by rocket. A rival director, Gaston Velle, sent a drunk to the moon on a chimney in *A Midnight Dream* (1905). The director Fritz Lang aimed for greater realism and drew on actual rocket research for *The Women in the Moon* (1929). This was also the first film to show a countdown and weightlessness in space.

The realism of *Destination Moon* (1950) gave sci-fi films a more serious theme. Despite a shoestring budget, every detail of the rocket, the spacesuits and the lunar surface was based on up-to-date knowledge. The painted sets and the stuffy semi-documentary tone have dated badly, but the film inspired a generation to believe that space was the next frontier to conquer, and that America was capable of doing it. Dozens of cheap imitations followed *Destination Moon*, including *Plan 9 from*

JURASSIC PARK

(USA, 1993) Director: Steven Spielberg

Jurassic Park was based on the best-selling novel by Michael Crichton. Advertised as the film 'you waited 65 million years' to see, it made over $120 million within ten days of opening in America and soon became the all-time box-office No.1.

Billionaire John Hammond (Richard Attenborough) is the owner of 'the most advanced amusement park in the world'. On show are dozens of living dinosaurs that have been genetically engineered from the DNA found in the blood of insects trapped for centuries inside amber stones. Shortly before the grand opening, he invites dinosaur experts Alan Grant (Sam Neill) and Ellie Satler (Laura Dern) to inspect the prehistoric creatures. Accompanying them are Hammond's grandchildren and Ian Malcolm (Jeff Goldblum), a mathematician who refuses to be impressed by anything on display. But their dream tour turns into a nightmare when the park's security system crashes and the dinosaurs go on the rampage.

Jurassic Park thrilled audiences with its heart-stopping story and its amazingly life-like special effects. But some critics complained that the dinosaurs were more lifelike than the human characters. Some of the dinosaurs were full-size, but many more were generated by the top SFX (special effects) company, Industrial Light & Magic, using 3-D computer scanners. The images were so spectacular that no-one seemed to mind that the dinosaurs in the park had actually lived in the Cretaceous Period and not the Jurassic!

△ Terrible acting and the cheapest sets and effects were typical in sci-fi B movies like the 1950s cult classic *Plan 9 from Outer Space* (1959), directed by Edward Wood Jr.

Outer Space (1959). Today these unintentionally hilarious films are considered 'cult' classics. As the American space programme of the 1960s turned science fiction into science fact, Hollywood lost interest in astronauts and concentrated on starships like the *USS Enterprise* in the *Star Trek* series. But film-makers have since returned to the subject of rockets to the moon in pictures like *The Right Stuff* (1983) and *Apollo 13* (1995), starring Tom Hanks.

◁ A decade before Yuri Gagarin's first manned space flight, *Destination Moon* (1950) managed to predict the look of space suits and rockets.

Robots and androids

The first screen robots were machines that either caused comic chaos or served fiendish criminals, such as the one encountered by legendary escapologist Houdini in the 1918 serial, *The Master Mystery*. *Tobor the Great* (1954) was the first space-age robot, but Robby, star of *Forbidden Planet* (1955), was a bigger hit with moviegoers. Apart from the cute Johnny Five in *Short Circuit* (1986), robots have more often been high-tech killing machines, like the holiday camp cowboys at *Westworld* (1973) and the man-machine *Robocop* (1987).

Androids are robots with human bodies. But *The Colossus of New York* (1958) was a robot with a human brain. Amiable robots like R2D2 and C3P0 in the *Star Wars* trilogy are again in the minority beside such ultra-violent 'droids as the replicants in *Blade Runner* (1982).

Time travel

Time travel is as old as cinema itself. H. G. Wells's landmark sci-fi novel, *The Time Machine*, was published just months before the first cinema show in 1895. However, the tale of the intrepid Victorian who travels to the year 802701 via 1917, 1940 and 1966 was not filmed until 1960. Thirty years later, *Total Recall* (1990) saw Arnold

△ Robby the Robot (bottom left of the poster) was the star of *Forbidden Planet,* a 1955 version of Shakespeare's play *The Tempest*. Robby was so popular with moviegoers that he was given a film to himself, *The Invisible Boy* (1956), and was a regular on TV sci-fi shows.

2001: A SPACE ODYSSEY

(UK, 1968) Director: Stanley Kubrick

2001: A Space Odyssey is based on a novel by sci-fi author Arthur C. Clarke. The complex storyline starts four million years ago, when peace-loving apes discover a black slab of stone, which somehow causes them to evolve into violent hunters, prepared to kill to protect their territory. Then, sometime in the distant future, the slab begins signalling from the moon and a craft, controlled by a computer called HAL, is sent to investigate. In mid-voyage, HAL starts to malfunction and wipes out the crew, before one astronaut manages to disconnect it and return safely to earth.

2001 transformed special effects and inspired many later sci-fi blockbusters. Viewed today, the effects are still startling. It took over three years to shoot at a cost of some £10.5 million. Echoing many of the themes popular in the 1950s, the film shows that although humanity has become increasingly greedy and brutish, it still has the power to reform. Audiences either loved or loathed *2001*, and to this day books and articles are published which try to explain its meaning.

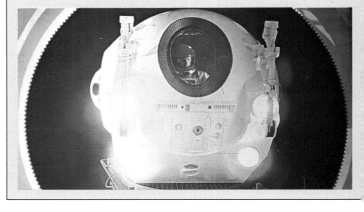

Schwarzenegger transformed into a Martian agent looking for revenge after visiting a company offering time-travel holiday memories. The film was a box-office smash, but it suffers from a problem common to many modern sci-fi pictures – an over-dependence on blood and guts and special effects to cover up weaknesses in the storyline. If trips to the future often required specially designed machines, journeys back in time apparently did not. Michael J. Fox, for example, went *Back to the Future* on three occasions (1985, 1989, 1990) at the wheel of a sports car.

▷ Astronaut Charlton Heston crashes through time to an earth centuries from now ruled by intelligent apes in *Planet of the Apes* (1968). Fine performances and the exceptional ape make-up made this unusual film seem believable.

STAR WARS

(USA, 1977) Director: George Lucas

Set 'a long time ago in a galaxy far, far away', *Star Wars* was originally intended to be the fourth in a series of nine films. As sci-fi was unfashionable in the 1970s, it was rejected by two studios before Twentieth Century-Fox took a risk with it. That risk has since been handsomely repaid. Lucas started work on the first three episodes in the series in the mid-1990s.

Leaving planet Tatooine, farmer Luke Skywalker takes up arms against the evil Empire and its military supremo, Darth Vader. Luke is trained in the art of 'the force' by Jedi warier Ben 'Obi-Wan' Kenobi, and he joins with androids C3P0 and R2D2, and mercenary sky-pilot Han Solo and his sidekick Chewbacca, to rescue Princess Leia from Darth Vader's ship, Death Star.

Star Wars was packed with references to classic movies of all genres. It was a thrilling combination of Oscar-winning special effects, a cast containing such star names as Sir Alec Guinness and Harrison Ford, and a plot straight out of a 1930s sci-fi comic strip serial like *Flash Gordon*.

THE EMPIRE STRIKES BACK

(USA, 1980) Director: Irvin Kershner

The Empire has trapped rebel forces on the ice planet, Hoth. Han Solo and Princess Leia escape to Cloud City to enlist the help of crooked Lando Calrissian, while Luke links with 'force' expert, Yoda, to prepare for a showdown with Darth Vader.

Star Wars was criticized for making war seem fun and *The Empire Strikes Back* is much darker in tone than *Star Wars*. The battle effects are so incredibly complex that a special computerized camera, the Empireflex, had to be invented to shoot them.

THE RETURN OF THE JEDI

(USA, 1983) Director: Richard Marquand

The last battle saw a return to the all-action adventure of the first film. Darth Vader has allied with Jabba the Hut while he builds an indestructible Death Star. But our heroes, in league with cuddly rebel warriors called Ewoks, eventually win the day. Despite another Oscar for the most brilliant SFX of the trilogy, *The Return of the Jedi* suffers from a thin plot, with its loose ends too neatly tied up at the close.

◁ Miniatures, models, animation, glass shots and computerized camera movements were just some of the effects that helped make the *Star Wars* trilogy the most successful sci-fi series of all time.

Aliens and space invaders

War of the Worlds was filmed in 1953, but 25 years passed before cinema technology made intergalactic warfare seem realistic. In many ways, these star wars movies are Westerns transferred to outer space, with lasers replacing six-shooters. The *Star Wars* trilogy (see box) sparked many imitations, such as *The Last Starfighter* (1984), but none could match its style, excitement or invention.

The first film to feature aliens was *Algol*, made in Germany in 1921. However, over 30 years passed before aliens became screen regulars, and many of them remained almost identical to earthlings apart from their bizarre costumes.

America's fears of an invasion by the Soviet Union grew in the 1950s, and both countries mass-produced nuclear weapons throughout this period of international tension known as the Cold War. Orson Welles had terrified America in 1938 when he simulated a real-life invasion in his radio broadcast of H. G. Wells's *War of the Worlds*, and cinema in the Cold War era exploited that reaction. In films like *The Thing* (1951), the aliens were really symbols of the Soviet threat – an unknown enemy bent on destroying the American way of life. *Invasion of the Body Snatchers* (1956) was a chilling film in which aliens plot to conquer earth by replacing humans with unfeeling lookalikes that hatch out of mysterious 'pods'.

Other aliens came to warn about the dangers of modern warfare, as in *The Day the Earth Stood Still* (1951). The third alien

△ *Alien³* (1992) ends a thrilling trilogy, set over 60 years, that blends sci-fi with horror as Sigourney Weaver does battle with the most terrifying of all space monsters. The films are notable for having a woman in the all-action role that Hollywood too often reserves for its muscular male stars.

wave began in the 1970s with equally kindly creatures in Spielberg's *Close Encounters of the Third Kind* (1977) and *E.T.* (1982). But the sense of menace was to return in *Alien* (1979) and its sequels, *Aliens* (1986) and *Alien³* (1992).

Worlds to come?

Science-fiction films tend to be most successful at times of international crisis, such as during the Cold War years. At that time the 'Bomb' movie was popular. Films like *Five* (1951) and *On the Beach* (1959) depicted life after a nuclear holocaust, while *Fail Safe* (1964) and the darkly comic *Dr Strangelove* (1963) showed how easily missiles could be launched accidentally. The most recent 'end-of-the-world' visions have been set after a global nuclear war, such as the Australian-made *Mad Max* trilogy (1979, 1985, 1989), starring Mel Gibson as the tough ex-cop Max.

Film-makers have regularly tried to predict how the future would look and what it would be like to live in. Using the most spectacular special effects of their day, they have conjured up worlds that have usually been both gloomy and sinister. Technology was used by evil masters to control the masses in future cities like Metropolis (see box) and Everytown in *Things to Come* (1936). In *Just Imagine* (1930), for example, the citizens were known only by their numbers, while in the film versions of George Orwell's novel *1984* (1955 and 1984) they were constantly spied on by the Thought Police

E.T. – THE EXTRATERRESTRIAL

(USA, 1982) Director: Steven Spielberg

E.T. owes a great deal to the magic created by Walt Disney and another 'no place like home' classic, *The Wizard of Oz*. However, the real secret of the film's success is E.T. himself, created by sculptor/inventor Carlo Rimbaldi.

E.T. is a 600-800 year-old alien who has been accidentally left on earth by his space-ship. He is discovered by a young boy, Elliott, who along with his pals helps E.T. 'phone home' to ask his people to come and collect him before scientists have a chance to experiment on him.

The film has a religious feel, thanks to E.T.'s ability to heal and even rise from the dead, but its emphasis is firmly on entertainment and the joy of childhood. Although the picture has its over-sentimental moments, audiences of all ages loved it, and *E.T.* remained the all-time box-office No. 1 for 11 years, before Spielberg's own *Jurassic Park* succeeded it.

▷ Three E.T. models were used at various times during filming. One was fully electronic and had 85 movements. Another was electro-mechanical and had 60. The third was a costume with radio-controlled parts.

and controlled by a cruel ruler called Big Brother. But since the 1960s the urge to rise up against such bleak tyrannies has also been a feature of sci-fi films like *Fahrenheit 451* (1966) and *Brazil* (1985).

The earliest sci-fi films tried to imagine what the future would look like, and to today's audiences they seem very old-fashioned. But directors of modern sci-fi pictures continue to present visions of future worlds and, perhaps, films such as *The Terminator* and *Judge Dredd* will be considered equally old-fashioned in a hundred years' time.

▷ The menacing Batmobile and the brooding atmosphere of Gotham City in *Batman* (1989), were inspired by *Metropolis* – made over 60 years earlier.

METROPOLIS

(Germany, 1926) Director: Fritz Lang

Life was hard in 1920s Germany and *Metropolis* was a warning that strict government was not the answer to its problems. Unfortunately the message went unheeded to the point that *Metropolis* was Adolf Hitler's favourite film.

Metropolis is an inhuman industrialized city, where slave workers are kept in caves beneath the streets. Fearing revolution, Fredersen, the city boss, plans to drown the workforce and replace it with robots made by the evil scientist, Rotwang. Although a robot identical to Maria, a woman trusted by the workers, nearly tricks the workers into their destruction, the action ends with a truce between the workers and their rulers.

The film took nearly a year to make and had a cast of over 37,500. The high-rise city, with its bright lights and sinister shadows, has influenced film-makers ever since, most recently in *Batman* (1989) and *Dick Tracy* (1990). Special effects photographer Eugen Schüfftan devised a special process for combining models with scenery painted on to glass, to give *Metropolis* a look that was both futuristic and realistic.

△ Metropolis, the city of the future, with its high-rise blocks, traffic jams and plane-filled skies.

FILMS TO WATCH

Films are made in the US unless otherwise stated

ROCKETS & SPACESHIPS

Conquest of Space (1955)
First Men in the Moon (UK, 1964)
Solaris (USSR, 1972)
Star Wars (1977)
Capricorn One (1978)
The Empire Strikes Back (1980)
The Return of the Jedi (1983)
The Right Stuff (1983)
2010 (1984)
The Last Starfighter (1984)
Apollo 13 (1995)

TIME TRAVEL

Time Machine (1960)
Dr Who and the Daleks (UK, 1965)
Island at the Top of the World (1974)
Time Bandits (UK, 1981)
Back to the Future & II & III (1985, 1989, 1990)
Bill & Ted's Excellent Adventure (1989)

LOST WORLDS

One Million B.C. (1940)
20,000 Leagues Under the Sea (1954)
Godzilla King of the Monsters (Japan, 1954)
Journey to the Center of the Earth (1959)
One Million Years B.C. (1966)
The Land that Time Forgot (1974)
The Land Before Time (Ireland/USA/UK, 1989)
Jurassic Park (1993)

FANTASY

Dragonslayer (UK, 1981)
Excalibur (1981)
Krull (1983)
The Dark Crystal (1983)
Legend (1985)
Labyrinth (1986)

ROBOTS & ANDROIDS

Robot Monster (1953)
THX 1138 (1971)
Silent Running (1972)
The Stepford Wives (1975)
Futureworld (1976)
Android (1982)
Short Circuit I & II (1986, 1988)
Robocop I & II & III (1987, 1990, 1993)

ALIENS & SPACE INVADERS

Invaders from Mars (1953)
Village of the Damned (UK, 1960)
The Day of the Triffids (UK, 1963)
Quatermass and the Pit (UK, 1968)
Alien, Aliens & Alien³ (1979, 1986, 1992)

E.T. (1982)
Enemy Mine (1985)
Explorers (1985)

FUTURE WORLDS

Metropolis (Germany, 1926)
Alphaville (France/Italy, 1965)
2001: A Space Odyssey (UK, 1968)
THX 1138 (1970)
Logan's Run (1976)
Dune (1984)
Brazil (UK, 1985)
Total Recall (1990)
Waterworld (1995)

COMIC STRIP

Batman (1966, 1989)
Flash Gordon (UK, 1980)
Supergirl (1984)
Teenage Mutant Ninja Turtles (1990)
The Rocketeer (1991)
Batman Returns (1992)
The Mighty Morphin Power Rangers (1995)
Tank Girl (1995)
Batman Forever (1995)

WEIRD SCIENCE

The Invisible Man (1933)
The Fly (1954)
The Incredible Shrinking Man (1957)
Fantastic Voyage (1966)
Altered States (1980)
Innerspace (1987)
Flatliners (1990)
Outbreak (1995)
Johnny Mnemonic (1995)

END OF THE WORLD

Seven Days to Noon (UK, 1950)
When Worlds Collide (1951)
Invasion USA (1952)
This Island Earth (1955)
On the Beach (1959)
The Day the Earth Caught Fire (UK, 1961)
Panic in Year Zero (1962)
Fail Safe (1964)
War Games (1983)
When the Wind Blows (UK, 1988)

SCI-FI FLOPS

Cat Women of the Moon (1953)
The Mole People (1956)
Attack of the 50-ft Woman (1958, 1993)
Wild Women of Wongo (1958)
The Brain from Planet Arous (1958)
Teenagers from Outer Space (1959)
Attack of the Killer Tomatoes (1980)

WAR

Cinema helped transform people's attitude to war by bringing the realities of combat to their local screens. At first governments were not keen to show such powerful pictures in wartime, for fear they would lower morale. But they soon came to realize that both factual and fictional films could stir up popular support for their war efforts.

Early film-makers were reluctant to make war pictures, mainly because they were so expensive. Battle sequences, like those in D. W. Griffith's American Civil War epic *The Birth of a Nation* (1915, see page 22), required hundreds even thousands of extras, and everyone had to be kitted out with an authentic uniform and equipment.

Battle scenes whether ancient, medieval or from the Napoleonic era usually looked spectacular, but period war films like *El Cid* and *Waterloo* have rarely done well at

the box office. One of the main reasons is that audiences are not always familiar with the historical background to the action and often find it difficult to identify with the characters, no matter how carefully they are introduced.

▽ Soviet director Sergei Bondarchuk made his name with an epic version of *War and Peace* in 1967. He followed Napoleon's retreat from Moscow to his final defeat in *Waterloo* (1970). Starring Rod Steiger as Napoleon and Christopher Plummer as the Duke of Wellington, the film needed 29,000 period uniforms.

◁ Audie Murphy won more medals than any other American soldier in World War II. After the war he bacame an actor. Yet in John Huston's Civil War story *The Red Badge of Courage* (1951) he plays a trooper who becomes a hero only after running from the enemy in sheer terror.

▷ *Wings* (1927) was the first and only silent film to win the Oscar for Best Picture. The flying sequences were shot in an early widescreen process called Magnascope, which used two projectors to fill the screen.

World War I

The combat film came of age during World War I. Few battle features were made in Europe itself (see page 28), but when America joined the war in 1917 Hollywood began to make war pictures designed to justify the cause, inspire hatred of the enemy and encourage recruitment. Among the more aggressive titles were *To Hell with the Kaiser* and *The Beast of Berlin*. But most of these wartime 'flagwavers' were sentimental dramas like *The Little American* (1917) and *Hearts of the World* (1918), in which such popular stars as Mary Pickford and Lillian Gish bravely resisted the 'beastly Hun'. Many Europeans resented Hollywood's version of World War I, particularly as its films suggested that American heroism brought about victory.

It was really only in peacetime that a more accurate account of the fighting began to emerge. Silent films like King Vidor's *The Big Parade* (1925) and sound features such as *All Quiet on the Western*

ALL QUIET ON THE WESTERN FRONT

(USA, 1930) Director: Lewis Milestone

◁ Lew Ayres (left) disapproved of war on moral grounds and declared himself a 'conscientious objector'. Yet during World War II he volunteered for medical service and often came under fire. But the studios felt his refusal to fight was unAmerican, and his career virtually came to a standstill.

All Quiet on the Western Front was adapted from a classic anti-war novel and follows the experiences of a timid German volunteer (Lew Ayres) during World War I. He is bullied throughout his basic training and sent to the Western Front in France, where his dreams of glory are soon replaced by the horrific realities of the trenches.

The film is full of dramatic camera movements that pitch the viewer into the heart of the battle. In addition to condemning war, it also shattered the popular image of the enemy as brutes by showing that the Germans had shared the same terrors and ordeals as Allied troops. But its sympathetic approach caused the picture to be banned in many countries. Hitler later had it suppressed believing, wrongly, that it was anti-German.

Front (see box above) and G. W. Pabst's *Westfront 1918* (both 1930) revealed the terrors of trench warfare. But audiences did not want to be reminded of what they had endured so recently, and the action adventure approach to war films soon took over. Pictures like *Wings* (1927) and *The Dawn Patrol* (1930), which focused on the most glamorous of the services, the air force, were especially popular.

GRAND ILLUSION

(France, 1937) Director: Jean Renoir

△ Von Rauffenstein (Erich von Stroheim) welcomes De Boldieu (Pierre Fresnay) and Marechal (Jean Gabin) to his escape-proof prisoner-of-war camp.

Set in a World War I prison camp, this complex film concerns the dilemma facing a French officer (Pierre Fresnay). While his patriotic duty is to escape with his fellow countrymen (Jean Gabin and Marcel Dalio), his personal code of honour tells him that he should not disgrace the camp commandant (Erich von Stroheim), who is an aristocrat like himself.

In an age of strong national pride the suggestion that people were less committed to their homeland than to their particular class, race or religion was highly controversial. By showing that enemies could have much in common, Renoir hoped to encourage a spirit of international co-operation and shatter for ever the 'grand illusion' of the title, that anything could be solved by war.

impact was strictly controlled in the nations under Hitler's rule. Pictures made in enemy countries were banned, and even those produced by their own film industries were strictly censored.

Over half of Britain's studio space was reserved for making propaganda documentaries and newsreels, while the rest was used for morale-boosting comedies and melodramas. British war features were particularly noted for their realism, whether dealing with battle, like *In Which We Serve* (1942) and *Western Approaches* (1944), or life on the home front as in *Went the Day Well?* (1942, see box opposite) and *Fires Were Started* (1943).

Theatres of war

After the Japanese attacked Pearl Harbor in 1941 America joined the war. As most American forces went to the Far East, the majority of Hollywood combat films were set in and around the Pacific. Events on land were described in such pictures as *Bataan* and *Guadalcanal Diary* (both 1943), while the war at sea and in the air was the focus of pictures like *Destination Tokyo* (1943) and *Thirty Seconds Over Tokyo* (1944).

Films were also made about the other main theatres of war. *The Immortal Sergeant* and *Sahara* (both 1943) dealt with the campaign in the North African desert; *Mrs Miniver* (1942) recalled the Dunkirk evacuation and the blitz; and *Action in the North Atlantic* (1943) and *Lifeboat* (1944) tackled the war at sea.

World War II

As war loomed again in Europe during the late 1930s, continental film-makers like Jean Renoir tried to warn people that civilization was on the brink of disaster in such features as *Grand Illusion* (1937, see box) and *The Rules of the Game* (1939). Shortly after the outbreak of World War II a number of Hollywood war films were made by British directors to alert Americans to the Fascist threat from Germany and Italy. Among the best were Alfred Hitchcock's spy thriller *Foreign Correspondent* and Charlie Chaplin's satirical assault on Hitler and Mussolini, *The Great Dictator*.

Cinema played a key role from the start of the 1939-45 conflict, even though its

◁ *In Which We Serve* (1942) tells the story of a British destroyer and its crew during World War II. Noël Coward wrote, co-directed and starred in the film, for which he also composed the music.

Several features like *Mission to Moscow* (1943) were made in tribute to the Soviet Union, and others applauded the courage of the peoples under Nazi rule. Fritz Lang's *Hangmen Also Die* and Jean Renoir's *This Land is Mine* (both 1943) failed, however, to recreate the atmosphere of fear and suspicion that existed in Occupied Europe. Instead they simply made romantic heroes out of the various anti-German resistance movements.

◁ Robert Walker leaps into action as one of the small group of American soldiers left to defend a Filipino peninsula against the invading Japanese in Tay Garnett's powerful film, *Bataan* (1943).

WENT THE DAY WELL?

(UK, 1942) Director: Alberto Cavalcanti

△ A Nazi paratrooper poses as a British soldier in a raid on a quiet English village. The story showed that everyone had to do their bit to help win the war.

Effective propaganda pictures were those that combined realism with entertainment, to make sure that their vital message made a lasting impression on wartime audiences.

A perfect example was *Went the Day Well*? Based on a story by Graham Greene, it showed how a single poacher liberated a sleepy country village after it had been captured by a platoon of Nazi paratroopers posing as British soldiers. This engrossing thriller was superbly paced and acted. It showed that in a crisis British calm would always triumph over German cunning, and also warned people to be on their guard against enemy agents.

In stark contrast, the first American war films were clumsy action adventures. They showed the Germans and Japanese as being no match for decent, clean-living American soldiers. B movies, and even better quality pictures starring Western heroes like John Wayne and Randolph Scott, kept this comic strip approach throughout the war. Most features eventually adopted a more responsible tone however.

CASABLANCA

(USA, 1942) Director: Michael Curtiz

Set in North Africa in 1942, *Casablanca* was easily the most popular film of World War II. Ilsa Lund (Ingrid Bergman) arrives at the Café Américain in Casablanca hoping to secure travel papers from her one-time lover Rick Blaine (Humphrey Bogart). These documents will enable her husband Victor Laszlo (Paul Henreid) to escape from the Nazis and fly to America to rally support for the underground cause in Europe.

Casablanca is still considered by most critics to be one of the masterpieces of the Hollywood studio era. Effortlessly blending dashes of romance, excitement, comedy, music and patriotism, it also had an exceptional cast including Peter Lorre and Sydney Greenstreet as a pair of shady villains, and Claude Rains as the crafty French police chief who helps Rick outwit the German police, led by Conrad Veidt.

In the winter of 1942-43, *Casablanca* came to symbolize a turning point in the war. It was released just weeks after the liberation of the city itself, which in the following year hosted the conference at which the Allied leaders planned the invasion of Italy. But over 50 years later the chief reason for the film's continued success is without doubt the Bogart-Bergman relationship, complete with its sentimental theme tune 'As Time Goes By'.

On to victory

The final stages of the war were described in such Hollywood films as *The Story of G. I. Joe* (1945) and *A Walk in the Sun* (1946), which explored the emotions of the Allied troops as they advanced towards Germany. These films were not based on true stories, but a number of later productions like *The Longest Day* (1972) and *A Bridge Too Far* (1977) attempted to reconstruct such real events as the Normandy landings and the battle for Arnhem.

Countless tales of personal courage began to emerge as war veterans returned home, and many were made into films like *The Pride of the Marines* (1945) and *Reach for the Sky* (1956). The quiet determination of prisoners of war to maintain the fight was revealed in *The Colditz Story* (1954) and *The Bridge On the River Kwai* (1957), while wartime espionage activities were made public for the first time in such features as *The Man Who Never Was* (1955).

Peacetime pictures such as *The Best Years of Our Lives* (1946) and *The Men* (1950) focused on the problems facing the wounded and the able-bodied as they tried to come to terms with their combat experiences. These pictures were among the most poignant. Any hopes that the next generation would be spared such misery, however, were quickly dashed by the outbreak of war in northeast Asia.

Korea and Vietnam

The Korean War (1950-53) was the first conflict to be covered in depth by television. As a result few films of any quality were made besides Samuel Fuller's *Fixed Bayonets* and *The Steel Helmet* (both 1951). The Vietnam War (1964-75) was also rarely out of the TV news. America's involvement in the region was so unpopular that with the exception of John Wayne's pro-war statement *The Green Berets* (1968), Hollywood largely avoided the conflict while it lasted.

Once the nation had begun to recover from the shock of defeat, film-makers started to examine the conflict from the viewpoint of the average soldier, many of whom were forced to join up while still in their teens. What emerged was a picture of war as a living hell, fought as much against the region's landscape and climate as against its elusive enemy. *Rambo: First Blood Part Two* (1985) opted for the comic strip approach, but blockbusters like *The Deer Hunter* (1977), *Apocalypse Now* (1979) and *Full Metal Jacket* (1987) used their violent content to show the gruesome nature of battle. Less explosive but equally thoughtful was *84 Charlie Mopic* (1989). A highly personal account of the war was provided by Vietnam veteran Oliver Stone. He recreated the horrors of the campaign and its impact on all caught up in it in *Platoon* (1986), *Born on the Fourth of July* (1989) and *Heaven and Earth* (1993).

APOCALYPSE NOW

(USA, 1979) Director: Francis Ford Coppola

△ The battle scenes in *Apocalypse Now* are among the most realistic ever filmed. Blank ammunition was used, but the action itself was shot to full scale as Coppola refused to use model helicopters, miniature sets or special effects photography.

At the height of the Vietnam conflict Captain Willard (Martin Sheen) is withdrawn from combat duty to cross into Cambodia and assassinate Kurtz (Marlon Brando), a renegade American colonel who is waging his own private war at the head of a local warrior tribe. In the course of his journey upriver Willard witnesses the full horror and madness of modern warfare. He also encounters many ruthless characters including an officer called Kilgore (Robert Duvall) who launches a napalm bomb attack on a beach so that one of his men can go surfing.

Apocalypse Now was filmed in the Philippines during a shoot that was almost as eventful as the film itself. The picture seemed cursed as a typhoon destroyed many of the sets, Martin Sheen had a heart attack, and an overweight Marlon Brando kept arguing about his part. The Filipino government even took back some of the helicopters it had rented to the production, to deal with a rebel uprising. These delays caused the budget to spiral from $12 million to $30 million and Coppola risked personal ruin to make sure it was finished. The film has always been considered a flawed masterpiece because its ending is rather confusing, in spite of a spectacular explosion that was then the biggest ever staged for the screen.

FILMS TO WATCH

Films are made in the US unless otherwise stated

EARLY WARS
The Red Badge of Courage (1951)
Spartacus (1960)
300 Spartans (1962)
War and Peace (1957 & USSR, 1967)
Waterloo (Italy/USSR, 1970)

WORLD WAR I – TRENCHES
The Four Horsemen of the Apocalypse (1921)
The Big Parade (1925)
Westfront 1918 (Germany, 1930)
All Quiet on the Western Front (1930)
Sergeant York (1941)
Paths of Glory (1962)

WORLD WAR I – ELSEWHERE
Wings (1927)
The Dawn Patrol (1930, 1938)
The Lost Patrol (1932)
Lawrence of Arabia (UK, 1962)
Oh What a Lovely War! (UK, 1969)

WORLD WAR II – OCCUPIED EUROPE
This Land is Mine (1943)
Mission to Moscow (1943)
Battle of the Rails (France, 1946)
A Generation (Poland, 1954)
Ivan's Childhood (USSR, 1962)
Mediterraneo (Italy, 1991)
Europa, Europa (France, 1991)

WORLD WAR II – THE HOME FRONT
Mrs Miniver (1942)
Since You Went Away (1942)
Went the Day Well? (UK, 1942)
Millions Like Us (UK, 1943)
The Life and Death of Colonel Blimp (UK, 1943)
The Way Ahead (UK, 1944)
Hope and Glory (UK, 1986)

WORLD WAR II – NORTH AFRICA
Casablanca (1942)
Five Graves to Cairo (1943)
The Immortal Sergeant (1943)
Sahara (1943)
The Desert Fox (1951)
Ice Cold in Alex (UK, 1958)

WORLD WAR II – WAR IN THE AIR
The First of the Few (UK, 1942)
Twelve O'Clock High (UK, 1949)
The Dam Busters (UK, 1954)
Reach for the Sky (UK, 1956)
633 Squadron (UK, 1964)
The Battle of Britain (UK, 1969)

WORLD WAR II – WAR AT SEA
In Which We Serve (UK, 1942)
Action in the North Atlantic (1943)
The Battle of the River Plate (1956)
Sink the Bismarck (1960)

WORLD WAR II – PACIFIC WAR
Bataan (1943)
Guadalcanal Diary (1943)
They Were Expendable (1945)
The Sands of Iwo Jima (1950)
Tora! Tora! Tora! (1970)

WORLD WAR II – P.O.W. CAMPS
Grand Illusion (France, 1937)
The Wooden Horse (UK, 1950)
Stalag 17 (1953)
The Colditz Story (UK, 1954)
The Bridge On the River Kwai (UK, 1957)
The Great Escape (1963)

WORLD WAR II – LIBERATING EUROPE
The Story of G. I. Joe (1945)
A Walk in the Sun (1946)
Attack (1956)
Patton (1970)
The Longest Day (1972)
A Bridge Too Far (UK, 1977)

WORLD WAR II DOCUMENTARIES
Target for Tonight (UK, 1941)
Why We Fight (1942-1944)
The Battle of Midway (1944)
Memphis Belle (1944)
The Negro Soldier (1944)
The True Glory (1945)
The Sorrow and the Pity (France, 1971)
Shoah (France, 1985)

THE KOREAN WAR
Fixed Bayonets (1951)
The Steel Helmet (1951)
Pork Chop Hill (1959)
*M*A*S*H* (1970)

VIETNAM
The Deer Hunter (1978)
Apocalypse Now (1979)
Full Metal Jacket (1987)
Good Morning Vietnam (1987)
Casualties of War (1989)

POSTWAR TRAUMA
The Best Years of Our Lives (1946)
Taxi Driver (1976)
Coming Home (1978)
Birdy (1984)
Gardens of Stone (1988)
Jacob's Ladder (1990)

THE WESTERN

Packed with stagecoaches, cattle stampedes, tribal raids, saloon brawls, lawmen, villains and gunfights, the Western represents a unique American contribution to the arts. Celebrating chiefly the 30-year period that followed the end of the American Civil War in 1865, Westerns often had similar plots, but their combination of breathtaking scenery, larger-than-life characters, distinctive costumes and exciting action made them popular with audiences worldwide.

The Wild West was still fresh in the minds of most Americans when the first cowboy picture, *Cripple Creek Bar Room*, was made in 1898. Indeed, famous true-life lawmen and cowboys like Wyatt Earp and Buffalo Bill Cody often appeared in films like *The Half-Breed* (1915) and *The Adventures of Buffalo Bill* (1917).

The first important Western was *The Great Train Robbery*, which was made in 1903 and played a key role in the development of film narrative (see page 21). One of its cast was G. W. Anderson, who became the first cowboy star in *Broncho Billy and the Baby* (1908). He played this 'good badman' in hundreds of shorts.

As the genre gained respectability important directors like D. W. Griffith began to produce such pictures as *The Battle of Elderbrush Gulch* (1913). More important was the contribution of Thomas Ince, who introduced many classic Western characters and situations in films like *The Narrow Trail*, made in 1917. He also discovered William S. Hart, who became the Western's first international hero. In France, for example, he was known as 'Rio Jim'.

Cowboy heroes

Although many sophisticated Westerns were made in the silent era, the genre became a mainly escapist entertainment in the 1930s. Action-packed B pictures with titles like *Riders of the Purple Sage* (1931) and *Pride of the West* (1938) stuck so closely to successful formulas that they often shared huge chunks of stock footage. This did not seem to bother their young audiences, who cared only that heroes like Tom Mix, Hoot Gibson, Gene Autry and The Three Mesquiteers triumphed over the villains in the last reel.

In 1939 *Stagecoach* restored the Western to A picture status and the genre reached the peak of its popularity over the next 20

JOHN FORD

John Ford once said: 'Westerns? I never look at them, but I love to make them.' Ultimately he directed over 60. Although he made his name with such silent Westerns as *The Iron Horse* made in 1924, he avoided the genre for almost a decade before returning with one of its undoubted classics, *Stagecoach*, in 1939.

Over the next 25 years he made some of the most popular and intelligent Westerns – including in the 1940s *My Darling Clementine*, *Fort Apache* and *She Wore a Yellow Ribbon*, in the 1950s *Rio Grande*, *Wagonmaster*, *The Searchers*, and in the 1960s *The Man Who Shot Liberty Valance* and *Cheyenne Autumn* – which were notable for the beauty of their composition and their insights into the hardships of frontier life.

As well as turning the Western into an art form, Ford also made hugely influential films in a range of other genres, winning Best Direction Oscars for *The Informer* (1935), *The Grapes of Wrath* (1940), *How Green Was My Valley* (1941) and *The Quiet Man* (1952).

▷ James Stewart, John Ford and John Wayne on the set of *The Man Who Shot Liberty Valance* (1962). Ford's first film was a Western, *The Tornado* (1917), as was his last – *Cheyenne Autumn* (1964).

△ Tom Mix (far left) was a champion rodeo rider before he made his first Western in 1910. He made over 160 movies over the next 25 years. William Boyd (left) played Hop-A-Long Cassidy in 69 films between 1935 and 1952.

Fading into the west

The decline of the movie Western coincided with an increase in the number of TV series like *Gunsmoke*, *Bonanza* and *Rawhide*. In the 1960s the making of Westerns switched to Europe, where a greater freedom to depict the harsh realities of frontier life resulted in violent Italian-made 'spaghetti Westerns' such as *A Fistful of Dollars*, *For a Few Dollars More* and *The Good, the Bad and the Ugly*, directed by Sergio Leone and starring Clint Eastwood. Similar pictures, known as 'sauerkraut Westerns', were made in Germany.

△ Clint Eastwood as 'The Man with No Name', the mysterious drifter at the centre of Sergio Leone's classic 1960s 'spaghetti trilogy'.

years. During the 1940s directors like John Ford and Howard Hawks began to concentrate more on character than action, a trend that was continued in the following decade by Anthony Mann and Budd Boetticher in a sequence of films that became known as 'psychological Westerns' because of their stress on motives and emotions.

COWBOYS AND THEIR HORSES

William S. Hart and Fritz
Tom Mix and Tony
Buck Jones and Silver
Ken Maynard and Tarzan
Gene Autry and Champion
William Boyd and Topper
Allan 'Rocky' Lane and Blackjack
Roy Rogers and Trigger
Tex Ritter and White Flash
Rex Allen and Koko
The Lone Ranger and Silver

STAGECOACH

(USA, 1939) Director: John Ford

This classic account of the dangers of frontier life tells of the clashes of class and personality that arise between the passengers of a stagecoach during its journey through a dangerous wilderness. At the outset the banker, the whisky salesman and the pregnant woman consider themselves superior to their companions. Yet at such moments of crisis as the birth of the baby and the

Apache attack, it is the social outcasts – the outlaw (John Wayne), the prostitute, the drunken doctor and the gambler – who prove to have the nobler qualities.

Stagecoach is widely thought to be the finest Western of all time, and it established a genre tradition in almost every scene. The film did not rely solely on the non-stop action recipe of the B picture, but instead used neat performances and skilful direction to make the characters' relationships every bit as fascinating as Geronimo's raid and the final shootout.

Several attempts have been made since the 1970s to revive the Western by exploring its familiar themes from new angles. Films like *Little Big Man* (starring Dustin Hoffman) and *A Man Called Horse* (with Richard Harris), for example, tried to paint more sympathetic portraits of Native American life, while *The Wild Bunch*, *McCabe and Mrs Miller* and *Unforgiven* stripped away much of the genre's traditional glamour. More recently, such features as *The Ballad of Little Jo* (1994) and *The Quick and the Dead* (1995), with Sharon Stone, have tried to present the West from a woman's viewpoint.

▷ A key element in the success of *Stagecoach* was Ford's use of Monument Valley in Utah. Its distinctive landscape was to appear in countless future Westerns.

◁ Daniel Day-Lewis as Hawkeye in the 1992 remake of James Fenimore Cooper's *The Last of the Mohicans*. Set in 1757, when foreign powers were fighting for control of America, it tells of the defence of a British fortress against the French and their Iroqouis and Huron allies.

'Go West !'

The pioneering era when America was a British colony has been curiously neglected by film-makers, even though it shares many of the themes central to the Western. *The Last of the Mohicans*, re-made as recently as 1992, is a rare exception. More popular, however, were tales like *The Covered Wagon* (1923) and *Wagonmaster* (1950) that depicted the perils faced by those who took up the challenge to 'go west' after the American Civil War. The problems posed by the bleak wilderness and hostile tribes were also key elements in pictures dealing with the making of communication links across the plains – the mail (*Pony Express*), the coach service (*Stagecoach*), the telegraph (*Western Union*) and the railroad (*The Iron Horse* and *Union Pacific*).

Native Americans

In 1973 Marlon Brando refused the Oscar for his performance in *The Godfather* in protest at the cinema's depiction of Native Americans as savages whose sole purpose was to be slaughtered in the name of 'progress'. Hollywood was certainly guilty of producing extremely anti-Indian pictures like *Northwest Passage* and *Arrowhead*, but in fact there were relatively few films like this. While the US Cavalry was regularly summoned to save settlers from raiding parties, it was almost inevitable that the braves had been provoked on to the warpath by a villainous 'White Man' wanting to drive prospectors away from a gold mine, steal valuable grazing land, or prevent the building of a railroad.

Broken Arrow (1950) is usually thought to mark a change in Hollywood's outlook, but many well-intentioned silent films made before World War I, like *Ramona* and *The Squaw Man*, had been made on the theme of peaceful co-existence. Although Westerns no longer show Native Americans in a demeaning way, it is still true that until Kevin Costner's *Dances with Wolves* (1990) film-makers were reluctant to cast them in leading roles.

The law of the West

True-life villains have been particularly romanticized in the Western. Although they lived by the gun, Billy the Kid, Jesse James and Butch Cassidy and the Sundance Kid were all portrayed as lovable rogues, and even the most brutal gang of all, Quantrell's Raiders, was seen in a good light in *Best of the Badmen*. Many fictional outlaws were also made out to be heroes, especially gunfighters who supported a just cause, as in *The Magnificent Seven* or *The Shootist*, or those who took the law into their own hands, either to find missing loved ones (*The Searchers*) or to avenge a killing (*The Man from Laramie*).

Similarly there was no guarantee of finding honest men on the side of justice. In addition to crooked or cruel sheriffs, there were deputies who betrayed their former partners, as in Sam Peckinpah's *Pat Garrett and Billy the Kid*, and bounty hunters who upheld the law purely for profit. But some were forced to practise such despised trades, like James Stewart in *The Naked Spur* who hoped to raise enough reward money to re-purchase the farm he had lost during the American Civil War.

▽ *Dances with Wolves* (1990) was only the second Western to win an Oscar for Best Picture. The first was *Cimarron* 60 years earlier. It took only another two years, however, before Clint Eastwood's *Unforgiven* won the same award.

◁ Randolph Scott (left) as an ageing bounty hunter in Budd Boetticher's *Ride Lonesome*. Together they made seven 'psychological Westerns', which helped transform the genre in the 1950s.

Lancaster, and Kevin Costner respectively), and have also inspired such fictional adventures as *Dodge City* and *Wichita* with Errol Flynn and Joel McCrea.

Earp usually kept the peace in the company of 'Doc' Holliday, but many Westerns have depicted the sheriff as a man alone, as in *High Noon*, starring Gary Cooper. Less conventional than most lawmen, but equally effective, was James Stewart's character in *Destry Rides Again*. He cleans up the town of Bottleneck without even firing a shot, for as he explained: 'You shoot it out with them, and, for some reason, they get to look like heroes. You put 'em behind bars, and they look little and cheap, like they are.'

JOHN WAYNE

△ John Wayne in John Ford's *The Searchers* (1956).

Having failed to capture the public imagination in *The Big Trail* (1930), John Wayne spent the 1930s in low-budget Westerns before finally achieving stardom as The Ringo Kid in *Stagecoach* (1939).

After a series of action-packed World War II pictures he returned to the Western in the late 1940s, usually playing larger-than-life figures whose tough heroism epitomized the pioneering spirit: *Fort Apache, Red River, She Wore a Yellow Ribbon, Rio Grande, The Searchers* and *Rio Bravo*.

As he aged, his characters in films like *The Man Who Shot Liberty Valance, El Dorado, The Cowboys* and *The Shootist* increasingly came to symbolize the passing of the West and its ideals. In 1969 he won a Best Actor Oscar for *True Grit*.

The lawman, although lacking the glamour of the 'good badman', has always been a Western favourite. Wyatt Earp was particularly popular. His exploits were frequently retold in films like *My Darling Clementine, Gunfight at the O.K. Corral* and *Wyatt Earp* (starring Henry Fonda, Burt

▽ Kirk Douglas, Burt Lancaster, John Hudson and De Forrest Kelly leave Tombstone to meet the Clanton Gang for the *Gunfight at the O.K. Corral* (1957).

Drifters and drovers

Many cowboys become lawmen only after eventful careers as frontiersmen, cattle-drovers, or simply as drifters. With the exception of Hopalong Cassidy, who rarely left the Bar 20 Ranch, the majority of cowboys in the 'horse operas' of the 1930s conformed to the 'saddle tramp' image. Yet a number of acclaimed A pictures like *Pale Rider* (with Clint Eastwood) have also used the theme.

As Greek myths and Arthurian legends used journeys or quests to prove a hero's courage and ingenuity, so too the Western relied on wagon treks, cavalry patrols, raiding parties, gold rushes, revenge quests and journeys by coach and rail to make its own mythology.

The most exhilarating expedition was the cattle drive, in which cowboys were made to live up to their names as they escorted huge herds across treacherous country. The first major trail movie was *North of '36*, made in 1924. Such was the

expense involved in gathering enough cattle to make the action look realistic that scenes from it were regularly re-used in other Westerns over the next 25 years.

Ranchers and sodbusters

Cowboys hit the cattle trail less frequently after Howard Hawks's *Red River* (1948). While B pictures turned their attention to rancher movies, with raids on ranches by rustlers and horse thieves, the emphasis in A features shifted to cattle barons, whose rivalries and family crises were more the stuff of melodrama than of the Western.

Rancher movies were always more popular than those about farmers. Farm features (nicknamed 'sodbusters') usually

told of toil and survival. Among them is *Shane* (1953), which is widely considered one of the great Westerns. Most sodbusters did not appeal greatly to audiences who preferred to escape to the plains or the lawless towns in order to forget the problems of their own lives. *Heaven's Gate* (1980) – one of cinema's biggest commercial disasters – was really a glorified sodbuster.

End of the trail

The settling of the wild frontier marked the end of the Western era. Yet there were many who were unwilling (or unable) to give up the cowboy lifestyle. Some, like *The Professionals* (1966) and *The Wild Bunch* (1969) became soldiers of fortune and accepted dangerous missions in Mexico. Others joined Wild West shows, as in *Buffalo Bill* (1944). This latter tradition survives today in the form of the rodeo, which has provided the background for pictures like *Junior Bonner* (1972), starring Steve McQueen.

Although Clint Eastwood has continued to make Westerns since the 1960s and there have been several attempts to revive the genre (most recently in 1994 with films like *Maverick*) it has struggled to find a new audience.

But its themes are far from dead. They now feature in other genres, with lawmen confronting villains on inner-city streets, gunfights now occurring in outer space, and cross-country journeys now happening in open-top automobiles. Whatever its future, the Western film can at least look back on the achievement of lasting over three times as long as the Wild West era it depicted.

HIGH NOON

(USA, 1952) Director: Fred Zinnemann

On the day of his wedding Marshal Will Kane (Gary Cooper) receives news that a killer he once jailed is coming to town for revenge. However, having agreed to postpone a fresh start with his new wife (Grace Kelly), Kane finds that the citizens of Hadleyville are too cowardly to stand by him and that he has to face the danger alone.

Considered the first 'psychological Western' (in which the emphasis is on the characters' motives rather than purely on their actions), *High Noon* was a carefully constructed picture that heightened the tension by telling its story in 85 minutes – almost the length of time the actual events would have taken. The film was also seen by many as an attack on those who abandoned their friends during the inquiries into Communism in Hollywood (see page 54). John Wayne was so disgusted with *High Noon* that he made *Rio Bravo* to counter what he reckoned was its unpatriotic tone.

◁ Brandon De Wilde recoils as his gunslinging hero Alan Ladd prepares to defend his parents' farm in George Stevens's *Shane* (1953).

▷ Mel Gibson and Jodie Foster in the comedy Western *Maverick* (1994), which was based on a hit TV series of the same name (1957-62).

UNFORGIVEN

(USA, 1992) Director: Clint Eastwood

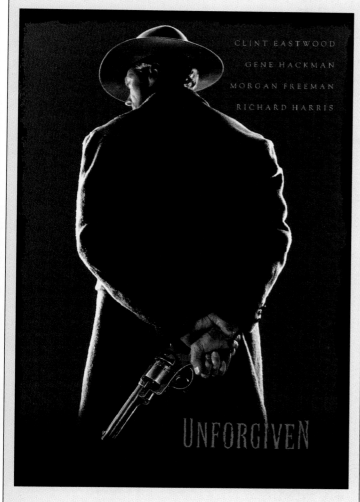

△ Starring in his 10th Western, Clint Eastwood played ex-gunfighter William Munny – 'a man as cold as the snow'.

When Sheriff 'Little Bill' Daggett (Gene Hackman) refuses to punish suitably an assault on a prostitute, her friends offer a reward for the capture of the culprits. Encouraged by the eager 'Schofield Kid' (Jaimz Woolvett), retired gunslinger William Munny (Clint Eastwood) reluctantly reunites with his former partner Ned Logan (Morgan Freeman) to undertake the mission. However, he soon comes into conflict with Daggett, who has already dealt brutally with 'English Bob' (Richard Harris), a rival gunman also on the villains' trail.

This tough, dramatic insight into the harsh realities of the old West has been acclaimed as one of the genre's finest films. By portraying Munny as a has-been forced into one last job in order to feed his children, Eastwood was trying to destroy the glamorous gunfighting legends of most Western books and films. Recalling many of his own films and other classic Westerns, he depicts the frontier as a cruel place where tragedy occurred every time somebody pulled a gun.

FILMS TO WATCH

Films are made in the US unless otherwise stated

THE PIONEERS

Drums Across the Mohawk (1939)
Across the Wide Missouri (1951)
The Big Sky (1952)
Silverado (1985)
Last of the Mohicans (1992)

WAGON TRAINS

The Covered Wagon (1923)
Brigham Young (1940)
Westward the Women (1952)
Bend of the River (1952)

THE CIVIL WAR

Virginia City (1940)
Santa Fe Trail (1940)
Rio Lobo (1970)
The Beguiled (1971)

COMMUNICATIONS

The Iron Horse (1924)
Union Pacific (1939)
Stagecoach (1939)
Western Union (1941)
Pony Express (1953)

NATIVE AMERICANS

Broken Arrow (1950)
Hondo (1953)
A Man Called Horse (1970)
Little Big Man (1970)
Dances with Wolves (1990)
Geronimo (1994)

THE CAVALRY

Fort Apache (1948)
She Wore a Yellow Ribbon (1949)
Two Flags West (1950)
Major Dundee (1965)

OUTLAWS

Jesse James (1939)
The Return of Frank James (1940)
The Left-Handed Gun (1951)
Butch Cassidy and the Sundance Kid (1969)
The Outlaw Josey Wales (1976)
Young Guns I & II (1988, 1990)

GUNFIGHTERS

The Gunfighter (1950)
The Magnificent Seven (1960)
Cat Ballou (1965)
The Shootist (1976)

LAWMEN

My Darling Clementine (1947)
High Noon (1952)
Gunfight at the O.K. Corral (1957)
Unforgiven (1992)
Wyatt Earp (1994)

DRIFTERS

Tumbleweeds (1925)
The Plainsman (1936)
The Westerner (1940)
Rio Bravo (1959)
High Plains Drifter (1972)
Pale Rider (1985)

REVENGE & QUESTS

Winchester 73 (1950)
The Man from Laramie (1955)
Two Rode Together (1961)
Hang 'Em High (1967)

CATTLE DRIVES

Red River (1948)
The Far Country (1955)
The Cowboys (1971)
City Slickers (1991)

RANCHERS

The Virginian (1929)
Broken Lance (1954)
The Big Country (1956)
McLintock (1963)
Big Jake (1971)

FARMERS

Apache (1954)
Shane (1953)
The Emigrants (Sweden, 1970)
Heaven's Gate (1980)

MEXICO

Rio Grande (1950)
Vera Cruz (1953)
The Professionals (1966)
The Wild Bunch (1969)

WILD WEST SHOWS

Buffalo Bill (1944)
Junior Bonner (1972)
The Electric Horseman (1979)
Broncho Billy (1980)

SPAGHETTI WESTERNS (all Italy)

A Fistful of Dollars (1964)
For a Few Dollars More (1965)
The Good, the Bad and the Ugly (1966)
A Bullet for the General (1966)
Once Upon a Time in the West (1969)

WESTERN WOMEN

Annie Oakley (1935)
Duel in the Sun (1946)
Rancho Notorious (1953)
Johnny Guitar (1954)
The Quick and the Dead (1995)

THE LIFECYCLE OF A MOVIE

The film is over and the credits begin to roll. Dozens of names and job titles appear in the list. Each one has played a part in making the movie, but who are they and what do they all do?

Film-making is a very expensive and time-consuming process. The average film costs $20 million. Many take over a year to make. How a film is made varies throughout the world, but most countries follow the Hollywood method, which breaks down the process into four stages.

These are Development, Pre-Production, Production and Post-Production and Distribution.

DEVELOPMENT

Every picture – whether it's a big-budget blockbuster or a small independent feature film – begins with an idea called a 'concept'. This is either an original story, or a book, play or TV series that already exists. These are known as 'pre-sold' works.

The person who brings together the people, the money and the equipment needed to make a movie is the producer. If they like the concept, they will ask a screenwriter (or scriptwriter), who will write the film script, to draw up a 'treatment' or short story. This gives details of the plot and the main characters, as well as suggestions for some key scenes.

△ Breaking the rule of 'never work with children or animals', *Free Willy* (1993) was an original story developed specially for the screen.

The producer

Producers look after all aspects of film-making, but are usually busiest during the early and the final stages. Once they have selected the film's subject and chosen the people who will work on it, their main task is to make sure that a film gets made on time and within the agreed budget. The best producers can combine an eye for a good story with an ability to handle the business side of a project. They are also skilled at dealing with creative artists, like the director and the performers, who can often be very temperamental and difficult to work with.

Howard Kazanjian, who produced the sci-fi blockbuster *The Return of the Jedi*, claims that the producer's job involves 'crossing art with arithmetic'. But most film producers are more concerned with creating popular, money-making entertainment than great works of art.

As producers have so many different tasks, they have a special team to assist them. The executive producer helps to raise the money for making the film. Many directors with 'sure-fire' box-office reputations, like Steven Spielberg, often take on this role. The associate producer usually has control of the day-to-day shooting in a studio or on location. They are helped by a production manager, who keeps the producer informed on a picture's progress.

The screenwriter

The screenwriter is involved in the making of a film from an early stage. Some screenwriters create the concept to offer to a film producer, others are hired to adapt a pre-sold work for the screen. Sometimes the producer asks the screenwriter for an 'outline script' to gain a better idea of the dialogue and action than the treatment has given. The outline gives details of the visual images or action on the left hand side of the page, while the dialogue, music and sound effects are given on the right. The producer uses the outline script to raise money for the project.

Once the money has been raised for the film, the screenwriter begins researching the story. In the case of a costume drama, they will study the historical background to a period, for example how people spoke and behaved at that time. For more modern movies they may visit the places where the action is set, to find locations with the right atmosphere.

The first duty of the screenwriter is to make the story flow. They also write the 'dialogue', the lines to be spoken by the performers. Dialogue not only has to sound like real speech, it also has to provide insights into the thoughts and emotions of the characters. Some directors write their own scripts, while others work with the screenwriter to ensure that the story is told through the visual images as well as through the words.

The movie package

The producer sends the treatment or outline script to a director (see below). In choosing a director, the producer has to ask some key questions: Does the director have a successful track record in the kind of film being planned? Are they 'hot' off a recent box-office hit? Can they be relied upon to complete the film on schedule and within budget?

Once the producer has hired a director, they decide together which performers

◁ Although Steven Spielberg is best known as the director of films like *E.T.*, he has also been executive producer on such hits as *Gremlins* and *Casper*.

△ Film-making can be very frustrating, even for experts like Woody Allen, who not only writes and directs his own films, but often stars in them, too.

PRE-PRODUCTION

With the budget settled, the producer and the director join together to put a project into pre-production. This phase of film-making often has the following key stages: casting, planning the shoot, researching details, making the sets, and costume and make-up.

Casting

It is vital to find the right stars for the leading roles, as big names normally persuade both backers and audiences to spend their money on a picture. It is also important that the 'principal players' are suited to their parts. Robin Williams, for example, would be rather miscast in an action-adventure film designed for Arnold Schwarzenegger. Sometimes if the director is undecided about a performer they will insist on a 'screen test', in which the performer plays a scene before a camera to give the director an idea of how they will look on screen.

△ John Travolta became a star after he was nominated for an Oscar for his performance in *Saturday Night Fever* (1977). But after *Grease* (1978), his career went into decline and he had only one hit, *Look Who's Talking* (1989), in the whole of the 1980s. Quentin Tarantino therefore took a risk when he cast Travolta as hitman Vincent Vega in *Pulp Fiction* (1994). But the film was a success and Travolta earned a second Oscar nomination. He is now back in demand with both directors and audiences.

would be best for the leading roles. Is the budget big enough to afford a megastar? Will a lesser-known performer reduce the film's chances of success at the box office? Do the performers and the director get along together? Are they free when the production is scheduled to start shooting?

The director might belong to a talent agency, which will also suggest some of the performers they represent for the key roles. The concept, the directors and the stars form what is known as a 'package'. As soon as the package has been agreed, the producer begins work on the deals that will provide the picture with its financial backing, or budget. The actual casting happens a bit later (see below).

Finding the budget

Film-making is a highly risky business. A major film studio might put 100 scripts into development each year, but only ten will make it as far as pre-production. Of those that are turned into movies only three will break even (recover their costs). Just one will become a box-office hit. There is no guarantee that a film will be successful, even with big-name stars or directors. So raising the money to make a film is very difficult.

Producers have all sorts of expenses to meet during the making of a movie. They have to estimate what these might be in a provisional budget. Once this is done they go to a major distribution company to ask for some of the money they need.

Distributors play a crucial role in the lifecycle of a movie. The distributor's main job is to persuade an exhibitor to show films in their cinemas, but they are also involved at the budget stage. Firstly, they have to decide whether a film is likely to be a box-office success. If they agree to distribute the picture they give the producer a 'front end' sum of money (an advance) which forms a large part of the film's total budget. In return the distributor will receive a 'back end' share or 'percentage' of the picture's box-office takings or 'receipts'.

Producers try to raise more money by selling their films to distributors in other countries, as well as to video and television companies. Once they have the backing of distributors at home and abroad, the producer will try to borrow the rest of the budget from a bank or big business corporation. This loan will be repaid from the box-office receipts.

A great deal of effort goes into making every aspect of a film as accurate as possible. The production designer and the costume and make-up designers spend a lot of time researching before they begin work. They use books, photographs, drawings, press cuttings and old films to find out what houses and furnishings looked like in a particular period, how people dressed and what they ate and drank. Every detail has to be correct – from the layout of a royal palace to the style of shoes common in 1820, or the design of a cereal box in 1961.

Supporting roles and minor or 'bit' parts are just as important. The performers for these are usually found by a casting director. The casting director also chooses the 'stunt doubles' (see page 140) and the people called 'stand-ins', who look like particular stars. They stand in for the stars while the lighting is being arranged for each shot. The extras for any crowd scenes also have to be hired. Extras are usually found by agencies based in the place where the action is to be filmed. Anyone can be an extra. Perhaps you could join an agency near you?

△ Over 300,000 extras were needed for *Gandhi* (1982), the record number for a single film.

▷ Robert De Niro is so dedicated to the art of acting that rather than use make-up he put on 22.5 kg in weight to play his part in *Raging Bull* (1980).

Planning the shoot

The scenes in a motion picture are not shot in the order in which they appear on the screen. All the action taking place in one location is recorded together, even though it may appear at different times in the finished feature. This is done to keep the costs down. Delays during shooting can be very expensive. A film unit working in the desert, for example, may have to wait days for a Foreign Legion uniform that has been sent to the wrong location. So, before shooting begins, a final or 'shooting script' is broken down into the different shots or 'camera set-ups' the director has chosen in order to tell the story. If the producer thinks that the picture will be too expensive to make, they might postpone it while they try to raise more money.

Once the shooting script is agreed, the associate producer draws up a plan called a 'shooting schedule' to show everyone where they should be at any time during production. Each member of the cast and crew is also given their own timetable known as a 'call sheet'. The associate producer also prepares a 'breakdown sheet', which contains details of the people and equipment needed for each scene to ensure that filming goes as smoothly as possible.

Many performers also like to research the role they are to play. They call on experts like doctors, scientists or musicians to get information about their jobs to help them 'get in character'. In *The Hard Way* (1991), for example, Michael J. Fox plays a star who joins a cop (James Woods) on patrol to prepare for his role in a crime film.

It is also vital to ensure that landmarks, streets, buildings or rooms to be used in a picture accurately reflect the period or mood of the film. Location scouts search for settings that will add to the drama or realism of the action. But it is not always possible or desirable to shoot on location. It might be difficult to get permission, or too expensive to shoot in a certain place. When this happens a production designer is hired to create sets that will have the same impact as the real places.

Sets and scenery

The production designer, or art director, is known as 'the architect of the film'. They work closely with the director to produce a sequence of 'storyboards'. These are a series of drawings that

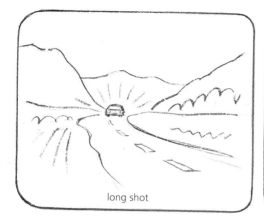
long shot

close-up

medium shot

△ Storyboards are used by directors to plan scenes in advance, right down to the last detail. This helps to reduce the amount of time it takes to shoot the action and keep the costs down.

break a scene down into the various close-ups, medium shots and long shots which the director will use to create the scene. The storyboards also help the designer work out the scale and shape of the sets and scenery, how they will be furnished and the sort of objects or 'props' that will feature in each scene.

Once the art director's designs have been finalised they are made into sets by a team of carpenters, plasterers, painters and electricians. As only one side of a set faces the camera, it is built out of 'flats' which are propped up by scaffolding hidden behind the scenes.

During the Golden Age of Hollywood (see page 36) the major studios had their own set stores. Many also had large areas behind the studio buildings called 'backlots'. Here complete sets of, for example, American city streets, European town squares or medieval castles were left standing for whenever they were needed. Some studios even had whole towns or ranches built out in the wilds for their Westerns. Today, however, most sets are only used for a single film. But because set building and location

◁ It takes teams of skilled workers many long hours to turn the art director's sketches into finished sets. You need some imagination to see how this building site inside a soundstage at Pinewood Studios will eventually become a magnificent set for *Interview with the Vampire* (1994).

▽ Based on careful historical research, this Roman street was built at Pinewood Studios for *The Last Days of Pompeii*. In the foreground you can see the scaffolding holding up the 'flats' from which the fronts of the different buildings have been constructed.

THE LIFECYCLE OF A MOVIE

shooting are expensive, a number of special effects have been created to allow film-makers to show a particular place without actually having to go there (see page 144).

Costumes and make-up

Clothes say a lot about the person wearing them, and so costumes play a key part in a film. The Hollywood studios used to have their own costume and wardrobe departments, full of period dresses, uniforms, hats, shoes and jewellery. But these have now gone, so the costume designer has to make, hire or buy costumes for each film. They also have to consult the director and the production designer to make sure their costumes contribute to the mood, as well as to the look, of a film.

▷ Lizzy Gardiner and Tim Chappel won the Oscar for Best Costume Design for the outrageous outfits they created for *The Adventures of Priscilla, Queen of the Desert* (1994), in which Guy Pierce, Terence Stamp and Hugo Weaving play 'drag queens' who make their living by singing pop songs dressed in women's clothes.

◁ △ A sketch for the costume worn by Katharine Hepburn in the part of Queen Eleanor in the historical drama *The Lion in Winter* (1968).

   First they find out how many costume changes each character has during the film. They then decide which styles and colours to use, making sure that these will suit both the performer and the mood of the scene. They may also have to provide costumes at different stages of 'decay', to show the result of gunshots, explosions, fights or falls. To prepare clothing for these 'tattered and torn' sequences, the designer treats the fabrics with chemicals, washes them and even brushes them with sandpaper. The 'key wardrobe' person is responsible for keeping the costumes in exactly the right condition during shooting.

▷ Marlon Brando's T-shirt was deliberately dirtied for his part in *A Streetcar Named Desire* (1951).

◁ △ Francesca Annis had to age many years to play the part of The Widow of the Web in the fantasy film *Krull* (1983).

whiskers, as in such costume dramas as *Little Women*. Sometimes a character's entire make-up can be composed of hair, such as the werewolf played by Michael J. Fox in *Teen Wolf*. A performer might spend up to five hours being made-up, and then a further two being cleaned up – and all this after spending ten to twelve hours shooting their scenes.

▽ Greg Cannom designed body make-up that was funny as well as convincing to turn actor Robin Williams into an elderly nanny in the comedy *Mrs Doubtfire* (1993).

All performers wear some form of make-up, known as 'street make-up', to make them look healthy under the bright lamps called arc lights that are used during shooting. But special effects make-up, particularly for horror and science-fiction features, requires much more creativity. An alien, for example a Klingon in the *Star Trek* films, not only has to have an original appearance, but also has to be suitably terrifying or friendly according to the story. It often takes the make-up artist several hours to put on make-up of this sort, as it is usually built up from several layers of specially shaped latex rubber. Once the face mask has been applied, it might be 'stippled' or coloured to add extra personality.

Make-up that ages a character, changes their sex or acts as a disguise can be just as complex. In *Little Big Man*, for example, Dustin Hoffman had to wear several layers of carefully moulded latex to convince the viewer that he was playing a 121 year-old man. Robin Williams had to be made to look like an elderly nanny in *Mrs Doubtfire*, while Jack Nicholson wore a huge painted smile to play the Joker in *Batman*. Realistic injuries are also the responsibility of the make-up artist. These range from a bruise or nose bleed after a fight, to a bullet wound, a sliced-off ear or a blown-off head. Sometimes a performer will need to wear total body make-up to play their character. In *The Fly*, Jeff Goldblum was dressed in latex designed to look like raw flesh oozing with fluids, to suggest that he was turning from a human being into an insect.

A hair stylist is also on hand to attend to any wigs or pieces of facial hair that are needed. These could be period hair styles or

PRODUCTION

Film-making looks very glamorous. But, in fact, it involves many early mornings and long working hours, often in uncomfortable conditions. There is a lot of waiting around while make-up is applied, sets are decorated and technicians prepare their equipment for a shot or a 'take'. In addition, there is the frustration of sometimes having to repeat a take ten or more times, until the director is satisfied.

Setting up a shot

Imagine it is eight o'clock in the morning on a studio soundstage. Some of the cast and crew have already been at work for two hours. One of the actresses is in the middle of a long make-up session that will transform her into a 96 year-old woman. The set decorator is putting the finishing touches to the set. One of the wardrobe department is fitting a 'squib' into the sleeve of an actor's shirt. This is a bag of fake blood wired up to a small explosive charge that will make the bag burst and create the illusion that the man has been shot in the shoulder.

The director now begins to organize the first take or 'camera set-up'. With the help of the performers' 'stand-ins', the director and the cinematographer (see below) decide where each character will stand during the action and how they will be lit. They also work out any camera movements. These need to be designed carefully to make sure none of the technical equipment appears in the shot, and that the camera itself is not reflected in a shiny surface. The sound recordist checks that it will be possible to record the dialogue without the microphone (held on a long arm by the boom operator) dipping into the shot.

The cinematographer

The cinematographer, also called the director of photography, is an important member of a film unit. They are responsible for selecting the camera, lenses, film stock, filters and lights that will be used during a shoot. They also act as the 'director of light', telling the chief electrician, known as the 'gaffer', where they want the various lights to be positioned or 'rigged' so that the light and shade around the set add atmosphere to the scene and glamour to the stars.

It is relatively easy to get the right patterns of light and shade inside a studio using arc lamps. Each lamp has four moveable flaps, nicknamed 'barn doors', to vary the amount of light and the direction in which it shines. But on location the cinematographer has to try to control natural light with flat screens called 'reflectors'. Sometimes coloured filters are fitted to the camera lens to keep the quality of light consistent from shot to shot.

Directors rely heavily on their cinematographers for their skill

at lighting or 'composing', the scene. Many directors try to work regularly with the same cinematographer. There have been several great teams in cinema history: D. W. Griffith and Billy Bitzer, William Wyler and Gregg Toland, Ingmar Bergman and Sven Nykvist, François Truffaut and Nestor Almendros, and Bernardo Bertolucci and Vittorio Storraro.

The camera crew

Meanwhile, an assistant to the camera operator, known as the 'clapper loader', is loading the film into the camera. Another assistant, the 'focus puller', works out the distance between any figures or objects in the shot so that they will be able to adjust the lens to keep everything in sharp focus. They also put down on the studio floor pieces of tape or chalk lines known as 'T-marks', so that the cast know where to stand during the action. A performer must always remember to 'hit their marks' while acting or the take will be spoiled.

◁ Two grips push the camera operator and the camera around on a dolly during the shooting of this sequence from *Kindergarten Cop* (1990), starring Arnold Schwarzenegger.

As the director wants the camera to follow the action during this take, the camera operator is arranging for it to be mounted on to a wheeled trolley called a 'dolly'. This will be pushed about the set by a team of assistants called the 'grips'. If the director decides to film looking down on the set, the camera will be placed at the end of a long arm fixed to a movable platform, known as a 'crane'. This is also moved around by the grips. On location the grips are also responsible for laying tracks on the ground to ensure the camera moves smoothly during 'tracking' shots. Sometimes these are filmed by the camera operator using a special support harness called a Steadycam. Another camera crew, the second unit, film some of the location scenes and the stunt footage.

Cue the performers

While the crew prepare the sets and equipment, the director works with the performers. Sometimes this brief period before a take is the only time the director and the cast have to discuss the best way of playing a scene. The actors and actresses will run over their lines and talk about the significance of the action and how their character should feel. Some directors will tell the performers exactly how they want them to act, others will allow them to improvise, or interpret the dialogue in their own way.

▷ Steven Spielberg and Harrison Ford discuss the best way to play a scene in *Indiana Jones and the Temple of Doom* (1984).

▷ While Miss Piggy has her hair brushed, the focus puller measures the exact distance between her and the camera to make sure the picture will be sharp and clear.

Screen acting is a fine art. The sequences that make up a film are not shot in the order in which they finally appear. So the players cannot give a continuous performance, as they would do on the stage. Instead they have to be able to throw themselves into the action each time the camera starts to roll. The director walks them through the take, showing them their marks and explaining where the camera will be positioned at any time. Perhaps they will have a final rehearsal. Then the director announces that they are ready to 'go for a take'.

△ This piece of action from *The Three Musketeers* (1993) shows how tough it is to play love scenes with so many people looking on.

'Action!'

The assistant director checks that the camera operator and the sound recordist are 'ready to roll'. They then shout, 'Quiet on the set! Give me a bell!' An alarm or a buzzer sounds and the studio doors are closed. A red light is switched on above the doors to warn people not to enter while a take is in progress.

As soon as there is silence on the set, the assistant director calls 'Roll 'em!' The sound recordist starts the tape machine and, when it is running at the correct recording speed, shouts, 'Speed!' The camera operator also turns on the camera. When it reaches a running speed of 24 frames per second, they call 'Mark It!'

The clapper loader stands before the camera and holds up the slate, or clapperboard. This is a small blackboard with an arm at the top held by a hinge at one corner. On the slate are written the names of the picture, the director and the cinematographer, as well as details of the action about to be filmed. Production begins with 'Slate One', no matter where this particular camera set-up occurs in the shooting script. The clapper loader shouts out the number of our take – 'Slate 30. Take 1' – and claps down the slate arm. This clap will later act as a signal to the editor (see page 142) to synchronize the sound tape and the film images. Nowadays most cameras and tape machines are electronically controlled to ensure they are 'in sync' throughout a take. The clapper loader ducks out of shot. The director shouts 'Action!', and the performers begin to act. At the end of the scene, the director calls 'Cut!'. If this is said in the middle of a take it means either that a performer has 'fluffed' their lines, the director is dissatisfied with the acting or that some technical problem has arisen.

Many modern directors shoot the action with a video camcorder, as well as a movie camera. This gives them the chance to play back a take instantly and judge its quality. In the past, they had to wait until the next morning to see the results of a day's shooting. These uncut sequences are called 'rushes' or 'dailies'. If the director is unhappy with the take, they will order the cast and crew to 'Go again', and do another take. But if all has gone well, they will announce, 'Print it'. Once the director has all the shots they need they will announce, 'That's a wrap'. It was once said, 'Do that often enough and you've got the makings for a movie.'

▽ While Timothy Dalton prepares to play James Bond in *The Living Daylights* (1987), the clapperboard is held in front of the camera to mark the scene.

STUNTS AND PHYSICAL EFFECTS

Many special effects (SFX) are added to a film in post-production to make the action seem more realistic or spectacular (see page 144). But many effects, known as 'physical effects', are needed during shooting itself.

MAKING WEATHER

It is impossible to control the weather during filming. As a result, many weather effects have to be specially created, either on location or inside a studio.

Huge fans are used to create strong winds, while swirling fog is made from a mixture of smoke and dry ice. Rain usually falls from sprinklers or giant watering cans fixed above the set. In *Singin' in the Rain*, the water had to be mixed with milk so that it showed up clearly on the screen. Nowadays snow is made from polystyrene, but in the past it was often a mixture of white sand, chalk and crystals known as water glass. If you look at the winter scenes in *Young Sherlock Holmes* you cannot tell that they were shot in the middle of summer.

▽ Giant wind machines are used to create a storm in this scene from *The Mosquito Coast* (1989).

A SMASHING TIME

Next time you watch a fight sequence, keep an eye on the number of things that break during the action. The bottles that get smashed are made out of a mixture of polystyrene and perspex, rather than real glass. Until quite recently, they were made from sugar and water. Tables and chairs that fall apart when a character lands on them are also carefully designed to prevent injuring the performers. The SFX unit also works

closely with the set builders to produce what are called 'breakaways'. These include walls, balconies and windows that will have to collapse or shatter convincingly when a performer or their stunt double crashes into them. Similar to breakaways are 'flyaways' or 'wild walls'. These are parts of the set that can be easily moved aside to allow a moving camera to follow the action – even through a solid wall.

DAREDEVIL STUNTS

Some action is too dangerous for the stars of a film to perform, so it is done by skilled stunt men and women. Although some actors and actresses insist on doing their own stunts, it is likely that anyone involved in a punch up, a car chase, a high-speed crash, or a fall from a high building is being played at that moment by a stunt double dressed to look like the star. In *Interview with the Vampire*, for example, Tom Cruise was replaced during the explosions, the fires and many other SFX sequences by a stunt double named Nick Gillard. At one point his character, Lestat, has to fly. This was achieved by launching Gillard into the air from a powerful springboard and holding him there using wires attached to a special body harness.

△ A stunt man hangs from the undercarriage of the plane in this dramatic chase scene from the Bond movie *Licence to Kill* (1989).

All stunts are carefully worked out by stunt co-ordinators, to make sure that nothing goes wrong. One slip during the scene in *Indiana Jones and the Last Crusade* in which Harrison Ford narrowly avoids a rotating ship's propeller, could have ended in tragedy if

△ Bruce Willis as cop John McClane surviving a spectacular explosion in the action adventure *Die Hard 2* (1990).

the stunt had not been planned in advance to the last detail. The best stunt co-ordinators have to be experts in explosives, chemistry, electronics, engineering, carpentry and model-making to make their stunts as realistic as they are safe.

Fires and explosions are among the most spectacular – and dangerous – effects to recreate. Petrol or kerosene is often used to keep screen fires burning, although gas is now widely used because it is easier to control. Setting a person alight, as in the fire brigade drama *Backdraft*, is one of the riskiest stunts and the stunt man or women is always protected by several layers of special clothing. Explosives are also handled with extreme care. Dynamite is used to create a big bang, while gunpowder is used for smaller scale explosions.

It is often too expensive to blow up real buildings, boats, planes or other vehicles. So film-makers are turning increasingly to miniatures and computer images to achieve the most dramatic effects. Although these are usually highly ingenious, many SFX experts and film fans still prefer the real thing.

▽ Members of the special effects team plan a World War II sea battle in the giant water tank at Pinewood Studios.

The end of the day

Although some of the cast and crew can now relax, others still have a lot of work to do. The director may view the rushes from the previous day. The grips have to pack away the camera equipment. The set decorators have to prepare the set for tomorrow's first set-up. The clapper loader records in detail what each reel of film contains, and sends them to the laboratory to be processed. Finally, the boom operator has to label the reels of sound tape and send them to another laboratory. Here they are transferred on to magnetic tape which has sprockets along its outer edge just like the celluloid strip. This is used by the editor to produce a 'rough cut' of the action.

Continuity

Perhaps the busiest person at this time is the script supervisor, who is also called the continuity assistant. Once shooting begins they act as a second pair of eyes for the director.

△ The continuity assistant sits beneath the performers preparing for a scene in *The Flight of the Phoenix*. The background scenery will be added later using a special effects process called a 'matte'.

The shots that make up a sequence have often been filmed weeks apart – some on location, some in the studio. But when they are edited together they have to look as if they are happening within a split second of each other in exactly the same place. In other words, the action has to seem continuous. Picture a soaking wet character in a blue dress dashing into a café to shelter from the rain. The action cuts from the location shot to one filmed in the studio. If the character comes through the door bone dry and wearing jeans there has been an error in continuity.

The script supervisor must prevent such slips, known as 'gaffes' or 'howlers'. Armed with the script, a stop-watch and a set of coloured pencils, they keep a record of everything that happens during a take. They write down any changes in the dialogue when a performer improvises their lines. They note on which words a character sits, stands or begins moving. They also have to keep an eye on many other details, like the time showing on a clock on a wall or the amount of food on a plate or drink in a glass. Finally, they have to know exactly where each character was standing, what they were doing and in which direction they were facing when the director shouted, 'Cut!'.

All these details, together with the director's comments on the quality of the take, are recorded on the daily continuity sheets. These are essential guides during the editing phase.

Foul-ups

The movies are a multi-million dollar industry. Vast sums of money are spent on every piece of equipment, every frame of film, and every second the cast and crew are on the set. Yet film-makers the world over still allow hundreds of glaring errors to slip past them and find their way on to the screen. Perhaps the greatest moment of movie muddle comes in *Captain Apache* (1971). The deputy sheriff of a town called Paradise walks out into the main street and is shot twice. Staggering back in agony, he collapses through the door of the jail – with a knife in his chest! Even the most famous are guilty of bloopers. In *Forrest Gump* (1994), Forrest says at Jenny's grave, 'You died on a Saturday'. But the date on the headstone is 22 March 1982, which was a Monday!

BECOME A BLOOPER DETECTOR

Continuity is a difficult job and mistakes do happen, but what is so amazing is that no one spots them in time. Here are a few common bloopers to keep an eye out for next time you watch a film:

- Microphones bobbing into shot from the top of the screen.

- People in cars or on carts who change seats from shot to shot.

- Reflections of the camera or the studio lights in mirrors or shiny metal objects.

- Pieces of scenery that are not quite long enough so you can see the studio at the edge of the screen.

- Props that bend, wobble, or fall over of their own accord or when performers bump into them.

- Modern-day items like cars, wristwatches, aeroplane vapour trails, and TV aerials in historical films.

- Back projection (see page 144) that suddenly changes direction or repeatedly passes the same landmarks.

POST-PRODUCTION AND DISTRIBUTION

Shooting is over, but there is still much to do before the film reaches a cinema screen. All that exist at the moment are thousands of metres of exposed film and used sound tape. During 'post-production' the best takes and the clearest soundtracks are selected and edited together to give the story its rhythm and continuity. Music, special optical effects and title sequences will then be added. In post-production a bad film can be rescued. But a good one can also be ruined!

Editing

Some directors would probably say that shooting is the key stage of film-making. But many others would claim that images recorded on film have no real meaning until they have been edited into a logical sequence.

D. W. Griffith (see page 22) and the film-makers of the Soviet montage era (see page 32) showed the importance of editing in screen story-telling. Today skilful editors still add to the pace, meaning and tension of a film by linking shots of varying lengths in an imaginative way. They can even improve an actor or actress's performance by selecting only the best shots from the different takes.

As soon as the reels of film and sound tape arrive from the processing laboratories, the editor matches them to make the rushes. The film and tape are threaded into a machine called a 'synchronizer'. The editor marks with a special pencil the place on each reel where the clapperboard arm clapped. The picture and sound are then fed through the synchronizer and stored on wire spools. The words spoken on the tape now match the lip movements of the performers on the film.

The director views the rushes and selects the takes they want to use for the final film. The unwanted footage is carefully stored, as parts of it might be needed later. The editor now begins to assemble a 'rough cut' of the film. The traditional method of doing this involved the editor cutting through the film strip and joining, or 'splicing' together the best scenes with sticky tape. Many editors today simplify this task by feeding the visual information into a computer. They number each frame and can then try out different sequences by keying in the necessary numbers.

When the location or stunt footage shot by the second camera unit has been added in, the editor shows the rough cut to the director. The film is often too long at this stage, and so the two of them work together to trim and tighten the action. Usually only a few shots are removed to increase the pace of the picture. But sometimes entire scenes are cut, if the director feels they slow down the story. The new version is called a 'fine cut'. Once it has been approved by the producer, the soundtrack can be edited.

◁ An editor watches the rushes on a viewing machine. Notice the celluloid strips hanging behind him in a 'trim bin' and the 'splicer' on the table to his left, which is used to join strips of film together.

△ The microphone boom hangs above Bill Murray during the shooting of *Groundhog Day*, although location dialogue is often re-recorded in a studio.

Sound and music

Only one part of the soundtrack has been recorded so far – the dialogue. But the words we hear in a cinema may not have been spoken precisely when the picture was filmed. Although sound taped in a studio should be fine, the quality of location sound might be poor. When working outdoors the sound recordist cannot always control the amount of background noise produced by traffic, crowds or the wind. As a result, the performers often have to record their lines again in a sound studio. This process is called 'looping', as the performers try to match the dialogue to their lip movements on short loops of film playing on a screen before them. This requires great skill, as they have to remember how they played the scene originally and repeat it exactly, down to the last laugh or sigh.

Many of the other sounds heard in a film will also have been 'dubbed', that is added, during post-production. Some sound effects are available from special sound libraries. But others like footsteps, a door slam, a car horn, a snapping branch, a body slumping to the floor have to be performed by a specialist called a

Foley artist, named after Jack Foley, who invented many sound recording techniques. Some effects require more imagination. The sound of ice in a drink is often made by rolling pen tops round a glass. Crackling fires are reproduced by crinkling cellophane. The sound of a sword or an arrow piercing a body is made by sticking a knife into a cabbage. In *The Karate Kid*, the noise of the flying kicks came from a swished badminton racket. The Foley artist often works with a 'looping group', who provide background voices. Listen to the customers in a restaurant scene or a crowd gathered on a street. Their chatter is really a looping group saying, 'walla walla walla'.

The last element to be added to the soundtrack is the music or 'film score'. Film music is most effective when it works with the audience's emotions. In some cases a music arranger scores a film using existing songs or pieces of classical music. The choice of music usually matches the period of the film. For example, *Good Morning, Vietnam* and *Dazed and Confused* were packed with rock hits from the 1960s and 1970s, while *The Madness of King George* used music by the 18th-century composer Handel.

But for most features the music is specially written by a composer. During what are called 'spotting sessions', the composer and director watch a rough cut of the film and decide on the mood and tempo suitable for each scene. They also agree on any incidents that might need special emphasis, like a kiss, a car chase or a moment of terror. A 90-minute film normally requires about 30 minutes of music. The composer usually has four or five weeks in which to write the score and to suggest the instruments needed to perform it. The music is then recorded in a sound studio. The conductor faces a screen showing the scene to ensure that the music and the action match.

The dubbing mixer now takes the three soundtracks – dialogue, special effects and music – and mixes them on to a single track. Each track is carefully balanced to make sure it does not drown out the other two. Once the final soundtrack has been mixed, the tape is sent to the laboratory. Here the sound waves are converted into light signals, which are fixed on to the soundtrack strip on the outer edge of the celluloid film.

▽ A mixing desk used to blend the different elements of a film's soundtrack.

THE MAGIC OF SFX

Special effects not only dazzle and entertain, but they can also turn fantasy into reality before our eyes. SFX are as old as cinema itself. Fades in and out, overlapping dissolves, super-impositions and stop-motion tricks were popular with pioneer film-makers like Georges Méliès (see page 20). The effects in modern movies are much more sophisticated and help make the action seem more lifelike and thrilling. The spaceships in the *Star Wars* films, the mix of humans and cartoon characters in *Who Framed Roger Rabbit?* and the dinosaurs in *Jurassic Park* were all created using the most advanced SFX technology.

Most special effects today are produced in a laboratory or workshop known as an optical house. But some SFX can be achieved during shooting itself.

FILM SPEEDS

Early film-makers soon discovered that they could create unusual effects by altering the speed at which the film passed through the camera. Slow-motion photography was achieved by 'overcranking' or running the camera faster than usual so that the film played at a much slower speed during projection. Slow motion is used to add to the drama of violent or sporting action, such as the athletes running along the beach in *Chariots of Fire*. It is also common to shoot SFX sequences with models or miniatures in slow motion to increase their realism.

Fast-motion photography was a feature of hundreds of silent comedies, as its exaggerated pace added to the craziness of the clowning. It was achieved by 'undercranking' or running the camera slower than usual. Car chases and other risky stunts are often shot in fast motion, with the action performed slowly and safely and then speeded up during projection to provide high-speed excitement.

SCENIC EFFECTS

Scenic effects can bring completely imaginary places into existence, and they too have been around a long time. The technique of 'back projection' was first used in the silent era. A projector cast a moving background on to a screen positioned behind the performers. It was often used, for example, to show the view through the window of a speeding car. These images were synchronized, or matched up, with the camera to prevent them flickering. The effect could look unconvincing, but a solution was found in 'front projection' (see diagram opposite).

To recreate convincing historical or futuristic backgrounds, film-makers use miniature or model sets, or what are known as 'glass shots' (see diagram). This technique was used in the classic films of the 1930s, *King Kong* and *Gone with the Wind*.

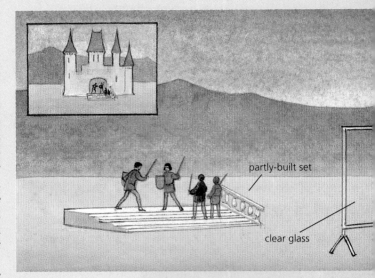

partly-built set

clear glass

Another cost-saving method involves building only the part of the set in which the performers will stand. The rest of the frame is filled by means of a glass shot or computer-generated scenery. Some experts claim that computer graphics will one day replace three-dimensional sets altogether.

All these systems require the background images to be available during the shooting of the action. But a process called 'matting' means that live action and artificial scenery can be joined into a single, or 'composite', shot. This takes place during post-production in special laboratories using a machine called an optical printer.

Today, more films than ever before are using computer-generated images to create the world in which the action takes place. In *Forrest Gump*, for example, the scenes in which Forrest meets famous people like President Kennedy were created by computer. Tom Hanks first acted out his part before a blue screen. These images were then converted by computer into thousands of small image points called 'prexels'. The footage of the president was computerized in the same way and then joined to the pictures of

▽ With artificial scenery behind him, Bruce Willis swings into action in *Die Hard* (1988).

◁ Glass shots allow directors to create breathtaking scenery or fantastic buildings without having to shoot on location or build expensive sets. Here, the turrets of a castle have been painted on to a sheet of glass positioned between the camera and a partly-built set, on which the actors perform. The camera films the action through the glass so that the painting and the set form a single image.

e painted on glass

camera

▽ In front projection, a projector casts pictures of the background scenery on to a semi-transparent mirror. This deflects the image on to a glass-beaded screen behind the performers. The camera films the reflection and the performers together, to form a single image.

glass-beaded screen

projected scenery   semi-transparent mirror

projector

camera

Forrest by 'morphing' or blending the prexels into a single image. Morphing can also be used to generate spectacular action, such as the moments when Jean-Claude Van Damme bursts back through time in *Timecop*, or when a hole appears in Goldie Hawn's stomach in *Death Becomes Her*.

CARTOONS AND MODELS

Animation is also a sort of special effect (see page 42). The sequence of pictures required for a particular movement, expression or gesture is drawn on to celluloid sheets called 'cels'. These are positioned over paintings of the required piece of background scenery and shot frame by frame by a camera operator. Many animated films today use computers, to reduce the number of illustrations that have to be drawn by hand. The stampeding zebras in *The Lion King*, for example, were produced in this way.

Most puppet and model films are also shot on a frame-by-frame basis. One of the best-known model animators today is Nick Park, who animated clay models for his Oscar-winning short films *Creature Comforts* and *The Wrong Trousers*.

Many science-fiction films also rely on models, particularly for their futuristic buildings and vehicles. Space flight and battle sequences also use light effects to give the impression of laser fire and spectacular explosions. The leading specialist in these optical effects is the American company Industrial Light & Magic. Among their many impressive achievements are *E.T. The Extraterrestrial*, *Back to the Future*, *Terminator 2*, *Jurassic Park* and *Forrest Gump*.

▽ Morphing was used to create this dazzling effect in the Jim Carrey comedy *The Mask* (1994).

△ Gizmo the cuddly Mogwai is just one of the many magnificent models and puppets that appear in Joe Dante's *Gremlins* (1984).

In the lab

The optical house is also responsible for a film's opening titles and closing credits. These too can often involve highly complex special effects and animation techniques. In the hands of a skilled designer like Saul Bass, who worked on the Hitchcock pictures *Vertigo* and *Psycho*, the credits can be a work of art in themselves. The title sequences for the James Bond films, for example, are always very inventive and atmospheric.

The finished optical effects are added to the fine cut. The original negative, which has been in storage since the rushes were made, is brought to the lab and trimmed so that it exactly matches the running order of the fine cut. The brightness and colour quality of the picture are checked. If the director and the cinematographer are happy with the look of the film, the visual images and the soundtrack are combined into a single print for the first time. This 'answer print' is shown to the producer.

'Coming to a cinema near you...'

Another print called a 'show print' is shown to members of the public at a special screening called a 'preview'. Everyone in the audience is given a list of questions to answer about the film. They might reply that a scene is too boring, a character is annoying, or the ending is unbelievable. Sometimes these problems can be solved by cutting entire scenes or re-editing others. But if the response is totally negative, the producer might even recall the cast and crew and insist that the director shoots new scenes to improve the picture.

The show print is also submitted to the film censors. They will view the picture and decide which age groups should be allowed to see it at a cinema, and later on videotape. In order to warn people about a film's suitability for younger viewers, the censors give it a 'certificate', or 'rating'. This rating system differs from country to country.

Once the producer has approved the film, 'release prints' are made for distribution to cinemas around the world. The 'preview reaction' usually gives the producer an idea of how a film will do at the box office. If the reports are mixed the movie will be given a 'limited release', with little advance publicity or advertising. But if they are enthusiastic the feature will be given a 'wide release', supported by an expensive promotional campaign.

Distributors naturally want as many people as possible to see a feature, to increase their share of any profits. So they often begin publicizing a film as early as the development stage. By announcing that, for example, certain big-name performers are going to star in an Oscar-winning director's adaptation of a best-selling novel, they create public interest. They keep this up during

▽ ▷ *Interview with the Vampire* (1994) hit the news long before its release when Anne Rice, the author of the original book, published a letter in the film paper *Variety* to deny reports that she disapproved of Tom Cruise in the leading role.

▷ ▽ An advertising campaign that succeeds in one country might not work in another. Notice the difference between the American and Japanese posters for *Four Weddings and a Funeral* (1994).

production with newspaper, magazine and TV reports of cast changes and rumours about arguments or romances on the set.

They also produce 'trailers', or short clips from the film, to give viewers a taste of what to expect from the full-length feature. They contain outline details of the plot and brief highlights of key scenes. They are usually screened at a cinema during the 'For Future Presentation' interlude, just before the big picture. Many exhibitors also put up posters to advertise the films that will shortly be showing at their cinemas.

Nearer the release date, advertisements start appearing in film magazines, and 'tie-in' products like T-shirts, games and sound-

▷ An audience wearing headsets fitted with special lenses enjoys the very latest in big screen entertainment at Sony's 3-D Imax cinema in New York.

▽ Magazines and newspapers dealing with all aspects of films and film-making have been popular with moviegoers from around the world since they first appeared in 1911.

track albums are put on sale. The distributors also send out information about the film to journalists, critics and TV presenters, hoping that they will give it a good review. The director and the stars sometimes go on 'publicity tours', giving interviews to the media. So by the time the film is given its first public showing, called a première, the audience will already know so much about it that it has become a 'must see' movie.

The lifecycle of a movie ends with you watching it on a screen. Wherever the film is screened, it is the duty of the cinema projectionist to keep the picture in focus and make sure every audience sees the same high-quality performance. But more people than ever before now watch films on TV or video at home.

In 1895 the Lumière brothers' film projector replaced Edison's peepshow viewer as the most popular way of watching moving pictures. One hundred years later, the best way to experience the magic of a movie is still to see it on the big screen.

▽ Millions of people worldwide watch films in multi-screen cinemas offering a wide choice of the latest movies. The biggest in the world is the Kinepolis in Belgium, which has 24 different screens under one roof.

FACTFILE

Who was Rudolph Valentino? Which film won the
Best Picture Oscar in the year that you were born?
How many movies can you name starring cats?
Which is the No. 1 box-office hit of all time? Is it the
same film that the critics describe as their No. 1? The
answers are all in this fascinating file packed with
film facts and figures. Plus there's an A-Z of the top
movie stars, from all periods of cinema history – so
you can look up your own favourites.

AN A–Z OF FILM STARS

ISABELLE ADJANI (born 1955) French actress whose performances in powerful dramas have made her an international star. *The Story of Adèle H* (1975); *One Deadly Summer* (1983); *Queen Margot* (1994).

WOODY ALLEN (born Allen Konigsberg; 1935) American actor and director who specializes in adult comedies with witty dialogue. *Annie Hall* (1977); *Manhattan* (1979); *Bullets over Broadway* (1994).

FRED ASTAIRE (born Frederick Austerlitz; 1899–1987) American actor best known for musicals, especially those made with Ginger Rogers. *Easter Parade* (1948); *Funny Face* (1957); *The Band Wagon* (1953).

INGRID BERGMAN (1915–1982) Born in Sweden, she was one of Hollywood's top dramatic actresses in the 1940s and 1950s. *Casablanca* (1942); *Gaslight* (1944); *Anastasia* (1956).

HUMPHREY BOGART (1899–1957) American actor who usually played tough guys on both sides of the law. *Casablanca* (1942); *The Big Sleep* (1946); *The African Queen* (1951).

MARLON BRANDO (born 1924) American actor whose method acting style helped transform screen acting. *A Street Car Named Desire* (1951); *On the Waterfront* (1954); *The Godfather* (1972).

◁ From top to bottom:
Marilyn Monroe,
Tom Cruise,
Marlene Dietrich,
Arnold Schwarzenegger.

JAMES CAGNEY (1899–1986) American actor who was a good comedian and dancer, but he specialized in tough guy roles. *The Public Enemy* (1931); *Angels with Dirty Faces* (1938); *Yankee Doodle Dandy* (1942).

JACKIE CHAN (born 1954) Hong Kong actor and director who specializes in action comedies and martial arts pictures. *Police Story* (1985); *The Armour of God* (1986); *Crime Story* (1993).

CHARLIE CHAPLIN (1889–1977) British actor and director whose comedies made him one of the biggest stars in cinema history. *The Gold Rush* (1924); *City Lights* (1931); *Modern Times* (1936).

MAGGIE CHEUNG (born 1965) Hong Kong actress who stars in serious melodramas, as well as action adventure movies. *As Tears Go By* (1988); *Days of Being Wild* (1991); *The Actress* (1993).

SEAN CONNERY (born 1930) British actor who became a star playing James Bond (see page 77), but has since played many varied roles. *Marnie* (1964); *The Man Who Would Be King* (1975); *The Untouchables* (1987).

GARY COOPER (1901–1961) American actor who played strong, silent heroes in many Westerns, dramas and comedies. *Mr Deeds Goes to Town* (1936); *The Westerner* (1940); *High Noon* (1952).

KEVIN COSTNER (born 1955) American actor and director who alternates between escapist blockbusters and more serious films. *Field of Dreams* (1989); *Dances with Wolves* (1990); *The Bodyguard* (1992).

JOAN CRAWFORD (born Lucille Le Sueur; 1904–1977) American actress who schemed or suffered her way through many Hollywood melodramas. *Grand Hotel* (1932); *Mildred Pierce* (1945); *Whatever Happened to Baby Jane?* (1962).

TOM CRUISE (born 1962) American actor who began in teenpix and is now one of modern Hollywood's major superstars. *Top Gun* (1986); *Rain Man* (1988); *Interview with the Vampire* (1994).

BETTE DAVIS (1908–1989) American actress who played both selfish characters and suffering heroines during her long career. *Jezebel* (1938); *Now Voyager* (1942); *All About Eve* (1950).

ROBERT DE NIRO (born 1943) American actor whose dedication to his art made him the finest screen performer of his generation. *Taxi Driver* (1976); *Raging Bull* (1980); *The King Of Comedy* (1983).

JAMES DEAN (1931–1955) American actor who has remained a teenage idol long after he was killed in a car crash. *East of Eden* (1955); *Rebel Without a Cause* (1955); *Giant* (1956).

GÉRARD DEPARDIEU (born 1948) French actor who has become an international star in a wide range of roles. *The Return of Martin Guerre* (1982); *Cyrano De Bergerac* (1990); *Green Card* (1990).

MARLENE DIETRICH (1901–1992) German actress who became one of Hollywood's most glamorous stars during the Golden Age. *The Blue Angel* (1930); *The Scarlet Empress* (1934); *Rancho Notorious* (1952).

KIRK DOUGLAS (born Issur Danielovitch; 1916) American actor who played both tough guys and likeable heroes. *Ace in the Hole* (1951); *Lust for Life* (1956); *Spartacus* (1960).

MICHAEL DOUGLAS (born 1945) American actor and producer. The son of Kirk Douglas, he has starred in many controversial box-office hits. *Wall Street* (1987); *Basic Instinct* (1992); *Falling Down* (1993).

CLINT EASTWOOD (born 1930) American actor and director who has made several police and action pictures, as well as many classic Westerns. *A Fistful of Dollars* (1964); *Dirty Harry* (1971); *Unforgiven* (1992).

DOUGLAS FAIRBANKS (born Douglas Ulman; 1883–1939) American actor who specialized in action-adventure pictures during the silent era. *The Mark of Zorro* (1920); *The Thief of Bagdad* (1924); *The Black Pirate* (1926).

HENRY FONDA (1905–1982) American actor who played occasional villains and comic parts, but was at his best as decent men fighting injustice. *The Grapes of Wrath* (1940); *Twelve Angry Men* (1957); *Once Upon a Time in the West* (1969).

JANE FONDA (born 1937) American actress. The daughter of Henry Fonda, she moved from comic and romantic parts to more serious roles. *Barefoot in the Park* (1967); *Klute* (1971); *Julia* (1977).

HARRISON FORD (born 1942) American actor who became one of the biggest stars of the kidpix era. *Raiders of the Lost Ark* (1981); *Witness* (1985); *The Fugitive* (1993).

JODIE FOSTER (born 1962) American actress and director. A former child star, she is now one of Hollywood's most respected performers. *Taxi Driver* (1976); *The Accused* (1988); *The Silence of the Lambs* (1991).

JEAN GABIN (born Jean-Alexis Moncorgé; 1904–1976) French actor who played many decent characters struggling against fate. *Grand Illusion* (1937); *Port of Shadows* (1938); *Daybreak* (1939).

CLARK GABLE (1901–1960) American actor who was known as the 'King of Hollywood'. He played action men and romantic leads with equal ease. *It Happened One Night* (1934); *San Francisco* (1936); *Gone with the Wind* (1939).

GRETA GARBO (born Greta Gustafsson; 1905–1990) Swedish actress who became one of Hollywood's biggest stars. She retired at the height of her fame in 1941. *Queen Christina* (1933); *Camille* (1937); *Ninotchka* (1939).

JUDY GARLAND (born Frances Gumm; 1922–1969) American actress. A former child star, she became one of Hollywood's most popular musical performers. *The Wizard of Oz* (1939); *Meet Me in St Louis* (1944); *A Star Is Born* (1954).

MEL GIBSON (born 1956) American actor who starred in many successful action adventures, dramas and comedies. *Mad Max* (1979); *Lethal Weapon* (1987); *Maverick* (1994).

LILLIAN GISH (1896–1993) American actress who was D.W. Griffith's favourite actress. Her career lasted over 60 years. *The Birth of a Nation* (1915); *Broken Blossoms* (1919); *The Night of the Hunter* (1955).

WHOOPI GOLDBERG (born 1949) American actress who has starred in serious dramas, but is best known for comic roles. *The Colour Purple* (1985); *Ghost* (1990); *Sister Act* (1992).

CARY GRANT (born Alexander Archibald Leach; 1904–1986) British actor whose many comedies, thrillers and melodramas made him one of the best-loved of all Hollywood stars. *Bringing Up Baby* (1938); *The Philadelphia Story* (1940); *North by Northwest* (1959).

TOM HANKS (born 1957) American actor who began in comic roles but now also takes major dramatic roles. *Big* (1988); *Philadelphia* (1993); *Forrest Gump* (1994).

KATHARINE HEPBURN (born 1907) American actress who was not always popular with audiences, but many of her films are now classics. *Bringing Up Baby* (1938); *The Philadelphia Story* (1940); *The African Queen* (1951).

DUSTIN HOFFMAN (born 1937) American actor who is known for his wide range of different characters. *The Graduate* (1957); *Marathon Man* (1976); *Rain Man* (1988).

ANTHONY HOPKINS (born 1941) British actor who has recently found screen fame after an acclaimed stage career. *The Elephant Man* (1980); *The Silence of the Lambs* (1991); *Shadowlands* (1993).

BUSTER KEATON (born Joseph Keaton; 1895–1966) American actor and director best known for his slapstick comedies. *Sherlock Junior* (1924); *The Navigator* (1924); *The General* (1927).

GENE KELLY (born 1912) American actor and director who made some of the finest Hollywood musicals. *On the Town* (1949); *An American in Paris* (1951); *Singin' in the Rain* (1952).

STAN LAUREL (born Arthur Stanley Jefferson; 1890–1965) & **OLIVER HARDY** (1892–1957) British and American actors who formed one of the most popular comedy teams in film history. *The Music Box* (1932); *Way Out West* (1936); *Blockheads* (1938).

GONG LI (born 1966) Chinese actress who usually plays strong-willed women. She often works with director Zhang Yimou. *Ju Dou* (1990); *Raise the Red Lantern* (1991); *Farewell, My Concubine* (1993).

MARCELLO MASTROIANNI (born 1923) Italian actor who starred in several films by director Federico Fellini and in romantic comedies with actress Sophia Loren. *La Dolce Vita* (1960); *8½* (1963); *Ginger and Fred* (1985).

TOSHIRO MIFUNE (born 1920) Japanese actor who starred in many films for director Akira Kurosawa. *Rashomon* (1950); *Seven Samurai* (1954); *Yojimbo* (1961).

MARILYN MONROE (born Norma Jean Mortenson; 1926–1962) American actress who remains a top pin-up idol today. *Gentlemen Prefer Blondes* (1953); *The Seven Year Itch* (1955); *Some Like It Hot* (1959).

DEMI MOORE (born Demi Guynes; 1962) American actress who began as a member of the 'brat pack'. She is married to the actor Bruce Willis. *About Last Night* (1986); *Indecent Proposal* (1992); *Disclosure* (1994).

PAUL NEWMAN (born 1925) American method actor who used to play cynical outsiders, but now usually takes character parts. *The Hustler* (1961); *Butch Cassidy and the Sundance Kid* (1969); *The Sting* (1973).

JACK NICHOLSON (born 1937) American actor who is best known for his larger-than-life performances in dramas and black comedies. *One Flew Over the Cuckoo's Nest* (1975); *The Shining* (1980); *Batman* (1989).

LAURENCE OLIVIER (1907–1989) British actor and director who went from playing romantic and Shakespearean leads to character roles. *Rebecca* (1940); *Hamlet* (1948); *Marathon Man* (1976).

AL PACINO (born 1939) American method actor who is at his best in hard-hitting dramas. *The Godfather* (1972); *Scent of a Woman* (1992); *Carlito's Way* (1993).

MICHELLE PFEIFFER (born 1957) American actress whose ability to play a range of dramatic roles has made her one of Hollywood's biggest stars. *The Fabulous Baker Boys* (1989); *Batman Returns* (1992); *The Age of Innocence* (1993).

MARY PICKFORD (born Gladys Smith; 1893–1979) American silent film actress who was known as 'America's Sweetheart'. *Rebecca of Sunnybrook Farm* (1917); *Pollyanna* (1920); *Little Lord Fauntleroy* (1921).

ROBERT REDFORD (born 1937) American actor who became a major star in such films as *Butch Cassidy and the Sundance Kid* (1969) and *All the President's Men* (1976). He also directed the hit films *Ordinary People* (1980) and *Quiz Show* (1994).

KEANU REEVES (born 1965) American actor who has switched from teen comedy to drama and adventure. *Bill and Ted's Excellent Adventure* (1989); *My Own Private Idaho* (1991); *Speed* (1994).

JULIA ROBERTS (born 1967) American actress who is one of Hollywood's top box-office stars. *Steel Magnolias* (1989); *Pretty Woman* (1990); *Flatliners* (1990).

GINGER ROGERS (born Virginia McMath; 1911–1995) American actress who came to fame in musicals with Fred Astaire. She also starred in many melodramas and comedies: *Bachelor Mother* (1939); *Stage Door* (1937); *Kitty Foyle* (1940).

WINONA RYDER (born 1971) American actress who has moved from teenage parts to a variety of dramatic roles. *Heathers* (1986); *Edward Scissorhands* (1990); *Little Women* (1994).

ARNOLD SCHWARZENEGGER (born 1947) Austrian-born actor who became one of Hollywood's most popular action men. *The Terminator* (1984); *Total Recall* (1990); *True Lies* (1994).

SYLVESTER STALLONE (born 1946) American actor and director who is best known for action-adventure movies. *Rocky* (1976); *Cliffhanger* (1993); *Judge Dredd* (1995).

JAMES STEWART (born 1908) American actor who was best known for playing shy, decent characters, although he also starred in Westerns and thrillers. *Desty Rides Again* (1939); *It's a Wonderful Life* (1946); *Vertigo* (1958).

▷ From top to bottom: Buster Keaton, Dustin Hoffman, John Wayne.

MERYL STREEP (born 1951) American actress who usually plays complex leading characters and is well known for her range of accents. *Sophie's Choice* (1982); *Silkwood* (1983); *Out of Africa* (1986).

ELIZABETH TAYLOR (born 1932) British-born actress who began in teenage roles before starring in many powerful melodramas. She was twice married to the Welsh actor, Richard Burton. *National Velvet* (1944); *Giant* (1956); *Who's Afraid of Virginia Woolf?* (1966).

SHIRLEY TEMPLE (born 1928) American actress who was the most successful child star of the Golden Age of Hollywood. *Curly Top* (1935); *Dimples* (1936); *Bachelor Knight* (1947).

SPENCER TRACY (1900–1967) American actor who was among the finest screen performers in Hollywood history. *Boys Town* (1938); *Adam's Rib* (1949); *Bad Day at Black Rock* (1954).

RUDOLPH VALENTINO (born Rodolpho Guglielmi; 1895–1926) Italian-born actor whose performances in romantic melodramas made him the biggest star of the silent era. *The Four Horsemen of the Apocalypse* (1921); *The Sheik* (1921); *Son of the Sheik* (1926).

DENZEL WASHINGTON (born 1954) American actor who often plays men of strong principles in powerful dramas. *Glory* (1989); *Malcolm X* (1992); *Philadelphia* (1993).

JOHN WAYNE (born Marion Morrison; 1907–1979) American actor who was best known for Westerns, but he also starred in many action adventures. *The Long Voyage Home* (1940); *The Quiet Man* (1952); *Hatari* (1962).

ORSON WELLES (1915–1985) American actor and director who was forced to go independent after many feuds with the Hollywood moguls. *Citizen Kane* (1941); *The Third Man* (1949); *Chimes At Midnight* (1966).

OSCAR WINNERS

THE ACADEMY AWARDS FOR BEST PICTURE

1927-1928: *Wings*
1928-1929: *Broadway Melody*
1929-1930: *All Quiet on the Western Front*
1930-1931: *Cimarron*
1931-1932: *Grand Hotel*
1932-1933: *Cavalcade*
1933: *no Oscar ceremony*
1934: *It Happened One Night*
1935: *Mutiny on the Bounty*
1936: *The Great Ziegfeld*
1937: *The Life of Emile Zola*
1938: *You Can't Take It with You*
1939: *Gone with the Wind*
1940: *Rebecca*
1941: *How Green Was My Valley*
1942: *Mrs Miniver*
1943: *Casablanca*
1944: *Going My Way*
1945: *The Lost Weekend*
1946: *The Best Years of Our Lives*
1947: *Gentleman's Agreement*
1948: *Hamlet*
1949: *All the King's Men*
1950: *All About Eve*
1951: *An American in Paris*
1952: *The Greatest Show on Earth*
1953: *From Here to Eternity*
1954: *On the Waterfront*
1955: *Marty*
1956: *Around the World in 80 Days*
1957: *The Bridge on the River Kwai*
1958: *Gigi*
1959: *Ben-Hur*
1960: *The Apartment*
1961: *West Side Story*
1962: *Lawrence of Arabia*
1963: *Tom Jones*

1964: *My Fair Lady*
1965: *The Sound of Music*
1966: *A Man for All Seasons*
1967: *In the Heat of the Night*
1968: *Oliver!*
1969: *Midnight Cowboy*
1970: *Patton*
1971: *The French Connection*
1972: *The Godfather*
1973: *The Sting*
1974: *The Godfather Part II*
1975: *One Flew Over the Cuckoo's Nest*
1976: *Rocky*
1977: *Annie Hall*
1978: *The Deer Hunter*
1979: *Kramer vs. Kramer*
1980: *Ordinary People*
1981: *Chariots of Fire*
1982: *Gandhi*
1983: *Terms of Endearment*
1984: *Amadeus*
1985: *Out of Africa*
1986: *Platoon*
1987: *The Last Emperor*
1988: *Rain Man*
1989: *Driving Miss Daisy*
1990: *Dances with Wolves*
1991: *The Silence of the Lambs*
1992: *Unforgiven*
1993: *Schindler's List*
1994: *Forrest Gump*

▽ The acting Oscars don't always go to the stars of the Best Picture. Peter O'Toole played the lead in the 1962 winner, *Lawrence of Arabia*, but failed to win an award.

▷ Woody Allen has been nominated for 9 Oscars, but he refuses to go to the glittering awards ceremony.

▽ Nick Park with the Oscar he won in 1990 for his animated film *Creature Comforts*.

OSCAR FACTS

The statuette is 13 inches tall and plated in 10-carat gold. It got the nickname 'Oscar' in 1931, when Margaret Herrick, the librarian at the Academy of Motion Picture Arts and Sciences claimed it looked like her Uncle Oscar.

- *Ben-Hur* holds the record for the most Oscars - with 11 wins.
- Walt Disney won 26 Oscars and 6 special Academy Awards.
- Only three films have won the 'Big Four' Oscars (Best Picture, Best Actor, Best Actress, Best Director) - *It Happened One Night*, *One Flew Over the Cuckoo's Nest*, and *The Silence of the Lambs*.
- *All About Eve* is the most nominated film with 14. It won 6.
- *The Turning Point* and *The Color Purple* were nominated for 11 Oscars each and won nothing.
- Katharine Hepburn was nominated a record 13 times. The male acting record of nine is shared by Spencer Tracy and Laurence Olivier.
- The youngest Oscar winner is Shirley Temple, who was just 6 when she received a special award for all her performances in 1934.
- The oldest winner is Jessica Tandy (80 years and 8 months).

THE LONGEST...

...Film - *The Cure for Insomnia* (USA, 1987) - 85 hours long!

...Title - *Un Fatto di sangue nel commune di Siciliana fra due uomini per causa di una vedova si sospettano moventi politici. Amore. Morte. Shimmy. Lugano belle. Tarantelle. Tarallucci a vino* (Italy, 1979). The English title was simply *Revenge!* The longest English-language title is *The Persecution and Assassination of Jean-Paul Marat as Performed by the Inmates of the Asylum of Charenton under the Direction of the Marquis de Sade* (UK, 1966).

...Single word in a title - *Schwarzhuhnbraunhuhnschwarzhuhnweisshuhnrothuhnweiss oder Put-Putt* (West Germany, 1967).

...Cinema name - Lentielectroplasticromomimocoliserpentographe, which was opened in Bordeaux, France in 1902.

THE SHORTEST...

...Title - A singer letter. Only *J, L, N, R, S, T,* and *U* have yet to be made. There have also been films called *3, $,* and *–*.

...Cinema name - In 1925, there was a cinema in Mattoon, Illinois, USA called K.

...Adult performer - Tamara de Treaux, who was 2ft 7in tall. Her best-known role was E.T. (who was also played at other times in the film by Pat Bilson and Matthew de Merritt).

FILM FIRSTS

Cinema show - Cinématographè Lumière in Paris, 28 December 1895

Feature film - *The Story of the Kelly Gang* (Australia, 1906)

Film made in Hollywood - *In Old California* (1910)

Film to use actors - *The Execution of Mary, Queen of Scots* (USA, 1895 - and Mary was played by a man, R.L. Thomas!)

Film star - Florence Lawrence (also known as 'The Biograph Girl' and 'The Imp Girl' after the studios she worked for).

Film director - L.J. Vincent (*The Passion Play*, 1898)

Animated film - *The Humpty Dumpty Circus* (USA, 1898)

Cartoon - *Humorous Phases of Funny Faces* (USA, 1906)

Film serial - *What Happened to Mary* (USA, 1912)

Colour film - *A Visit to the Seaside* (UK, 1908) in Kinemacolor by G.A. Smith of Brighton.

Sound films - Unknown titles by Oskar Messter in Germany in 1896, using discs played along with the film.

Widescreen film - *The Robe* (USA, 1953)

3-D films - Untitled country scenes shown in New York in 1915.

Holographic film - Untitled film of a girl putting jewellery into a glass box, shown in Moscow in 1977. It lasted just 30 seconds.

△ A clever shot capturing the mystery at the heart of Alfred Hitchcock's *Vertigo* (1958), considered by many critics to be one of the finest films of all time.

ALL-TIME TOP 10 BOX-OFFICE HITS

1 *Jurassic Park* (1993)
2 *The Lion King* (1994)
3 *E.T. The Extraterrestrial* (1982)
4 *Forrest Gump* (1994)
5 *Ghost* (1990)
6 *Star Wars* (1977)
7 *The Bodyguard* (1992)
8 *Indiana Jones and the Last Crusade* (1989)
9 *Terminator 2* (1991)
10 *Home Alone* (1990)

A box-office blockbuster means great entertainment but it does not necessarily mean great cinema. Every ten years the British film magazine *Sight and Sound* invites international critics to select their Top 10 films of all time. The list is very different to the box-office chart.

CRITICS' ALL-TIME TOP 10

1 *Citizen Kane* (1941)
2 *Rules of the Game* (France, 1939)
3 *Tokyo Story* (Japan, 1953)
4 *Vertigo* (1958)
5 *The Searchers* (1956)
6 *L'Atalante* (1931)
= *The Passion of Joan of Arc* (France, 1928)
= *Panther Panchali* (India, 1953)
= *Battleship Potemkin* (USSR, 1925)
10 *2001: A Space Odyssey* (UK, 1968)

▷ Macaulay Culkin made his stage début at the age of four, and appeared in his first film four years later. *Uncle Buck* (1989), *Home Alone* (1990) and *Home Alone 2: Lost in New York* (1992) made him one of the best paid child stars of all time.

THE BIGGEST...

...Film industry - India (with an average of some 800 films a year).

...Cast - *Days of Treason*, a 1972 Czech film, lists 260 performers in the credits.

...Cast of extras - 300,000 in *Gandhi* (UK, 1982).

...Cinema - The Roxy in New York (1927-1960) could hold 6,214 customers.

...Single audience - 110,000 saw *Boots*, directed by D.W. Griffith, at the Oval Amphitheater, Colombus, Ohio on 4 July 1919.

...Film set - The Forum was reconstructed for *The Fall of the Roman Empire* (1964). It measured 1,312 ft by 754 ft.

...Box-office flop - *Orphans* (USA, 1987) cost $15 million to make and took only $100,000 in the USA.

THE SMALLEST...

...Film industry in the world - Iceland, which only got its first studio in 1988, averages 3 films a year, although Uruguay had produced less than 30 films throughout the entire century.

...Cinema - The Miramar in Cuba had 25 seats, although only 17 can squeeze in at the smallest of the six screens at the Biohoellin in Reykjavik, Iceland.

...Film set - The boat used in Alfred Hitchcock's *Lifeboat* (USA, 1944).

ANIMALS IN THE MOVIES

- Strongheart refused to howl before a camera and had a double to do his howling for him.
- Rin Tin Tin was such a superstar of the silent screen that he had his own valet, chef, and chauffeur - and a five-room dressing room!
- There was only one problem with *The Courage of Lassie* (1946) - Lassie wasn't in it.
- A dog was once nominated for the Best Screenplay Oscar - Robert Towne so disliked the film made from his script of *Greystoke: The Legend of Tarzan, Lord of the Apes* (1984) that he insisted the writing credit was given to his sheepdog, P.H. Vazak.

CAT MOVIES

1 *That Darn Cat* (USA, 1965)
2 *The Three Lives of Thomasina* (USA, 1963)
3 *Harry and Tonto* (USA, 1974)
4 *The Incredible Journey* (USA, 1963)
5 *Rhubarb* (USA, 1951)
6 *The Cat from Outer Space* (USA, 1978)
7 *Cat's Eye* (USA, 1978)
8 *The Adventures of Milo and Otis* (Japan, 1986)
9 *Gay Purree* (USA, 1962)
10 *The Aristocats* (USA, 1970)

DOG MOVIES

1 *Owd Bob* (UK, 1938)
2 *Old Yeller* (USA, 1957)
3 *Greyfriars Bobby* (UK, 1960)
4 *The Spy with a Cold Nose* (UK, 1966)
5 *Benji* (USA, 1975)
6 *Digby: The Biggest Dog in the World* (GB, 1973)
7 *Turner and Hooch* (USA, 1990)
8 *Lady and the Tramp* (USA, 1955)
9 *One Hundred and One Dalmations* (USA, 1961)
10 *Beethoven* (USA, 1992)

- Only four fiction films have been made with all-animal casts:
  1 *Bill and Coo* (USA, 1948) - Love Birds
  2 *Perri* (USA, 1957) - a squirrel
  3 *Jonathan Livingstone Seagull* (USA, 1973) - a seagull
  4 *The Adventures of Milo and Otis* (Japan, 1986) - cats, dogs, farm animals

THE MOST . . .

...Expensive film - *Waterworld* (USA, 1995) which reportedly cost $180 million to make.

...Cinema screens in the world - China has 152,000 - and has the biggest annual audience, each inhabitant going to the pictures, on average, 20 times a year.

...Films in acting career - Tom London made over 2,000 films from 1903 to 1959.

...Starring roles - Indian comedy actress Manorama has been top-billed in over 1,000 films.

...Films as director - American William Beaudine made 182 feature films and over 120 shorts, some 300 films in all.

...Roles by a single performer in one film - 27 by Rolf Leslie in *Sixty Years a Queen* (1913).

...Retakes for a single scene - 342 for one brief moment of Charlie Chaplin's *City Lights* (USA, 1931).

...Filmed fictional character - Sherlock Holmes (204).

...Filmed real character - Napoleon (194).

...Filmed author - Shakespeare (300 adaptations of his plays to date).

...Filmed story - Cinderella (94 versions so far).

...Paid to a child performer - $4.5 million to Macaulay Culkin for *Home Alone 2: Lost in New York* (1992).

△ Film stars are usually advised never to act with children and animals. Yet dozens of animal movies have been made and training animals for the screen takes a great deal of skill. This shot from *Beethoven's 2nd* shows the troublesome St Bernard with his family. Over 100 different dogs were used to play the puppies at different stages of the action.

GLOSSARY

(for an explanation of who does what to make a film, and other technical film-making terms, see *Lifecycle of a Movie*)

animation The process of using a movie camera to photograph drawings, puppets, clay models, silhouettes, or abstract shapes one frame at a time so that they appear to move when the film strip is run through a projector.

art-house film The name given to artistic or intellectual rather than commercial films (often in a foreign language).

avant garde A French term used to describe non-commercial or experimental films and film-makers.

biopic A film based on the true story of a famous person.

blockbuster A film that is a huge box-office hit, or one that cost an enormous amount to make and to publicize.

box office The place at the front of the cinema where tickets are sold. The term 'box-office hit' is used to indicate a successful movie.

B picture A cheap, quickly made film shown before the main feature.

camera angle The position of the camera in relation to the object being photographed.

censorship The act of banning entire films or cutting scenes from them to prevent viewers from seeing obscene, violent or politically dangerous material.

CD-i The popular name for interactive compact discs which enable viewers using special computer software to alter or interact with images stored on the disc. Some feature films are now available on CD-i.

choreography The art of inventing and arranging dance routines.

cinematography The proper term for motion-picture photography.

close-up A camera shot in which an object fills most of the screen.

credits The list of the cast and crew shown at the beginning or end of a film.

cross-cutting An editing technique whereby action from two or more sequences (happening in different places) are edited together to give the impression they are all taking place at the same moment.

cutting The way in which a film is edited to move from one shot to another.

distributor The person or company that persuades the exhibitor to show in their cinemas the films made by the producer.

documentary A film that deals with events, persons, places, or abstract themes in a factual rather than a fictional way.

dubbing A process of adding new sound-effects or dialogue to a sound-track after filming has been completed. It is also used to correct mistakes or add dialogue in a foreign language (instead of subtitles).

editing The task of selecting a variety of shots and joining them together into an order that tells the story of a film.

exhibitor The person or company that shows films to the public at movie theatres ranging in size from multiplexes to small independent cinemas.

expressionism An artistic movement which expressed thoughts or emotions by means of exaggerated or distorted images. The term is usually applied to films made in Germany in the 1920s.

feature A full-length moving picture usually lasting over 90 minutes.

film d'art The name given to the lavish costume dramas made in France in the 1910s by the Film d'Art company.

film gauge The width of the film strip, usually measured in millimetres from 16 mm to 35 mm to 70 mm.

film noir A French term meaning 'dark film' applied especially to moody black-and-white films of the late 1930s and crime films of the 1940s.

film stock The strip of film, coated on one side with light-sensitive chemicals, on which a movie is photographed.

flashback A scene which goes back in time to show events that took place before the present action of the story.

focus The way in which a camera keeps an image sharp and clear. With soft focus a blurred or softened image is used for a romantic or dreamy effect. When the camera lens and lighting are used to keep both close-up and distant objects in clear focus this is called deep focus.

frame A single shot on a strip of film.

freeze frame A shot in which the action suddenly stops and remains as still as a photograph.

genre A group of motion pictures which have storylines, characters, settings, themes and film techniques in common. Among the most popular genres are the Western, horror, the musical, science fiction and comedy.

independent film A motion picture made by a film-maker without the financial backing of a major studio or production company.

jump cut A rapid cut made in a scene in which the sense of the action continues but the position of the performers or their background suddenly changes.

kidpix Feature films produced to appeal specially to younger audiences.

location work Any filming that happens outside a studio.

long shot A shot in which objects or views are shown at a distance from the camera.

melodrama A film genre which heightens the themes found in drama. Often used to describe sensational, romantic films with simply drawn characters and improbable events.

mise-en-scène A term, which literally means 'putting in the scene', which describes everything contained in a camera shot – the action, set, props, lighting, costumes and make-up.

montage An editing technique whereby a number of images are combined in quick succession for greater impact.

morphing A modern special effect in which computers merge two separate images into a single picture.

neo-realism This term, meaning 'new realism', was applied to films made in Italy after World War II which used real locations, natural lighting and non-professional performers.

newsreel A film showing footage of news or sporting events, usually lasting 10 to 20 minutes. They were often shown before the main feature. Sometimes film-makers would edit such footage into their fictional films.

new wave The name given to any film-making movement that dares to be different and breaks away from tradi-tional methods of screen storytelling. The best-known is the French New Wave (1959–1963).

offscreen Any event or sound that is not actually shown on the screen, but still affects the action of a scene or the story in general.

optical toys Any toy that entertains the user with visual images, for example the magic lantern.

pan A shot in which a camera, fixed to a stand called a tripod, follows the action from one side of the screen to the other.

persistence of vision The eye's ability to retain an image for a split second after it has been removed from direct sight – without this we would not see moving images.

première The first showing of a motion picture to the public. These openings are often glittering occasions with large crowds, the press and television cameras watching the famous stars who attend.

propaganda Films designed to persuade viewers to accept the film-maker's point of view on social or political issues.

prop Any object needed to make a scene more realistic. Small items like cups or guns are called hand props, while larger objects used to decorate a set are called set props.

remake A new film version of an earlier motion picture, usually keeping the same title but sometimes with minor changes to the plot.

sequel A follow-up to a successful picture, often with a number after the original title. Sequels often continue the original story, with the same stars repeating their roles.

set The film equivalent of a stage, complete with scenery and props.

short A film lasting no longer than 30 minutes.

slapstick A term applied to fast-moving physical comedy which relies on char-acters falling over or hitting each other with objects like custard pies.

soundstage A huge, soundproofed room in which the film set is built.

special effects Also called SFX, a term for the various technical tricks, models, make-up and costume devices, stunts, fires and explosions used in films.

subtitles The dialogue printed in the viewer's own language at the bottom of the screen.

superimposition A camera trick in which two or more images are recorded on a single frame of film.

synchronize The process of precisely joining together the soundtrack and the visual images so that the voices heard match the lip movements of the charac-ters on the screen.

take When a shot or complete scene is recorded by the camera.

talkies The nickname given to the earliest sound films because they contained characters talking rather than miming as they had done in the movies of the silent era.

teenpix Movies made for teenagers.

vaudeville Another name for a variety theatre show (also called music hall) in which singers, dancers, comedians, magicians and acrobats performed their acts one after the other. Many performers found fame in silent films.

widescreen A film screen larger than the standard size, made possible by new processes such as CinemaScope and Panavision.

zoom A lens that remains in sharp focus while giving the impression that a stationary camera is moving towards or away from an object.

INDEX OF FILMS

General Index

ACKNOWLEDGEMENTS

The author would like to thank James Harrison, Charlotte Lippmann and Keith Shaw for their work on the book. Also Bob Allen, Bob Angell, Kevin Brownlow, Fred Chandler, Albert Critoph, Peter Cushing, Rosamund Davies, John Gainsborough, Connie Hacquart, Steve Jaggs, Walter Lassally, Christopher Lee, Ann Moody, Christine Payne, S. T. Taylor, Emma Valentine, Kate Wheeler and Nigel Wooland, for their generous assistance.

Design: Keith Shaw
Picture research: Charlotte Lippmann

Abbreviations: t=top; b=bottom; l=left; r=right; c=centre

Photographs
The publisher would like to thank the following for permission to reproduce the following photographs:

A.F.E. Corporation, Kobal: 44/45tc
Akira Comittee: 66t
Albatros, Kobal: 31b
Alma-Afa Studio: 47c
Amblin Entertainment: 148b; *Kobal*: 112/3
Amblin/Universal, Kobal: 70bl
Andre Paulvve Productions: 50b
Anglo Amalgamated Productions: 103t
Apple Corporation Limited: 110b
Archers Film Productions: 51b
Artemis-Hallelujah-Argos/New World, Kobal: 58t
Avco Embassy: 136l, 136c
Bunuel-Dali,Kobal: 31t
Cady Films: 48t
Carolco International: 82bc; *Kobal*: 70t, *The MovieStore Collection*: 132t
Channel Four: 67t
Colorific!: 132b,145br,150, 150-4, 151

Columbia, Kobal: 61, 88tr, 134l, 69tr, 83r, 151b *The Moviestore Collection*: 30/31, 143tr,60
Contemporary Films, Kobal: 63b
Cristaldi Film/Film Ariane: 1, *Kobal*: 34/5
Culver Pictures Inc.: 25bl
Daiei Motion Picture Company: 49b
Daily Variety: 146c
Dinode Maurentiis/Cinematografica Mos Film, Kobal: 118b
© *The Walt Disney Company*: 43br
Douzhenko Studios: 62b
Eagle Lion, Kobal: 113b
Ealing Studios: 85t; *Kobal*: 96b, 121l
Elton Corporation: 38t
Edison, Kobal: 21t
Empire: 147bl
Eon Productions, Kobal: 77l
Era International: 66b
Felix the Cat Productions, Kobal: 4bl, 42bl
Films Cisse: 64b
First National Pictures/Charles Chaplin Corporation, Kobal: 80t
Fox Film Corporation: 91tr
Gaumont/British Picture Corporation, Kobal: 45b
Gordon Company/Silver Pictures, Kobal: 138l, 141t
The Ronald Grant Archive: 5cr, 27bm, 83l, 150a, 150d
Greenwich Film Production: 1br, 90l
David W. Griffith Corporation: 23t
Guild Film Distributors, Kobal: 4/5, 69tl, 78t
Hal Roach Studios: 82t
Hammer/Columbia: 101,103b
Hepworth Manufacturing Company: 21br
Histronic Film, Kobal: 28/29
Horizon Pictures/Romulus: 76
Huntly Archive: 28b
I.T.C., Kobal: 139tr
David King: 32b, 33t
The Kobal Collection: 8/9, 22b, 25br
Live Entertainment, Kobal: 94t, 98t
London Film Productions, Kobal: 46t
Longroad Production/Penthouse Productions/ Paramount, Kobal: 133tr

Lucas Film Limited/Paramount, Kobal: 77r
M.G.M. 36t, 38b, 57t, 88, 106t, 108/109b, 114t, 114c; *Kobal*:12r, 36, 42tr, 53tl,118t, 118/9, 148t, ,151b; *The Moviestore Collection*: 139b
Marc Wanamaker/Bison Archives: 27br
Méliès, Kobal: 20/1
Metro Goldwyn, Kobal: 27t
MGM/UA: 69br
Miramax Films, Kobal: 64t, 65c
Minerva Film: 48b
Morgan Creek/Warner Brothers: 75cr
New Line Cinema: 105
Olympia-Film, Kobal: 44t
Omni Zoetrope : 123
Orion, Kobal: 104b, 126b
Orion Pictures Corporation/Strong Heart/Demme, Kobal: 104b
Orion Production/United Artists: 95c
Paramount: 84c,91tl,97l,98b,99,119t,150-2, 150c,151d; *Kobal*: 53tr, 53b, 68b , 70c, 86b, 87, 93 ,107r ,111, 124b,127b,128c *The Moviestore Collection*: 139tl
Philips: 71b
Pinewood Publicity: 135bl, 135br, 141c, 141b,143,143b
Polygram: 67c; *Kobal*: 67c
Prana Film: 100/1
Precitel/Terra Film, Kobal: 59b
Producoes Cinematograficas Mapa; 62t: 62t
Productions Georges de de Beauregard
Produzione De Sica: 49tl
R.K.O.: 84t,107-1; *Kobal*: 89t
Range Pictures/Bettmann/UPI: Cover, 54b, 74,148/9, 152t/1
Rank Film Distributors: Kobal: 104t
Rank Laboratories: 18bl
Réalisations D'Art Cinématographique: 120
Samuel Goldwyn Company: 88b
Satyajit Ray Productions
Science and Society Picture Library: 10t, 11t,12b, 13, 16t, 16r, 16/17
Sedif les films de Carosse/Janus, Kobal: 58b
Selznick International Pictures, Kobal: 89b
G.A. Smith: 21bl
Société Générale de Films: 29br

Société Générale de films/Gaumont/MGM, Kobal: 5t,32/33t
Société Nouvelle Pathé Cinema, Kobal: 47b
Frank SpoonerPictures: © *Benali- Gillord Liaison*: 3, 147t
Starling/Famous Film Productions, Kobal: 112b
Swedish Film Institute: 29tr; *Kobal*: 50t
Triangle/Keystone, Kobal: 80b
Tristar/Columbia: 18bc, 18br
Twentieth Century Fox: 2, 30, 40, 69m, 92b, 110tl, 126t, 30, 40, 69m, 92b, 110tl, 126t; *Kobal*: 79t, 137b, 144, 153b
Two Cities Films:120b
U.I.P.: 138r; *The Moviestore Collection*: 140l
UIP/Universal: Kobal 151
UFA: 44, 117; *Kobal*: 28t
United Artists: 25t, 74, 84b, 25t, 74, 84b, 86t, 110tr, 125b, 128l; *Kobal*: 55b, 79b, 94b, 125c, 134r, 151c, 152l
United Artists/Charles Chaplin Corporation, Kobal: 81t
Universal: 70br, 100, 102t, 11b, 119b, *Kobal*: 39, 51b, 68t, 78b, 102t, 116c
Universal/International: 92t; *Kobal*: 85b
Mike Vaughan: 147 br
Villealfa Film Productions: 67b
Wade Williams: 113t
Wark Producing Company, Kobal: 23b
Warner Brothers: 37, 56 75tr, 97r, 92m, 95t, 116/7, 122, 124, 129, 132b, 148-1; *Kobal*: 42bl, 58br, 72/3, 96t, 106b, 142, 145
Warner Brothers/Seven Arts: 95b
Warner/Pathé, Kobal: 60t

Cover
Front Cover and Spine: *Range Pictures/Bettmann/UPI*
Back Cover: l *Guild Film Distributors, Kobal*; r *MGM/Selznick International*

Illustrations and Diagrams
Nick Hawken: 14, 15, 16b, 19t & b
Bob Hersey: 24, 55, 135,144-145,145t